PRINTHOUSE BOOKS PRESENTS

Super Senior

Inspired by true events

Lorenzo "EL GEE" Gladden

VIP INK Publishing Group, Incorporated

Atlanta, GA.

Lorenzo "El Gee" Gladden

© Copyright 2016, Lorenzo T. Gladden
All rights reserved.
No part of this book may be reproduced, stored in a retrieval system, or
transmitted by any means, electronic, mechanical, photocopying, recording, or
otherwise, without written permission from the author.

PrintHouse Books, Atlanta, GA.

Published 5-15-2015

www.PrintHouseBooks.com

VIP INK PUBLISHING GROUP; INCORPORATED

Cover Art designed by Beyond Graphix.

Editor: Cheryl Hinton

Isbn: 978-0-9970016-48

Library of Congress Cataloging-in-Publication Data

#2016932008 LORENZO 'EL GEE' GLADDEN

1. Fiction-African American-Romance
2. Fiction-African American-Urban Life
3. Lorenzo 'El Gee' Gladden

PRINTED IN THE UNITED STATES OF AMERICA

Contents

Class of '94 5

Senior Week 26

Hurt Feelings 50

Hell on a Hill 65

In Da Club 86

Simply Red 100

Holidaze 121

Snapped 151

Just in Time 172

Keep it Moving 196

Conspiracy Theory 222

Reunited 247

Beginning of the End 267

The Sweat Box 309

Blue Splash '97 325

Burning Sands 345

Certified Intensity 361

Reality Check 374

Thunder Buddies 390

Settled Down 411

Ain't that a Snitch 421

Movin' On 430

1
Class of '94

June's heat blanketed the hundreds of people that sat in attendance at Kelly Stadium, home of the Hargrove High Red Foxes. Even after the sun had gone down, the night's temperature was still in the mid-80's. The keynote speaker's words that blared through the public announcement system weren't enough to drown out the sway of the programs people used to fan themselves. Situated on, what was normally, the fifty yard line was the graduating class—all 306 of us. We impatiently waited for the speaker to finish so that we could begin the rest of our lives. Whoever he was finished his long, drawn out lecture to polite applause as our principal took his place behind the podium once again.

"Ladies and Gentlemen," Principal Spooner began. "It gives me great pleasure to present to you…the graduating class of 1994!"

Shouts, screams, and whistles rang out from the crowd as we stood and tossed our caps into the air before the procession. For most of us, that night symbolized the end of four of the best years of our lives. It was also the start of a new journey in search of higher education. Of my graduating class, about fifty percent of us went on to college. Out of that fifty percent, only a small number experience another commencement ceremony. Some completed their journey in the allotted four years but many of us gained the ever-so-popular title of Super Senior.

Before I go any further, allow me to introduce myself. My name is Andre Marcellus Marshall. All my friends and family call me Dré. In 1994, I was 5'8" and on the heavier side of the scale but I was not sloppy with it. I wore my weight well. I always considered myself to be a bit of an "Overweight Lover" and the ladies will agree with me. I wasn't the tall, light-skinned kid with the light eyes and good hair, and I wasn't the chocolate kid that was starting to get a little recognition with the emergence of actors like Wesley Snipes and the death of Al B. Sure and El DeBarge. I was in the middle—a cup of coffee with just the right amount of cream.

After I took pictures with my friends and family, I found Jocelyn, my girlfriend, so I could take her home to get ready for the after party at Lakeisha Maynard's house. We had been anticipating this party since her birthday party the summer before. Only the coolest of the cool would attend. When I caught up with Jocelyn, she was talking to her best friend. I remember how beautiful she was that night. Her long black hair sat on her beige shoulders that were exposed by the blue sundress she wore. Even from a distance I could see that twinkle in her eye. To that point in my life, she was the best thing that had happened to me. I just wished she was a part of my graduating class. Jocelyn had one more year to go. When I got to her, she gave me the coldest hug and the most unenthusiastic greetings. She said goodbye to her friend then we walked to my car.

"I can't believe two years went by that fast," I began as I started the car. "It seems like I just got here."

"Yeah," she replied with no emotion.

"This is a big night for me. You're supposed to be happy right along with me. What's wrong?"

"Nothing."

"Don't tell me nothing. I've know you too long to know when something's bothering you."

"I said its nothing," Jocelyn snapped. "Just drop it."

"My bad."

We sat in silence for the majority of the ride. I wanted to know what was going on in my baby's head. If I knew Jocelyn like I thought I did, it had everything to do with me graduating.

"Are you still going to Lakeisha's party?" I asked turning down the radio.

"Dré," Jocelyn paused. "This is not going to work out."

"Excuse me?"

"I think we should go our separate ways."

"Where is all of this coming from? How long have you been feeling this way?"

"I've been feeling like this for a while. I just didn't know when I was going to tell you or how I was going to tell you."

"So you wait to drop this bomb on me on what is supposed to be one the happiest nights of my life?"

"I'm sorry, Dré. I didn't want to tell you tonight but I guess the sooner I told you, the better."

"Well thanks. Good lookin' out."

"Please don't be mad. I'm really just tryna look out for you. In a couple of months you leave to go to school. You'll be on the other side of the state. I want you to enjoy yourself and not have to worry about trying to stay faithful to some girl back home that's still in high school."

"But you're not just some girl. You're my girl."

"Trust me, Dré. It's for the best. You may not see it now but you will."

When I arrived to Jocelyn's house, her mother and father were just pulling into the driveway. When she tried to lean over and kiss me, I turned my face to the window. She bid me one more goodbye and got out of the car. I couldn't bear to look at her. I backed out of the driveway and sped off as her father tried to approach my car. I really don't know how I felt as I drove home. All I remember was my instincts led me home. My grandmother and grandfather were sitting on the couch when I walked in. I tried to walk past them and into the kitchen but my grandmother noticed the look on my face.

"Baby," she called from the den. "What's wrong?"

Super Senior

"Nothing, Mom; I'm fine."

Since my grandparents raised me, I called them Mom and Dad instead of Grandma and Pop Pop like the rest of the grandchildren did.

I fixed a glass of iced tea and walked into my room. After I placed the glass on the nightstand, I flopped down on the couch that was in my room and put my arm over my face. I sat in silence for a moment until Mom knocked on the door then came in.

"Dré," she called as she sat down on my bed. "Talk to me, Baby. This is supposed to be one of the happiest nights of your life. You should be getting ready to go out and enjoy yourself with your friends. What's wrong?"

Without removing my arm from over my face, "Other than not being able to graduate from high school in North Carolina?"

"We're not having that conversation."
"Jocelyn broke up with me."

"It may not seem like it now but that was the best thing that could've happened to you. Next month you turn 18. You become a man. You're entering college. You shouldn't be worried about keeping up with some high school girl back home."

"That's the same thing she said," I explained as I sat up.

"That girl is crazy about you and you know it. She cares enough about you to let you go so that you can live your life freely and not have to worry about hurting her or running around behind her back."

"I guess you're right." Mom repositioned herself from the bed to beside me on the couch.

"Momma's always right." Mom wrapped her loving arms around me and rocked me like she used to when I was younger.

"Speaking of mother's, did mine call?"
"No she didn't."

"What about my father?"
"Yes. He called last night but you were still at work. He called back right after you left. He told me to tell you that he loves you and he's proud of you. He also said to be expecting something in the mail this week."

"Okay. I really wished he coulda made it but I know he just moved to St. Louis."
"You know he would've been here if he could've."
"I know."

"Now are you going to sit here and talk to me all night or are you going to go have a good time with your friends?"

"I'm getting ready to change in a minute."
"Your grandfather said you can stay out as late as you want to but it has two conditions."

"Which are?"
"I don't have to tell you this but no drinking."
"And number two..."
"You don't have to get up for Sunday school but you must be in morning service on time."

"I can handle that."
"I know you can. Have fun, Baby."
"I love you, Mom."
"I love you, too."

My grandmother was such an amazing woman. She always knew the right words to say to cheer me up when I was down. We had a great relationship. I could talk to her about any and every thing. It was like she understood me more than anyone else could.

My grandfather was my Pastor and the reason my life was moved from North Carolina to South Carolina in the middle of my sophomore year. He and I were just as close as my grandmother and I, but it was on a different level. He was from the old south. Dad was the breadwinner and the provider of our family. I knew he loved me more than anything in this world, other than God and his wife, but he didn't openly express it like Mom did. I was cool with that because I knew where my place was in his heart.

    My grandparents raised me in the church but they did not force religion down my throat like the parents of some of my friends. They gave me freedom and allowed me to make my own decisions. I was the only one of my friends that didn't have a curfew but I wasn't a fool. They only had one rule. If I went out on Saturday night, I had to be in church on Sunday. That wasn't a problem because I was in the choir and I loved singing on Sunday mornings. If I was not working or in church, I spent what time I could with Jocelyn. Since she was no more, I had to find something, or someone, else to occupy my time.

    It was almost eleven o'clock when I got to Lakeisha's house. The street was lined with cars all the way to the corner on both sides. Lucky for me somebody left me a parking spot right in front of the house. I stepped out the car looking fresh to death in black jean shorts, my red Class of '94 t-shirt and my red and black Nikes. Mrs. Maynard greeted me at the front door. Lakeisha's mother was the mother that all young boys were in love with. I didn't know how old she was but she was beautiful. The way she looked, dressed, and carried herself one would not think that she had a seventeen-year-old daughter. Mrs. Maynard was the black version of Stifler's mom from the *American Pie* movies.

"Hey Dré!" Mrs. Maynard greeted. "What took you so long? Everybody's been asking about you."

"You know I always have to make a grand appearance," I laughed.

"Everyone's out by the pool. You have a good time."

"Yes, ma'am."

I walked through the house and out the back door. As I said before, only the coolest of the cool attended. My boy, Twist was the DJ for the night. On the mic keeping the crowd hype as always was my best friend, Nick Arthur. Twist was the tall light-skinned brother with the light eyes and good hair that I spoke of earlier. His real name was Felix Robinson. We started calling him Twist during our junior year when he came up with this funky dance move at a party. Nick was my ace. He and I were about the same height and he was slightly darker and slimmer than I was.

Twist and Nick were the first cats I met when I moved to South Carolina. We were all in the band together until we quit during band camp this year. We didn't see eye to eye with the new band director. The thing that brought us all together was music. We were all rappers with three different styles that blended perfectly to form what we called Triple Threat. I guess I clicked with them because they kept me tied to music like my boys back home did.

"Uh oh!" Nick shouted on the mic. "Trouble is in the house! What up, Dré Smoove!"

I was greeted with daps and pounds from the guys and hugs from the ladies as I made my way through the crowd towards my fellas. I dapped Twist and gave Nick one love.

"What took you so long?" Nick asked as he put the mic on the stand.

"Long story… I'll fill you I later."
"Nope…You are gonna fill me in now. Walk to the car wit me."

Right before Nick and I got to the wooden gate that led out of the backyard, I was intercept by Tommy Girl, Chelsea Bridges. Tommy Girl was a gorgeous 4'11". She was small but her body was amazing. Her caramel covered frame was perfectly proportioned, with just enough booty and chest. Her hair was long and curly, and her eyes were a beautiful shade of light brown.

Tommy Girl was the one that got away from me. She was the first girl that I met when I moved to South Carolina. Her pastor came to preach at our church shortly after we got settled in. I didn't see her until the choir took the stand to sing. From the time they put the mic in her hand, I could not take my eyes off her. Not only was she beautiful but she had the voice of an angel. I'll never forget that night. She led *Goin' Up Yonder* by Walter Hawkins. I got a chance to talk to her after service that night but didn't get a chance to see her again until school started that January. To make a long story short, she and I became close friends but I waited too long to make my move. That's when Mike Barrett stepped in and scooped her up. For two years I'd been kicking myself for taking too long.

"Where you goin'?" She asked as she hugged me.
"I'm steppin' out to the car with Nick for a minute. I'll be right back."
"Don't take too long. I wanna dance."
"I don't think ya boy would be too happy about that."

"That's what happens when you don't keep in touch…you miss things."
"What's that supposed to mean?"
"You'll find out. Just don't take too long like you did before."

Tommy Girl winked at me then walked away. When I got to the street, I looked for Nick's hooptie but did not see it.

"Yo Nick!" I called.
"Down here." He replied from the shadows. When I got to him, he was leaning on a black, convertible Mustang 5.0.

"Oh snap! …This you?"
"Yup…Pops got it for me for graduation."

"Word up?"
"Guess what else."
"What?"
"Mom's lettin' me drive it to the beach next week."
"Stop playin! You know how many girlies we can pull rollin' down the strip in this bad boy?"

"Exactly… Wait a minute. Where ya girl at?"
"We called it quits."
"For real?"

"She said that it just wasn't gonna work out with me goin' off to school and her still being here."

"Trust me. That's the best thing that could 'a happened to you right now."

"Why does everybody keep saying that?"
"Cuz it's true. Now hit this." Nick handed me a blue plastic cup.

"You know I don't drink."
"I know. I was just checkin'. Now let's get back to the party before Tommy Girl come out here lookin' for you."

"Very funny."
"I'm not laughin'."
"You know something I don't know?"
"Yup."

"What?"

"She made me promise not to tell you. She wanted to tell you herself."

Nick and I walked back to the party. Once inside, we mingled with our classmates, spit a few rhymes back and forth on the mic and got up on some girls.

I enjoyed myself more than I thought I would; considering how the night began. Even though we all knew that that night was probably going to be the last night we would all be together, it didn't bring the mood down. We enjoyed our last time together. I tried to leave the dance floor after being held hostage for forty-five minutes by Sonya Thomas, a girl that had had a crush on me since the middle of junior year. As Twist slowed it down for some slow grinding, I tried to walk off the dance floor but once again was intercepted by Tommy Girl.

"I've been waiting patiently for you all night," Tommy Girl explained as she took me back onto the dance floor. "It's my turn."

Tommy Girl wrapped her arms around my neck as I put mine around her waist and locked my finger behind her. The music controlled our bodies as we danced to *Comforter* by Shai.

"Are you going to fill me in about…," She took her finger and pressed to my lips.

"Later." After she put her arm back around my neck, she laid her head on my chest.

We continued to dance for about two more songs until we were rudely interrupted by her being snatched away from me.

"Get your hands of me, Mike!" she yelled as she snatched away from him.

Mike was her ex-boyfriend and a high school drop out. He was supposed to graduate with us but quit at the beginning of the year.

"What are you doing here? I told you to stay home!"
"Come on, man. Don't be grabbin' her like that."
"This ain't got nothin' to do with you, Dré. This is between me and her."

"True dat but you don't have to put ya hands on her like that."

"Nigga, this my girl. I can put my hands on her any way I feel like it."

"I'm not you're girl! You threw that away when you screwed Vonda."

"Who you think you talkin' to? I ain't one of these punks out here. I'll knock your head off."

"So you one of them," I interrupted. "A punk ass bitch scared to hit a man so you put ya hands on females."
"What you say?"
"You heard me."

Mike had me outsized but I wasn't going to back down. He turned as if he was getting ready to walk off then tried to swing at me. He swung so hard that when he missed, it threw him off balance. Had he hit me, he probably would have knocked me out but somehow, I got out of the way.

I didn't really want to fight him but there was no turning back. I had to do something before he caught his balance. I remembered that he had not to long been in a car accident and had a bad right knee. Thinking quickly, I kicked him in the side of his right knee. It buckled and he went to the ground. By that time, Mr. Maynard got there, escorted him outside, and waited until he drove away. Twist quickly got the party back on track as I walked Tommy Girl over to the picnic table and sat down beside her.

"I'm sorry about that, Dré."
"That wasn't your fault. I just couldn't let him grab on you like that. Has he done that to you before?"

"Mike may act crazy but he ain't no fool. Those boys on the Southside got his head gassed up like he somebody so he been frontin' like he's a thug."

"What did you see in that dude?"
"Mike wasn't always like that. When he was in school, he was sweet. Something just snapped inside of him after his Mom died a few months ago."
"Is that what you wanted to tell me?"

"If you woulda took your head out of Jocelyn's ass long enough you woulda known that me and Mike broke up a couple months ago."
"That's cold but as I recall, you chose Mike over me."

"Cuz you took too long. I liked you just as much as you liked me but I wasn't going to wait forever for you to tell me."
"I guess we can't see what's right in front of us sometimes."

"Can you see me now?"
"Crystal clear…"
"What about Jocelyn?"
"She broke up with me tonight."
"Stop lyin', Dré…"

"Okay ladies," Nick began on the mic. "If you didn't know, my man Dré is back on the market. You betta get at'em while you can. Some girls ain't wastin' no time."

"Told you," I laughed.
"How much longer do you wanna stay here?"

"What you got in mind?"
"I just want to chill. You know, how we used to chill."
"Let me holla at my boys and say my goodbyes then we can go."

"I'll meet you out front in fifteen minutes."
"Word." I walked back to where Nick and Twist were.

"You leavin'?" Nick asked.
"Yeah. Tommy Girl ain't feeling too good. She asked me to take her home."

"Alright, I'll be at your crib bright and early Monday morning to pick you up. Be ready."

"You know it." I dapped up my boys and said goodbye to everyone. As I was leaving, I apologized to Lakeisha and her parents for the minor altercation. Once I finished talking to them, I met Tommy Girl out front and we left. Fifteen minutes later, we were at our favorite spot.

There was a lake near my house. We used to go there to talk all of the time.

As we sat on the dock and talked, Tommy Girl and I caught up on the things we'd missed due to having other people in our lives. Talking to Tommy Girl that night made me remember what it was I liked the most about her. I loved talking to her. She and I were always on the same level. That was something that I just didn't have with Jocelyn. For an hour and a half, the two of us reconciled a friendship that we allowed to get lost. Neither of us was ready to jump into another relationship but it felt good to have my friend back.

"Are you going to the beach next week," I asked.
"I was but my girls couldn't get they money right."
"Come down anyway. You can chill wit me."
"You still goin' down with Nick and Twist."
"Of course…"

"Thanks but I'll pass. I don't wanna cramp nobody's style. You know how Nick is."

"It ain't even like that."
"Seriously though…I would but I start school next week."

"How is that possible? We just graduated."
"I'm not goin to college. I'm goin' to cosmetology school."

"For real?"

"I ain't got four years to waste. I need money now especially with all my clients getting ready to go off to college."

"I feel you."

"What about you? You still going to school in Greenville? You and Nick supposed to be roommates, right?"

"Nick straight turned his back on me," I laughed. "He changed his mind and decided to go to FMU."

"Why would he wanna go there? If he wanted to stay in the area, he might as well went to Coker."

"I think it has a lot to do with his mother still working out of town. He wants to be around for his grandmother."

"Don't his brother go to Coker?"

"Yeah but he's too busy chasin' white girls to go home and check on his family."

"Some things never change," Tommy Girl laughed as she put her shoes back on.

"I'll be alright though. I need to take some time to be by myself and meet some new people."

"Well just don't forget about me this time."

"I was a fool to let you get away from me before. It's times like this that I missed the most by not having you in my life, even as a friend. Besides, we got a whole summer to kick it before I leave."

"I'd like that." I stood up then helped her up. She put her arms around me and gave me a hug. "Thank you for a great night."

I looked down at Tommy Girl as she looked up at me. Her beautiful, white teeth were exposed when she smiled at me. I leaned my head towards her. She closed her eyes as she accepted my lips to hers. We stood engaged in a deep kiss for what seemed like an eternity.

"I think we better go before we don't make it to church in the morning," she laughed as she took her thumb and wiped my bottom lip.

"I think you're right."

We sat in silence as I drove her home. She gave be a kiss on the cheek as she got out of the car and thanked me for a wonderful evening. I thought about her the whole way home. Though it took us a couple of years to gain back our friendship, everything happened when it was supposed to happen.

Super Senior

2
Senior Week

In the Carolinas, the week after graduation was dubbed as Senior Week. Every year, thousands of newly graduated seniors from across the two states flooded into Myrtle Beach, South Carolina. For one whole week, there would be nothing but parties, fornication and who knows what else an out of control teenager could get into. Most of the rooms on the strip would be overloaded with multiple people in each room. It wasn't cheap to spend a week at the beach in the summertime. Knowing this, my boys and me started saving the previous summer so it would just be us—three friends in a three bedroom villa in North Myrtle Beach. We weren't on the strip but with accommodations like we had, it wouldn't be hard to find some company.

Because of Twist, we got a late start and got stuck in traffic about twenty minutes from the beach. We didn't mind because we were having a ball. Traffic was at a stand still for almost an hour. We turned the car off and started roaming around in traffic trying to get a head start on the rest of the dudes. You shoulda seen us that day. We had on our *Triple Threat* t-shirts that had our stage names on the back and our logo airbrushed on the front. As a graduation gift to myself, I bought a nice Gucci Link, gold chain with a microphone medallion hanging from it. On the hip was the Motorola Sky Pager—with the 800 number. You couldn't tell me shit.

Twist and me had just finished talking to four girls from Columbia when I spied this fine ass girl standing on the passenger side of a Honda Accord. She had a light brown complexion with her long hair pulled back into a ponytail. Judging by how she was dressed and her jewelry, she couldn't have been from South Carolina. As I got closer, I could see that she had on a bikini top and some denim Daisy Dukes. The thing that set it off was that she had on Timberland boots. That was some straight up north style.

"What's up, ladies?" I greeted as I approached the passenger side of the black, Honda Accord.
"Hey cutie," she responded.

"Where y'all from?"
"I'm from North Carolina but my girls from Dillon."

"You from North Kak, fa real?" What part?"
"Fayettenam baby! Ain't no other place to be from."

"Stop lyin! I'm from the Ville. What school you graduate from?"
"I graduated from Smith. What about you?"

"I was supposed to graduate from Oak Forest but I moved here a couple years ago."

"That's what's up. Where you stayin' at?"
"Me and my boys got a villa on the Plantation."

"It must be about 30 of y'all if you on the Plantation," the girl in the back seat laughed. The Kingston Plantation was a resort that was known for being expensive.

"We don't roll like that, Sweetheart. It's just the three of us."

"Daaayum!" The driver interrupted. "Y'all doin' it like that?"

"We do alright."

"Where the rest of ya boys at?" The back seat passenger asked. I stood up and looked around to see if I could see Twist.

"Yo Twist!" I shouted. His tall ass popped up from between the cars. I motioned for him to come to where I was. I continued to talk to the girls as I waited for him to get there.

"Ladies, this is my man, Twist."
"Twist?" the back seat passenger laughed. "What kinda name is that?"
"I can't tell you," Twist began. "I have to show you…but we have to be laying down." She didn't say

anything to his reply. She just smiled as he got in the back seat with her. I noticed that traffic was starting to move again.

"Come on, Twist. Traffic startin to move." I turned my attention back to the front seat passenger. "Where y'all stayin at?"

"We at the Holiday Inn on the south end of the strip."

"My bad," I laughed. "Nah…I'm just playin." I reached into my pocket and pulled out one of my cards I had made. "Here's my pager number. Hit me up when you get a minute."

"Maybe…"

"I'll take that answer. It's that no thing that gets me." She laughed as she tucked my card between her breasts. We exchanged goodbyes and headed back to the car. An hour later, we finally hit Ocean Boulevard. That is what the tourists called it but to those of us that were from the Carolinas, we knew it as *The Strip*.

Traffic on the Strip was just as bad as the traffic going down. The only thing about being on the strip was that you couldn't get out and roam around in traffic. You got locked up for stuff like that. The only thing that was allowed was that you could get out of a car in traffic and go to the sidewalk and vice versa. Nick dropped the top right as we pulled onto the strip. Twist sat up on the back seat like we were in a parade as I got my lean on. We were bobbin' our heads to a mix tape that Twist put together. It took us another hour to get to the south end of the Strip. Just as we got in front of the Holiday Inn, I saw the girls that we were talking to in traffic walk out of the lobby and remembered that I did not get her name.

"Scoop me up when you come back," I told Nick as I got out of the car. "I forgot to get her name."

"Alright," Nick replied. I worked my way through traffic and approached the girl from Fayetteville.

"Excuse me," I called to her. She stopped and laughed. "What's so funny?"

"All I gave you was conversation and you stalkin' me already."

"Girl Stop," I laughed. "We saw y'all comin out the lobby and I realized I forgot to ask you ya name."

"You woulda found out when I hit you up."

"In a few hours this pager's gonna be puttin in overtime. A lot of pages might get ignored. A lot of people I won't remember when I call back if I call back. I just wanna make sure you don't get lost in the hype."

"So it's like that?"

"I'm just keepin' it real wit you. My girl broke up with me on graduation night so I'm ready to hang loose and have some fun."

"I feel you on that. Me and my dude broke up a couple weeks ago so I feel the same way."

"Maybe we can have some fun together."
"Depends on what kinda fun you talkin about…"
"Real fun…like we do it in the 'Nam."
"I'm wit dat."
"What's ya name?"
"Lena."
"Nice to meet you…I'm Dré."

"Where ya boy at?" The girl that was in the back seat asked.

"They rode down the strip. They'll be back though."
"Good."

I walked with the three girls down the street. Me and Lena engaged in some pretty good conversation as we strolled. By the time Nick came back up, we were standing in front of the Pavilion—a small amusement park and arcade on Ocean Blvd. Nick pulled to the side of the curb and blew the horn.

"Come on," he shouted. "We gotta go check in."

"Who is that?" The driver inquired.

"That's my boy Nick." I replied. "Y'all wanna roll?"

"Nah," Lena answered. "We're gonna chill for a minute then we'll probably go back to the hotel until tonight. We're in 527 if you make it back down that way."

"Just hit me on the hip when ya'll get ready to get out for the night and we'll meet you somewhere."

"That's what's up."

I hopped in the car just as a police officer was approaching to tell Nick to move along. Once we got off the strip we were good. Not too many people ventured toward North Myrtle Beach during that week.

We got to the Plantation around 3:30 and checked in. The villa was all that. It was in the middle of four other villas in a cul-de-sac. Twist had an aunt that lived at the beach. She had already been there and stocked the place with food for us. I did not realize how tired I was on the way down. I didn't get any sleep the night before and I was too hyped up to sleep on the ride down. Once we looked the place over and inspected all the amenities, we crashed until the sun went down. We knew it wasn't going to be much sleeping going on that week.

Around 8:30, my sleep was disturbed by the sound of my pager going off. When I looked at the number, it read: 8035550527-910. It took me a minute but I figured out who it was. The code 910 let me know that it was Lena because that was our area code in North Carolina. I wiped my face and picked up the phone. She picked up before the first ring stopped.

"May I speak to Lena?" I asked groggily.
"How did you know it was me?"
"Cuz I ain't gave nobody else from the 910 my pager number."
"You think you're smart," she laughed. "Did I wake you up?"

"It's cool. I needed to get up anyway."
"What y'all getting into tonight?"
"Nothin' planned as of yet. We'll prolly come down that way, park and hit the strip."

"My girls said that these guys from their school throwin' a party at the Wyndham."
"That's where ya'll goin?"
"That's the plan."
"Well check this out. Meet me in front of the Pavilion around 10:30."

"Why so late?"

"Cuz its three dudes that take just as long as females do to get dressed. Then we gotta make our way through traffic."

"Aight," she laughed. "See you then."

When we finally got dressed and got back to the Strip, it was almost ten o'clock. We parked a couple streets over on King's Hwy and walked to Ocean Blvd. As expected, it was live. People were everywhere. Teenagers ran in and out of hotels and up and down the streets. We were barely on the strip for five minutes when we saw the police with about four guys in handcuffs sitting on the side of the curb. Nick saw that and immediately handed me his keys. He knew he was going to be drinking and I was not. We did not want to have to call his mother to come get him out of jail.

In my mind, we had to be the three freshest brothers on the strip. Girls called down to us from the balconies of hotels, from cars on the street and some of everywhere else. I was on a mission to go and meet Lena. I hollered at a few girls, gave out a few cards but I kept it moving. It was just the first night but nobody had caught my eye the way that she did. Nick noticed that I wasn't lingering to long with any of the females that we met.

"Why are you in such a rush?" he asked. "You walkin' like them old white ladies in the mall."
"I told Lena I'd meet her at the Pavilion at 10:30."

Looking at his watch, "It's only ten after."
"I know."
"Don't get down here and fall in love on the first night."

"You are trippin'..."

"I'm trippin'? How soon we forget what happened when we went to DC last summer. You met ol' girl the first night we were there and left ya boy hangin the whole trip. To top it all off, you didn't even get the ass."

"If somebody woulda took one for the team I woulda got the ass but noooooo. You dissed her home girl and we got stuck wit'er."

"Are you serious? That chick looked like a damn sea monkey on crack."
"But her body was flawless."

"So you tellin' me you woulda hit that."
"Hell no! I don't do ugly chicks."
"And I do?"

"Tomekia Jackson."
"That's a low blow. We were fourteen and as I recall, I was takin' one for the team back then."

"And I appreciated it."
"As a matter of fact, you still owe me for that one."

"No I don't. I repaid my debt on that one."
"When?"
"Back in October when we went to Raleigh to visit your Pops."

"That girl wasn't ugly, she was just chunky."
"Soup is chunky. That girl was fat."
"But she was cute."
"Debt paid."

"Alright, we can go round and round all night. I'm just sayin'. You just got out of a two-year relationship. You will probably never see any of these girls ever again in life. Just enjoy yourself."

"I plan to…with Lena."

"You're hopeless. Where's Twist?" When we turned around to look for Twist, he was about ten feet behind us walking with his arm around two girls. "Yo man…lemme get one of them up off ya."

"Oh no my brother," Twist laughed. "You got to get your own."

We stopped and chopped it up with the two girls that Twist was walking with when Nick grabbed me and Twist and started to walk back in the direction we'd just come from.

"Where we goin?"

"Stop asking questions and don't look back. When I say cross the street, we cross the street. Cross the street." We darted across the street at the intersection of 8th Avenue North and Ocean Blvd. "Stop right here."

"Who are you running from?" I asked as I caught my breath.

"I'm not running from anybody. I just saved your life."

"What?"

"Tommy Girl at three o'clock." I looked directly across the street and sure enough, Tommy Girl was walking up the street with her cousin and best friend.

"She told me she wasn't coming. She was supposed to start school this week."

"Well she's here now and I refuse to let her lock you down for the week. Does she have a code?"

"A code?"
"Yes a code. A pager code."
"Nah."

"From here on out…when you give a chick your number, give her a code. When you get a page with no code, don't answer it."

"What about the girls I gave my number to earlier?"
"Spoils of war."
"War?"

"Yes. The war of me keepin' you from gettin' locked down this week. You can get at Tommy Girl when you get home. Not this week."

"I'm not hidin' from her. If she finds me she finds me."

"I'm not sayin' hide. Just don't be so visible."

"You stupid…I just wanted you to know that. I gotta get to the Pavilion."

"Then let's go cuz I know she got home girls."
"And they just as fine as she is."

"Then why are we still standing here?"

The three of us laughed and cracked jokes all the way down the strip. Lena and her girls were surrounded by six guys when we arrived. Her eyes lit up when she saw me. Either she was happy to see me or I was her way out from the guys.
"Hey baby!" she greeted as she hugged me and kissed me on my cheek. "Just play along. Please." That she said through her teeth. The other two girls followed suit and did the same to Twist and Nick.

"Y'all out here cheatin' on us already?" I laughed.
"Of course not, Boo. You know you're the only man for me."

"You fellas have a good evening." The guys mean mugged us as we walked off with the three ladies. "You know you owe me for that one, right?"

"I know. Thank you so much."
"Forgive me for being rude, this is my boy Nick and y'all met Twist earlier."

"Twist that's Shonda and the big headed girl with you, Nick, is my cousin Stacey."

"Why I gotta have a big head?" Stacey laughed.
"Because you do."

"Where the party at?" Nick inquired. "As a matter of fact, forget the party, where the drinks at?"

"Some of our friends from school throwin' a party at the Wyndham," one of the girls interjected.

"They got drinks?"
"And smoke."
"Well I know where I'm goin'," Twist chuckled.

"You down, Dré?"

"We can check it out for a minute."

"Where y'all from?" Nick asked.
"We're from Dillinger."

"Dillinger? Oh hell no. I'll just find my drinks somewhere else."
"You got somethin' against Dillinger?"

"Baby girl, I'm from Harts Vegas.
"Hargrove. Ewwwww! I touched a Red Fox."
"So how does it feel to have your arms on a real man?"

"What are y'all talkin' about?" Lena inquired.
"Hargrove and Dillinger are rivals in football," I explained.

"Girl please. I been to ya city and ain't no niggas this fine there. Besides, don't nobody care where y'all from. Its time to party like we do in Gotham City."

"Well Miss Gotham City, you better have Batman on speed dial just in case it gets ugly," Twist joked. By the time we got to the party, the police and hotel security had already broken it up.

"Now what?" Shonda exhaled in frustration.
"Don't even sweat it," Nick comforted. "We got drinks at the crib."

"And smoke," Twist added.

"And a Jacuzzi." I topped off.

"Count me in," Stacey approved. "How do we get there?"

"Since y'all gotta go back to ya hotel and get your car, meet us at the Citgo gas station on the corner of 8th Avenue North and King's Hwy in about 20 minutes."

"See you then." The three girls crossed the street and walked towards their hotel. Me and the fellas walked back to the north end of the strip to get the car. I had my eyes peeled for Tommy Girl as we moved in the direction of our destination. To keep from running in to her, I suggested that we cross over and walk up the street that ran parallel to Ocean Blvd. We made it to the car free and clear. When we got to the store, the girls hadn't got there yet. While we waited, I decided to go inside and pick of a few more contraceptives just in case. The trio pulled into the parking lot as I was walking out of the store. I hopped in the car and they followed us to our spot.

"Wow," Shonda said in awe. "This place is unbelievable. I know y'all parents put out some money for y'all to be up in here."

"We paid for this ourselves," I replied.

"You damn Skippy," Nick co-signed. "When we do it, we do it big."

"I see." After we gave the girls a tour of the spot, they kicked off their shoes and got comfortable. Nick served the drinks, Twist put on some music and commenced to rolling up some of his glaucoma medication, then we hit the Jacuzzi.

"I noticed y'all had on matching shirts earlier today," Lena began as she sipped her drink. "Y'all a group or something?"

"Yeah," I answered. "Triple Threat. We're the hottest rap group to come outta the low country."

"Rappin's cool but I love a man that can sing."
"Me too, girl," Stacey agreed. The three of us looked at each other then jumped into the three part harmony of Boyz II Men's, *Its So Hard to Say Goodbye to Yesterday*. Twist took the high note, Nick came with the middle and I brought in the bass. They were hypnotized by the way our voices blended together. I could hear the panties getting wet even with us already in the water. When we finished they gave us a standing ovation.

"I thought you said you were rappers?" Lena asked.
"That don't mean we can't sing. I was a singer before I was a rapper."

Super Senior

"I haven't heard you rap yet but I think y'all might need to stick to singing."

"We incorporate it all. You've probably never heard a hook sung in three part harmony on any rap song you've ever heard."

"Never." We continued to talk as Nick got up to fix another drink. When he came back, he had two cups in his hand. He handed one to me before he got back in the Jacuzzi.

"What is this?"
"Gin and Orange Juice."
"You know I don't drink."
"C'mon man. You can be a PK when you get back to the Ville."

"What's a PK?" Stacey asked.
"A preacher's kid." I explained.

"Just have a drink wit ya boy. We just graduated; we're at the beach and…"

"And in a hot tub with three fine ass hotties," Twist interrupted.

"Who wouldn't drink to that?"
"You know what," I began as I raised my cup. "I'll drink to that. To the class of 1994."

"To 1994!" They answered together.

The six of us had a good time. It was far better than being cramped up in a hotel room with a whole bunch of people.

As time moved on and the party favors started to escalate the mood, couples started to go their separate ways. Before long, Lena and I were by ourselves in the hot tub. Throughout the night, I noticed that she kept staring at me. It was as if she was trying to figure something out.

"Why you keep staring at me like that?" I asked as I sipped my drink.
"I don't know. I feel like I've seen you somewhere before."

"Fayetteville's not that big. I'm sure we've seen each other before in passing."

"It's nothing like that. I feel like I've seen you on stage before."

"I used to rap back in junior high."
"With a girl?"
"Yeah."
"Victoria?"
"You know Vickie?"
"Yeah, I know that bitch."
"Wow."

"She graduated from Smith this year."
"Why you don't like her?"
"She couldn't stay away from my ex who, at the time, was my boyfriend."

"Sounds like Vickie," I laughed. "But anyway, enough about her; I wanna talk about you."

"What do you wanna know?"
"Now that you've graduated, what's your next move?"

"I'm going to Johnson C. Smith in the fall."
"To major in?"
"Marketing. I've always dreamed of owning my own advertising agency like Angela from *Who's the Boss*."

"That's hot."
"What about you?"

"Football was supposed to take me to college but I got hurt and couldn't play my Senior year. I had good grades but not good enough for a full academic scholarship. Money's tight so I had to accept a partial scholarship to a Southern Baptist junior college in Greenville, South Carolina. The only reason they gave me the scholarship was because my Dad is a preacher. I had to take it or I wouldn't be going anywhere."

"That may not be where you want to go but at least you're going to school. Some people don't even make the effort. You'd be surprised at how many of our classmates are still going to be in the same cities after we've made it and come back to visit."

"That's true."
"Do you know what I love more than a man that can sing?"
"What's that?"
"A smart man."

Lena leaned towards me and pressed her soft lips to mine. She let out a soft moan as our tongues intertwined. She put her cup on the side of the Jacuzzi and put her arms around my neck. I put my arm around her waist that was submerged in the water and pulled her to me. When she was close enough for me to reach her with my other arm, I pulled her into my lap. She straddled me as we continued to kiss. We paused for a moment and gazed into each other's eyes.

"You are so pretty," I whispered as she smiled. "When I saw you earlier, I knew you couldn't be from down here. They don't make girls like you down here." Lena pressed her forehead against mine then gave me another peck on the lips.

"Let's go to your room."

I exited the hot tub then grabbed Lena's hand to help her out. She dried off then wrapped the towel around her body as I gathered the cups to throw them away. Once I tidied up a little bit. I led her upstairs to the master bedroom. When we got there, I gave her a t-shirt to put on. She went into the bathroom to change. While she was changing, I slid into a pair of basketball shorts and a tank top then waited for her in the bed. I opened the box of condoms and placed them in the drawer of the nightstand. I thought she was just going in to change but she took a shower. I dozed off waiting for her. I woke up when I felt her crawl into the bed.

"I'm sorry," she apologized. "I didn't mean to wake you."

"I didn't realize I dozed off." We got under the covers as Lena cuddled up next to me.

"Listen, Dré," she began placing her head on my chest. "I know things got heated in the Jacuzzi a little while ago but I don't want you to think I'm a hoe or nothin' like that."

"Why would I think that?"

"I don't know. It's just that I'm really feelin' you but I don't get down like that on the first night."

"To be honest, I didn't expect you to. I'm just glad we had a chance to chill and get to know each other."

"For real…?"

"Yes."

"So you're not mad that your boys might be gettin' some and you're not?"

"I'm a different breed of dude. Besides you are a North Carolina Queen and I hold my women from back home to a higher standard. Trust me. I'm cool." Lena lifted her head up and kissed me on my lips once again.

"You must be trying to make me fall in love with you."

"Loving me is not that bad."

Super Senior

3
Hurt Feelings

The next morning I woke to an empty bed but a room filled with the smells of those morning cuisines. I walked downstairs to find Lena and her girls putting it down in the kitchen while they danced to the music that was on the radio. I stood at the bottom of the steps and watched them work. Lena looked so at home in the kitchen. When she saw that I was there, she trotted over to me.

"Morning, Boo!" she greeted as she hugged me. She tried to kiss me but I pulled away.

"Not yet. I haven't washed my face or brushed my teeth."

"Boy, stop playin and gimme a kiss." I bent down and kissed her on the lips.

"Y'all really didn't have to do this."

"I know but we just wanted to thank you guys for a fun night."

"Well, you're welcome and thank you for breakfast."

"Now hurry up and get it together. The food'll be ready in about ten minutes."

"Okay."

"And wake your boys up."
"Yes ma'am."

I walked back upstairs in shock. I woke Twist and Nick then went into the bathroom to wash my face and brush my teeth. When I walked back down, everyone was sitting at the table waiting for me. I took my place at the table beside Lena. Twist tried to pick up his fork and start eating but Shonda made him put it back down.

"We have to say grace first," Shonda scolded.

"Will you say grace, Dré?" Lena asked. We all grabbed hands and bowed our heads as I blessed the food. Once it was over, we dug into a meal of bacon, eggs, pancakes, and home fries.

"I didn't know my aunt put all this food in here," Twist said as he paused from inhaling his food.
"She didn't," Stacey replied. "We went to the store."
"How much do we owe you?" I asked.
"Thirty…"

"Nothing," Lena interrupted. "It was our pleasure."

The six of us ate and engaged in small talk over a delicious meal. We looked like three couples the way we carried on. Once the meal was over the girls cleared the table and washed the dishes. They hung out for another hour then headed back to their hotel. I headed back upstairs to go back to sleep. Before I laid back down, I looked at my pager. I had seven missed pages from the same number. It had to be Tommy Girl. I put the pager back on the nightstand and drifted back off to sleep—full and content.

For a brother that just got out of a relationship three days prior, I felt no effects. It was almost like it never happened. I knew that once I was back home and away from all the scattered ass running around at the beach, it would finally set in. Until it did, I planned to enjoy every minute I spent at the beach. This was my last hoorah before I went off to college. I decided to take Nick's advice and enjoy myself. That didn't mean that I was out to try to conquer as much ass as I could but I was going to get it in. After I took my shower and put my shorts and socks on, I walked downstairs. Twist was rollin' up and Nick already had a cup in his hand.

"What up, fellas?" I greeted. "One day down, six more to go."

"I gotta tell you, Dré," Nick paused from his drink. "My hat goes off to you. You outdid yourself when you found that crew."

"Word up," Twist added. "Shonda is a straight up freak. I ain't get no sleep."

"Stacey tried to give me a run for my money but I held my own. She almost got me a couple times. How was Lena?"

"Amazing..." I chose the broadest word that I could find that didn't indicate whether I did or didn't have sex.

"That's what I'm talkin' bout, boyeee!" Nick turned to Twist. "That's why we N.F.L... Niggaz For Life."

"True indeed...So what's the plan for the day?"

"I told Stacey I'd take her to Broadway at the Beach then we hittin' up the outlets."

"Whooooa! Twist call 911 cuz this dude must be sick. You chillin' wit the same girl two days in a row?"

"Hey man...I get's my share of booty but you know my motto: Never give up sho' ass for mo' ass."
"Cuz then you wind up wit no ass," Twist added as he laughed.

"I'm diggin' Stacey. She's mad cool."
"What's the catch?"
"She goin to FMU."
"I knew it!"

"What can I say? I gotta keep one in the hip pocket."

"I don't blame you one bit, homeboy."

Around two o'clock, we met the girls and took them to Broadway at the beach. We started out playing miniature golf then we took them to lunch at the Hard Rock Café. After lunch we walked around for about an hour more then headed to the outlets. Once at the outlets, we agreed on a meeting place and time and then went our separate ways. Lena and I went in and out of stores laughing and talking like we'd known each other for years.

"I'm serious," I laughed. "People that go to Fayetteville State do not graduate…ever."

"It's not that bad."

"My cousin started at State when I started was in junior high in 89. It's '94 and he still ain't graduated."

"That's just yo cousin."

"That's everybody. Let's go in the Hilfiger store."

That was the worst mistake I could have made. We weren't in the store ten minutes before she walked in. I saw her before she saw me. For about ten seconds, I couldn't move. When I was finally able to, she saw me and walked right toward me.

"Hey Dré," she greeted.
"What's up, Chelsea."
"Oh, so I'm Chelsea now?"
"Chelsea this is Lena. Lena this is Chelsea."
"Nice to meet you," Lena replied.
"Uh huh. Can I talk to you for a minute, Dré?"
"Yeah. What's up?"
"Alone."

"Excuse me for a minute, Lena. I'll be right back." I followed Tommy Girl outside.

"I guess that's why you can't return my calls. I paged you 7 times last night."

"My pager was off."
"Now I see why."

"You told me you weren't coming down so how was I supposed to know that was you?"

"If you woulda took time to call me back you would've know that I was here. If somebody pages you more than once, that might mean they want to talk to you."

"Look…my bad. I shoulda called you back."

"I was tryna see you last night since I had to go back today."

"Why you goin' back already?"

"I told you. I start school tomorrow. My cousin and me rode down just so I could surprise you. I guess I was the one that got surprised."

"Don't act like that."

"Anyway. I gotta go. We might come back down this weekend. If you can get ya head outta her ass for a minute, I might wanna see you."

"Just hit me."
"I hit you last night." Tommy Girl turned to walk away.

"I can't at least get a hug?"

"If you woulda called me back last night you might've got more than that."

Tommy Girl walked off. As long as I'd known her, I was still never able to figure her out. When I walked in the store, Lena was at the register. She paid for her items then left.

"Was that your ex?" she asked."

Super Senior

"Nah...just a friend."

"Okay Biz Markie. The stress she had in her face made it look like she was more than just a friend. I explained me and Tommy Girl's relationship as we walked to the next store. I was really feeling Lena so I didn't want her to feel like I was lying to her or hiding anything. At 5:30 we met the rest of our crew at the Food Court. After we had ice cream, the six of us headed back to the Plantation to chill until the sun went down. That night was spent with the girls but after that we all decided that we would take a break from each other and do our own things. Over the next three days we ran wild on Myrtle Beach. It was nothing but girls, parties, and non-stop fun. I'd never had that much fun in my life.

That Friday night, the fellas and I decided to go our separate ways to scout out some prospects for the party we were planning for Saturday night. Since we didn't want it to be too outta control, it was exclusive and invite only. I was about 3 hotels down from the Holiday Inn when I got a 910-911 page. I didn't bother to try to find a phone; I went straight to her room since I was so close. I got there and Lena opened the door. It was dark. She wrapped her arms around me and broke down into tears.

"What's wrong?" She didn't answer. I held onto her as she cried like a baby in my arms for about twenty minutes until I was able to calm her down enough to sit down. When I turned on the lamp that was beside the bed, I saw that her hair was messed up and her clothes were mangled. "What happened?"

"Me and my girls were out on the strip when these three guys rolled up on motorcycles asking us if we wanted to ride. We jumped on the back like dummies. The dude I was with turned off the strip and headed up the highway towards where y'all at. I kept telling him to take me back but he kept ridin'. He didn't stop until we got to the Plantation. I told him again to take me back. He said that he had to change his shoes and that he would take me back after that. I tried to wait for him outside. After about 10 minutes another guy comes to the door telling me that his boy was on the phone and to come in the house. When I walked in, it was two more guys in there besides him and the other guy that came to the door. I sat down on the couch and they were just staring at me whispering to each other. The next thing I know, the guy that I came with came up behind me and grabbed me. I did everything I could to get away from him but he would not let me go. I finally kicked him in his nuts and ran in the bathroom."

"How'd you get out?"

"I climbed out the window and ran over to your place but you weren't there. I saw a white lady pull up at the spot next door. I walked over there and asked her if I could use her phone to call a cab. I guess she saw by the way I was acting that I was scared so she offered to take me where I needed to go. That's how I got back. The first thing I did was page you when I got here."

"They didn't hurt you, did they?"
"Nah…I'm alright. I'm just a lil' shook."

"You gotta be careful out there baby. These niggaz is crazy down here." I stood up from the bed and moved to the couch. Lena curled up in my lap like a frightened child as I put my arms around her and rocked her like my grandmother used to rock me when I got scared as kid. Twenty minutes later Stacey and Shonda walked in the room with the two other guys that were riding with. All the laughing ceased when they saw that Lena was crying.

"What's wrong, Cuz?" Stacey asked with concern as she walked over to the couch.

"I don't wanna talk about it?" she sniffled.
"Excuse me for a minute." Lena stood up so that I could get up. "Can I talk to y'all for a minute outside?" The two guys that looked to be in their early twenties followed me outside. "I don't have no beef wit y'all cuz I don't know you but I got a problem with whoever was on the bike that she was on."

"What you talkin' about, Dog?" The taller of the two guys inquired.

"Ya boy tried to rape my girl."

"What?"

"I'm serious and I gotta problem wit that?"

"To be honest with you, we don't really know that dude. He's friends wit one of our homies that came down wit us."

"If that's the case, then ya boy was probably there too. She said it was about four of'em."

"I'm sorry for what happened to ya girl. Like I said, we don't even know him like that. If we knew he was that type of dude we wouldn't even fuck wit'em."

"I'm stayin out at the Plantation too. If I see him, his shit is over."

"Trust me, Cuz. His shit is already over. We don't fuck wit cats like that. We'll handle it."

"I appreciate it."

"For real man…a thousand apologies to ya girl." I walked back in the room to check on Lena. She was lying across the bed when I got there.

"You need anything?" I asked as I sat down on the side of the bed.

"I'm okay. What did they say?"

"They said they would handle it for me."

"Yeah right…they're probably just goin back to clown his ass cuz I got away."

"I don't think so. The way they looked when I told'em what happened told me that they got just as pissed off as I did when you told me. They said they didn't even know him. He was the friend of a friend that came down with them." Lena sat up in the bed and positioned herself beside me.

"Whether they handle it or not, I shouldn't have jumped my ass on the back of that bike."

"We all make mistakes. Just be thankful nothing more than hurt feelings came out of it."

"You're right. Thank you for coming." Lena put her arms around me and kissed me on my cheek. "It really means a lot."

"I gotta look out for my people. You from the crib… You want me to go so you can get some rest?"

"I don't want to ruin your night but I'd rather you stay."

"I can hang out for a little while."

"Thank you." I kicked my shoes off and laid back on the bed.

Lena put her head on my chest. In a matter of moments, she was fast asleep. I'm glad she asked me to stay because I was having too many crazy thoughts running through my head. It gave me a chance to calm down. My pager went off with a number I didn't recognize but the 007 behind the number let me know it was Nick. I called him back and told him to come down to scoop me up. I went back to the bed, kissed Lena on her cheek and walked outta the room. When I got in the car I told Nick and Twist what happened. I tried to convince him to take me back to the Plantation but he wouldn't.

The next night, our spot was crazy. There were about thirty people there—twenty females and about ten dudes. We kept everybody in the house and music to a minimum to keep anybody from calling security or the police. Despite the previous night's events, Lena was there having a good time. Around midnight I stepped outside to get some air. Two guys pulled up in a red Honda Prelude. I didn't recognize them until they got out and started walking towards the spot. One of the guys had his arm in a sling and his hand was wrapped up.

"This where the party at?" The shorter of the two asked.

"What's up fellas? Come on in."

"I handled that little problem for you as you can see," The guy with his arm in the sling laughed.

"What happened?"

"Let's just say that homeboy won't be eatin' no solid foods for awhile."

"True indeed…Go on in. Drinks are in the kitchen and it's plenty females to go around."

"Thanks, Dog."

"I didn't catch ya names. I'm Dré."

"I'm Gary and this is my boy, Irv." Irv walked in the house as Gary paused for a minute. "The same thing happened to my sister a couple years back at Bike Week. She wasn't so lucky though."

"Sorry to hear that."

"It's a fucked up situation cuz dude got away and I didn't get a chance to put my hands on him. Ol' boy caught it for both of'em." I followed Gary back into the house and introduced him to Nick and Twist.

After they got some drinks, we all sat at the table to bust some Spades. There were so many women there that Nick and Twist didn't mind that Gary and Irv were there to see Shonda and Stacey. The night turned out to be a good night. Everybody had a good time, there was no trouble, and by the end of the night, everybody had somebody.

When it was all said and done, that night Lena and I finished what we started in the Jacuzzi the first night we met. It was just as amazing as I thought it would be. We spent all day that Sunday together. I hated that when the week was over; Lena was going back to the Ville. Fayetteville was only two hours away though. Once I got to school in August, Charlotte would be just as close. I guess I had to make a few road trips to see Lena at school.

Tommy Girl never made it back like she said. When I got home, it took some major apologizing but she forgave. She told me that she was so caught up with the fact that both of us were single at the same time again; she got jealous when she saw me with Lena even though she and I weren't together. She and I spent the summer together. I noticed as the second week in August rolled around, she started putting space in between us because she knew that I would be leaving soon. She tried not to show it but Tommy Girl fell hard for me that summer. She would've been a good girl for me but the timing wasn't right. I didn't want us to get too heavily involved right before it was time for me to go.

4
Hell on a Hill

The summer was over and I had enjoyed it. On a Monday morning in mid-August, my grandparents and I pulled onto the campus of New Grove College in Tigerville, SC. Tigerville was a small town on the outskirts of the city of Greenville. The campus was quite small. At first sight I saw that there were two main buildings besides the administration building, the library, and the gym. When the campus ambassadors took us on the grand tour of the campus, I found that the only building that I missed was the Student Center which I later learned was where I would be doing my work-study. Across from the student center and down the hill a piece was the girl's dorms. On the other side of the campus which was only a very short walk were the boy's dorms.

There was one main dorm, Brice Hall. To the right of Brice were about 7 smaller two-story buildings. These buildings were called the Units. Most of the freshmen lived in Brice Hall. That is where I would be calling home for the next year. Brice had three floors. On each floor were five main doors. Once you went through those doors, there were four rooms—two on each side joined by a bathroom. My room was on the far end, on the first floor. My grandfather helped me get the things that were in their car into my room.

"Well baby," my grandmother exhaled. "This is it."

The look on her face was that of a mother tying to hold back tears because her baby had finally left the nest.

"Please don't cry, Mom. You know if you start cryin' then I'ma start cryin'."

"I'm not gonna cry." As soon as she said that, tears rolled down her cheeks. "You just don't know how proud we are of you, Dré."

"Thanks, Mom." I put my arms around her and gave her a big hug. "I love you."

"Alright," my grandfather began. "You be safe and take care of yaself. Don't let these Baptist folk get tuh'ya. You know the truth."

"I won't."

"You got some money?"

"Yes sir." He reached into his shirt pocket and handed me a small, brown envelope.

"All year I been telling people my son was gradjatin and goin' off to college. These are gifts from those people. I know you gone get you a job but this should hold you 'til you do. Don't go spend it all up in one place. You gotta have gas money and stuff."

"Thank you, Dad." I hugged him.

Super Senior

"We gotta get up da roid. Call us when you get settled in."

"I will." My grandmother hugged me again then they walked to the car. I watched as the drove off. I couldn't believe it. I had made it to college. I walked up the small hill to my car to get the rest of my things to take into the room. My roommate hadn't arrived yet so I got the chance to pick what side of the room I wanted. From the outside, it didn't look like the rooms would be that big but they were.

When you first walked in, there was a bed against the same wall the door was on. On the adjacent wall with the window was the other bed. The beds were attached to the wall so that you couldn't move them. On the wall in front of the door were closets built into the wall on each end. Under the closet were three drawers. In between the two closet spaces were our desks. They were also built in to the wall. In the middle were six smaller drawers—three beside each desk. On the left when you walked in was the door that led to the bathroom. We had a sink and a mirror inside the room and we shared the toilet and shower with our suitemates.

I finished settling in around noon. I had the stereo, the TV and the Sega Genesis hooked up, my clothes were put away and my bed was made. I started getting hungry so I walked up to the cafeteria. When I got my food and sat down by myself, I noticed that I was the only black person there at the time. While I was eating a tall, blonde girl and a short white guy walked up to my table. They were chipper as ever.

"Hi!" The girl greeted as she handed me a pamphlet. "My name is Holly Holloman."

"And I'm Chad Wellington. What's your name?"

"I'm Dré."

"Well nice to meet you Dré," Holly responded with her deep southern accent. "I'm the president of the Baptist Student Union and we'd like to invite you to our first meeting of the year this Thursday night. When you get a chance just look over this pamphlet and it'll tell you all about us."

"Okay."

"Okay then! We'll let you get back to your lunch. Hope to see you Thursday. God bless you."
"God bless you, too." I continued eating as I skimmed through the pamphlet. As I read, somebody else came up to my table.

"Mind if I sit down?" a voice asked. I looked up into the prettiest brown eyes. This being was around 5'1", with a smooth brown complexion. Her long, black hair was pulled into a ponytail and through the back of a khaki hat that displayed the school's letters on them. She had the build of a cheerleader—small frame with a small but perky chest.

"No, not at all."

I noticed that the red shirt she wore also had the school letters on the left side over her heart.

"Thanks."

"You must really love this school," I laughed.

"Why you say that?"

"Cuz you got on a hat and a shirt with the school letters on them."

"Oh," she giggled. "I'm a campus ambassador."

"Oh okay. How long you been here?"

"Last year was my first year."
"That's what's up. I'm Dré." I extended my hand.

"I'm…"
"Beautiful? Yes."

"Thank you," she blushed. "I was going to say Zoë."

"It's a pleasure to meet you." We sat and chit chatted as we ate. Zoë had the cutest little voice with a slight rasp to it. She also had a beautiful smile and an adorable laugh.

"So, where are you from?"

"Before I answer that, can I ask you a very important question?"

"What is it?"

"Are there going to be more black people here than just us?"

"Wow," she laughed. "Yes, but not too many more. Most of the freshmen will be here by tonight and early tomorrow. The upperclassmen will start coming in tomorrow as well."

"Whew! I was nervous. I'm used to being around a lot of white people but this is ridiculous."

"You so crazy. Now answer my question."

"I'm from North Carolina originally but I spent my last two years in high school at Hargrove High."

"Oh okay. I was looking at some of the student profiles and noticed that there were students coming from

Florence and one from Darlington. I didn't see your profile."

"You're familiar with the area?"

"Yes I am. I have family in Lake City."
"Where you from?"

"I'm from Charleston."

"No you're not."

"Why does everybody keep saying that? Yes I am."

"You're not Geechie."

"I went to Bishop England."

"That explains it."

"That is not funny."

While we were talking a tall, black guy came and sat down beside Zoë. "Hey baby."
"What's up?"

"Baby, this is Dré. Dré, this is my boyfriend, Fly. He's on the basketball team."

"I ain't never seen you around here. You must be a fresh fish."

"A fresh fish?" I asked with confusion in my voice and disapproving look on my face.

"Yeah. That's what we call freshmen 'round here."

"It's all in fun," Zoë added.

"So Fish, where you from?"

"He's from North Carolina but..."

"I was talking to him," Fly snapped.

"Like she was saying, I'm from North Kak but I graduated from Hargrove High."

"Then you from South Carolina."

"I spent two years there. I'm a North Carolinian to the heart. What about you?"

"I'm from the Metro?"
"I wasn't aware that there were any Metropolitan cities in South Carolina."

"The Metro is what they call Columbia," Zoë explained.

"He was talking to me," Fly scowled. I was starting to get annoyed by the way he was talking to her.

"You don't have to let him talk to you like that."

"How I talk to my girl is not your concern, Fish."

"You know what? I gotta bounce. I got something to do. It was nice to meet you, Zoë. I'll see you around."

I could tell that there was potential to be some problems between me and Fly. For my own sake, it was best that he and I just steered clear from each other.

Needless to say, I was heated as I walked back to my dorm room. I never understood why women continued to deal with guys that treated them like they were less than queens—especially a girl like Zoë. As I approached Brice Hall, more people were moving in. I started seeing a few more black faces. When I got to the door of my room, I heard voices inside. I opened it to find a short, dark skinned guy with a low fade, talking to his parents. We all exchanged pleasantries as they readied themselves to go.

"Okay, Sweetie," the woman began. "We're getting ready to go."

"Okay, Mom. I love you." My roommate hugged his parents and walked them to the car. Fifteen minutes passed before he came back in the room.

"What's up, Man?" I greeted as he came back in. "I'm Dré."

"I'm Kevin. Where you from?"

"I'm from North Carolina but I graduated from Hargrove."

"Oh okay. I'm from Union."

"Union," I paused. "Why does that sound familiar?"

"I'm from the same place as the crazy white lady that drowned her kids and said that a brother kidnapped them."

"That's right. She put ya'll on the map."

"I know, right," he laughed. "Is it just me or are there not a lot of black people here."

"It's not just you. From what I heard, it's not going to be too many more than what you've probably seen so far."

"Anybody next door?"

"I hadn't seen or heard nobody since I've been here."

Super Senior

Kevin and I continued to talk and get acquainted as he put his things away and got settled in while I sat on my bed looking through the rules. I opened the window and turned on the stereo to see if I could attract more of our kind. The only thing I managed to attract was a security officer telling me to turn my music down.

"Dog…did you know that we can't where hats in the building?"

"Are you serious?"

"No loud music, no smoking on campus and there's an eleven o'clock curfew on weekdays."

"What about weekends?"
"One o'clock."

"They don't' tell you this type of shit when you come to visit."

"They know they wouldn't have no students here if they did. They wait 'til they got ya money then spring this shit on you."
"Peep what I heard though…no co-ed visitation. Girls can't even be over the curb on the grass in front of the dorm. They'll get kicked out."

"What! Hell nah! I coulda stayed at the crib for that."

"Don't trip though. There's a hotel right down the hill called the Cricket Inn. They give us a nice discount."

"That's what's up."

"I'm ready to find the clubs. My cousin told me about a few spots in the area. He said there's a club over by the mall that does College Night on Wednesdays. I think he said the name of it was Images. Then there's another spot called the Foxhole downtown."

"Did he say what the crowds were like?"

"Knowing him, they're probably mixed crowds. He's one of those brothers that like white girls so those are his kinda spots."

"Ain't nuttin' wrong wit a white girl every now and then..."

"I don't discriminate either. I know where the spots are. I just gotta find somebody wit a car."

"That's all taken care of. I got Da Bean parked outside. We good..."

After Kevin got all his stuff put away, we played some video games then walked toward the student center hoping to get a glimpse of some honeys. All we saw were white girls until we got inside the student center. Standing at the counter looking at the menu were two black girls. They were about the same height with different complexions and builds. One was light-skinned and thick in all the right places and the other was a milk chocolate with a slim frame.

Leaning over to my roommate, "Which one you want?"

"It don't matter to me. I'll take Slim Goodie."
"Good cuz I like'em light and thick."

The ladies ordered their food and sat down at a table. After we ordered, we approached their table. "Excuse me, ladies. My name is Dré and this is my roommate, Kevin. Due to the fact that it's two of you and two of us, we were wondering if we could join you." The girls laughed.

"What did he just say?" the darker of the two asked as she continued to laugh.

"He said do you mind if we sit down?" Kevin clarified.

"Why didn't he just say that?"

"Because anything else would be uncivilized," I replied. We joined the ladies.

"You can't be from anywhere in South Carolina talkin' like that." Thick and light skinned remarked.

"I'm originally from up North but I spent my last two years of high school in Hargrove."

"For real? I'm from Florence. I graduated from South Side."

"True indeed… What's ya name?"
"Tiffany but all my friends call me Red."
"Can I call you Sexy Red?"
"I like that even better," she smiled. When she smiled I noticed two of the cutest dimples and a small gap between her two front teeth.

"What about you, Dark and Lovely," Kevin inquired. "Where you from?"
"I'm from Marion…and my name is Taneika."
"Where's that?"
"It's not too far from Florence."
"I'm from Union."
"Union? Ain't that the same place the white lady drowned her kids and said that a black man kidnapped'em?"
"Yeah."
"I bet you have to answer that question every time you meet somebody," I chuckled.

"You have no idea."

"What made y'all come here?" I asked the girls.

"We play softball." Red replied.
"Oh okay. That's what's up."
"What about ya'll?"

"My chorus teacher went here and she told me about it. Next thing I know, they were willing to throw a little bit of money my way so I'm here."

When the food was ready, we continued to talk as we ate. We shared stories from our senior years and found that we knew a few of the same people. Time slipped away and before we knew it, we had sat there for three hours. I was really diggin' Sexy Red but it was too early for me to make any type of move or show interest. I wanted to see what else NGC had to offer in the female department. After being put out because the restaurant part of the student center was closing, we walked the girls to their dorm. Once we bid them goodnight, Kevin and I returned to our side of campus. We played a few more games of football then called it an early night because we'd both been up since the crack of dawn.

The next day, despite the fact that I'd already had my schedule, me and my roommate went to the gym to check out open registration after we hit the cafeteria. From first sight, the gymnasium looked like a huge bowl of rice with very few specks of pepper mixed in. At first we sat in the bleachers just to survey the room. We greeted our people as they approached or walked by. While we were in the gym, we met our neighbors from across the hall. La'vell Hunt and Reese Fordham were from Myrtle Beach. They were recruited by NGC to play baseball. La'vell was the taller of the two by about four inches. They were about the same complexion with the same athletic builds. Just by conversation, I could tell that they grew up around a lot of white people by the way they talked and the things they said. Further along in the conversation I learned that they loved gray girls—white girls that dated black guys.

They told us they would catch up with us later and headed for the exit. As I surveyed the scene a little closer, all I saw was a few corny-looking black guys and a few scallywags. So far, Zoë and Red were the best looking females I'd come in contact with but it was still early in the week. Classes hadn't started yet. Even though Tommy Girl and I got pretty close that summer, she was the furthest thing from my mind. After meeting girls like Zoë and Red, I realized that my grandmother was right. The break up between me and Jocelyn was the best thing that could have happed to me. There was no way that I would be able to maintain a relationship with her and still remain faithful.

Later that night, I bumped into Red in the TV lounge that was downstairs in the student center. She was watching some show I didn't recognize. She was stretched out on the couch wrapped up in a blanket.

"You look comfortable," I said as I walked over to the couch.

"I am," she replied without taking her eyes away from the television.

"What are you watching?"

"The Young and the Restless." Red finally looked away from the television and up at me. "Hey Dré...I didn't realize that was you. You wanna sit down?" Red moved her legs for me to sit down on the couch. As soon as I did, she stretched them out across my lap.

"Excuse me, Ma'am?" I laughed. "Do I look like an ottoman?"

"Shhh!" I didn't say anything else. I knew how women were about their shows. I sat quietly and watched it with her. To my surprise, the show was actually pretty good. Forty-five minutes later, the show ended and the conversation began. "What you been up to all day?"

"Me and Kev went to open registration for awhile. After that I talked to my grandmother. So pretty much nothin'. What about you?"

"Me and Tanieka worked out this morning then we hit a few balls. After we ate, I went to the room and chilled out. I was there until I came in here."

"Why didn't you watch it in your room?"

"Tanika brought the TV. Her brother dropped it while they were moving in. I won't be able to go home and get mine until Fall Break in October."

"You should see if Tanieka can convince Kev to let her get his TV. We don't use his cuz mine is bigger."

"She been talkin' 'bout that boy since last night."
"He's been talkin' about her, too."

"She was on the phone with him when I left to come down here."
"So that's who he was talkin to. I figured it was a girl cuz he was in straight Mack Daddy mode."

"You goin' out tomorrow night?"
"Goin' out where?"

"Some of our teammates told us about this club behind the mall that does College Night on Wednesday."

"Images. Kev was tellin me about it yesterday. You goin'?"
"We might. If we can find a ride."
"Don't worry about the ride. If you wanna go just let me know."

"You got a car?"

"I wouldn't be tellin' you not to worry about a ride if I didn't."

"What kind?"

"Don't worry about all that. It gets me from point A to point B."

"My bad," she laughed. "My teammates said they were leaving around 9:30. We can follow them."

"True indeed..." We talked for a little while longer then I walked her to her dorm. "You got a boyfriend back home?"

"If that's what you wanna call it."
"What's that supposed to mean?"

"Before I left, he suggested that instead of breaking up that we should do our own thing while we're apart."

"And you went for that?"

"Me him been together since freshmen year. I guess I'm just used to him being in my life."
"I can understand that but if a man is not willing to maintain while you're apart and let you be the only woman in his life, then maybe its time to get used to being with someone else."

"Wow...I never thought about it like that."

"My girl did me a favor. She broke up with me graduation night. Now I don't have to worry about whether or not I could stay faithful to a girl back home."

"If she hadn't broken up with you, would you have stayed faithful?"

"I would have for as long as I could. If I felt that it wasn't working out with us being apart, I would have done the right thing by letting her go instead of having her believe that she's the only one in my life and I'm up here with somebody else."

Red stopped under a streetlight.

"Either you're too good to be true or you're runnin' hellah game on me."

"I don't consider it game. I just know what women want."

"What do women want?"

"Most women want a man just like them but is still a man at the same time."

"What does that mean?"

"They want a man that they can talk to like they talk to their girlfriends; someone that listens and'll talk back. In the same breath they want him to also be that provider, protector and lover."

"Is that so?"
"It's a fact."
"How do you know?"
"My grandmother told me so," I laughed.
"Your grandmother's a smart woman."
"She's been right so far."

Once we got to her dorm, Red wrapped her arms around me and hugged me. As she held onto me, she pulled her head back and looked into my eyes.

"Will I see you tomorrow?"
"Only if you want to be seen..."

"You are somethin' else, André Marshall."
"We just met. The best has yet to come."

5
In Da Club

The Chronic blared from my speakers as I readied myself for the night's events. Kev was hogging the bathroom so I decided to go ahead and iron my clothes. Some clubs were crazy about dress codes so I chose a casual ensemble to be on the safe side. As I was putting a razor sharp crease in my khaki's the phone rang.

"Hello?" I answered as I put the phone to my ear and held it with my shoulder.
"May I speak to Dré?"
"This is he."
"Hey, this is Red. Did I catch you at a bad time?"
"I was just ironing my clothes. What's up?"
"Nothing. I know I hadn't seen or talked to you all day. I was calling to see if your offer for a ride was still good."

"Of course it is. I'll be leaving in about an hour and a half."

"You got room for one more?
"Yeah. I got room for one more. Who is it?"

"It's my suitemate. She was supposed to ride with her roommate but her roommate changed her mind so now she's not goin'."

"That's cool. Tell'er she can ride."

"Thanks," Red paused for a minute. "I shouldn't be tellin' you this but I been thinkin 'bout you since last night. You really got me wondering about you."

"Wondering what about me?"
"Whether you're all talk or not."
"Don't wonder about it. Find out for yourself."

"It's all you, Dog," Kev said as he exited the bathroom with a towel wrapped around the lower half of his body. "My bad...I didn't know you were on the phone."
"It's all good."
"Who dat?" he whispered.
"Hold on a sec, Red." I put my hand over the bottom half of the receiver, "Its Red."

"Her and her girl ridin wit us?"
"Yeah."
"Cool."
"Alright...I'm back."
"I'm not gonna hold you cause I know you're gettin' ready. Where you want us to meet you?"

"I'll call you right before I walk out the door and y'all can just meet me outside your dorm."
"Okay, Baby. See you in a little while."
"Baby?"
"You got a problem with that?"

"You can call me whatever you want to call me…as long as you call me."

"You so silly," she laughed. "Bye."

Around 9:30, we picked up the girls and were off to Images. The parking lot was filling up fast. Being from a smaller city, we didn't have a club like Images. All we had were small clubs and holes in the wall. Images was huge. When you first walked in, you had to go through a turnstile then you were patted down by a bouncer that looked like Larry Blackmon from Cameo. The next step was to the counter to pay and get your hand stamped if you were under twenty-one or receive a wristband if you were over. After you paid, you were then able to walk through two large doors that led inside the club.

By the time we got in, it was around 10:30. We all stood in amazement at how plush Images was on the inside. We were all from small cities so none of us had ever been in a club like this before. To the right as you walk in, there was a bar surrounded by people ordering beers, shots and mixed drinks. To the right of the bar was a section that had couches against the walls. Directly in front of us was the large, hardwood dance floor placed in front of a stage where the DJ was set up. It was still early so there weren't that many people on it yet. I glanced up and noticed that there was a second floor that overlooked the main floor of the club. Up there were tables, couches and small bar. Colored lights danced around the club as the DJ was starting to get the club jumping. The five of us walked around the club until we found a table. Once we found a good spot, we sat down.

"Yo!" Kevin shouted over the music. "This place is live as hell!"

"True indeed…!" I shouted in response. The girls spotted their teammates and informed us that they would catch up with us later.

I'd never seen so much diversity in a club besides Union Station back home in Fayetteville. There were all kinds of people from white to black, Hispanic to Asian. We sat and shot the breeze as the club's vibe continued to escalate. Once it was just Kev and I, we began to check out the scene. About twenty minutes after we got there, La'vell and Reese fell in the groove with two snow bunnies.

"There go ya boys," I pointed out to Kev as I laughed.

"These cats don't waste no time!" They spotted us, came, and sat down.

"What up, fellas?" La'vell greeted in his best portrayal of a black person. "This is Bethany and Katie. We went to school together. They go to Furman." Before long, the DJ dropped *Back and Forth* by Aaliyah and the dance floor started to fill up. Another thing I wasn't used to seeing coming from a small city in the south was a lot of interracial dating and interacting. It was different in Fayetteville because of the two military bases. There were people from everywhere. When I got to South Carolina, it went from being diverse to somewhat segregated. Of course the schools were integrated but after the bell rang in the afternoon. We all went back to being separated.

Before long, Red and Taneika came and got Kev and I and led us to the dance floor. The club went to another level when the first note of Bell Biv DeVoe's, Poison blasted out of the speakers. I tried to hold in my laughter watching Kevin dance with Tanekia because she was a lot taller than he was. Her ass was damn near to his chest. Me and Red were almost the same height. She was a tad shorter than I was. It was a magical experience to dance with Red. She had the softest ass I'd felt to that point in my life and she kept backin' it up on me. At that age, we could dance for hours without stopping. After a good forty-five minutes of non-stop hit after hit, the DJ decided to slow it down.

Tanekia and Kevin left Red and me on the dance floor. She turned around to face me. The lights danced in her eyes before the dance floor got dark and the disco ball started to spin. Red smiled as she wrapped her arms around my neck and pressed her body against mine. The halter top she wore that night allowed me to feel her soft, yet damp, skin as I locked my fingers in place and rested them on the small of her back right above her back side. *I'm Ready* by Tevin Campbell controlled our bodies. Chest to chest and pelvis to pelvis, Red and I danced. She sent chills down my back as she lightly raked her fingernails on the back of my neck.

"You better stop," I laughed. "I'm not responsible for my actions if you keep doin' that."

"That must be your spot."
"One of 'em."
"Where another one?" I pressed a semi-erect friend against hers.

"You so nasty," she laughed. Every girl had a song that made her loose her mind. When that song came on, it brought something out of her that only that song could bring out. For Red, that song was *Stroke You Up* by Changing Faces. After Tevin Campbell went off and that song came on, Red repositioned herself with her back to me and her ass right on my manhood. She took my hands and placed them on her hips and held on to them as she grinded all over me. The move that drove me crazy was when she slide her ass all the way down my legs then slowly slid it back up until she was where she started. I can't front, that made me hard as hell. When she felt it, she looked back at me with a sly grin on her face and continued to dance. La'vell and the girl he was with were close by.

"You need a condom!" he laughed.

"I might!" At the close of the song, Red wrapped my arms around her waist and led me to a table. When I sat down, she sat in my lap.

"You cool?" she asked.

"I'm good…I think. And you called me nasty."

"That wasn't nasty."

"Then what was it?"

"I was expressing myself through dance." She laughed as she hugged me. As she did, she must've seen something. "Come on."

Red grabbed me by my hand and led me upstairs to the second level. We found a spot in a secluded corner and she sat me down on a couch. She straddled my lap then pressed her lips to mine. Our tongues got acquainted with each other as we engaged in one of the best things that the French could have given us. In mid-kiss, I heard a commotion coming from the first floor. We paused to see what was going on. I looked over the rail to see my roommate involved in a scuffle.

"Oh Shit! It's Kev. Come on!" I rushed down the stairs to aide my roommate but by the time I got there, security already had him hymned up. We followed them through the doors and outside the club. Something must've really pissed him off because Kevin didn't strike me as the fighting type.

"Calm down!" the bouncer commanded.

"I'm cool, man. Let me go."

"This is a warning. We do not allow fighting in the club. The next time, you won't be able to come back."

"I told you, I'm cool." The bouncer walked back in the club.

"What happened?" I asked.

"This dude kept grabbin' all on Tanekia while they were dancin'. She kept telling him to stop but he wouldn't. That's when I walked on the dance floor and told him to chill out. Then he pushed me."

"Where's my girl?" Red inquired.
"She gotta still be in the club."

"Go get her and your other girl so we can ride out." I told Red. She walked back in the club to round up her crew. "You good?"

"Yeah, I'm straight."

"I'm tryna figure out why they didn't make the other dude leave."

"Prolly cuz he was a white boy." By the time I got Kev calmed down, Red and the other two girls came out of the club.

"What in the hell was that all about?" Tanieka yelled as she approached.

"Dude wouldn't stop grabbin' on you even after you kept tellin' him to stop."

"I can handle myself. I don't need you to fight my battles for me. You're not my man."

"Calm down, Tanekia," Red pleaded. "I'm sure Kevin didn't mean no harm. He was just tryna look out for you."

"Exactly!" Kevin co-signed.

"Did you not hear what I just said? I don't need you or anybody else to fight my battles for me."

"Take her to the car, Red. Please." I handed Red my keys.

"Okay. Come on, girl." The three girls walked toward the car as I sat down on a bench that was in front of the club.

"I didn't mean to fuck ya night up, Homie."
"It's all good."
"We cool?"
"Yeah. We cool. Truth be told, I woulda prolly did the same thing."

"I can't figure out why she trippin' like that. Since we been talkin' on the phone she been actin' like its all about me. We get out here and she flipped the script."

"That's something you'll never be able to figure out."

I sat for about ten minutes to give Red a chance to calm Tanekia down then we walked towards the car. When we got about 30 feet from the car, we saw the same white boy Kevin had just got into it with at my car talking to Tanekia. When they saw us coming, they walked away, she got into a car with him, and another guy then drove off.

Kevin didn't say anything the entire ride back to campus. For the most part, nobody really said anything. Once we got to campus, I dropped Kevin off in front of the dorm then rode to take Red and her friend to their dorm. When we got there, Red's friend thanked me for the ride then got out. Red told her that she didn't have to wait for her because she wanted to talk to me for a minute. I waited until she was inside her dorm then pulled off. There was limited parking by my dorm so after a certain time, the only parking spaces that were open were behind the student center. I backed into a parking spot and turned the car off.

"Wow," I exhaled. "What a night."
"I know right," Red agreed. "I don't know what got into Tanekia tonight."

"Did you know her before you came?"

"Nope... We met this summer when we came to visit the campus. She seemed like cool people, that' why I suggested that we be roommates. I can't believe she left with that guy like that."

"There's only so much you can learn about a person in a couple days."

"I guess you're right. I hope she's okay."
"She'll be alright. Don't worry too much about it."
"I just hate that it interrupted what we were gettin' into."

"And exactly what was that?"

"Lemme refresh your memory." Red leaned over and laid those soft lips on mine once again. I enjoyed the taste of sour apple that was on her tongue from the gum she was chewing. Just as we were getting into it, a light flashed in my car and a tap came at the window. It was campus security. He motioned for me to let the window down.

"Okay you two," he began as he shined the light on us. "It's after curfew. You need to be in your rooms."

"Yes sir," we answered simultaneously.
"Can I walk her to her to her dorm?"

"Walk her to her dorm then get to yours. If I come back through and see you still out, I'll have to give you a citation." The security officer watched as we exited the car and walked towards her dorm.

"I had a good time tonight," Red began. "Even if it was cut short…"

"How about I make it up to you this weekend?"
"What you got in mind?"

"I don't quite know yet but I'll have it figured out by then."

"Okay," she laughed. "I'll see you at breakfast." I watched as Red walked into her dorm. I smiled as I walked back to mine. I thought Kevin would be in either the bed or the shower by the time I got there. Instead he was coming out of the door as I was coming down the hill.

"I need you to take me somewhere or let me borrow you car," he said with stress in his voice.

"What's up? What's wrong?"
"I need to go get Tanekia."
"What?"
"The guy she left with put her out at a store by the club."

"You gotta be kidding me. Did she say which one?"
"She's at the Exxon right off the exit."

"Damn it! Hold on." I ran in the room to call Red to tell her what the deal was. By the time I was walking in the room, the phone was ringing. It was Red. I told her that I already knew what was going on and to meet me at my car. I went back outside and we ran to my car. Red was already there when we got there. The three of us jumped in and headed back toward the city.

Tanekia was standing inside the store talking to the lady behind the counter when we pulled up. Kevin got out and walked toward the door. When she saw him she rushed out and wrapped her arms around him. They stood locked in that hug for about five minutes. I could see her saying something but I could not make out what it was. She finally let him go and they got in the car.

"Thank you so much, Dré. You don't know how much I appreciate this."

"You okay?"
"I'm cool. Sorry about the way I acted tonight."

"We good..." We all silently agreed that there was no need to bring up the night's past events. Instead, I turned up the music and we rode back to campus.

Classes started the next day. I felt like I was back in elementary school again because just like the 80's, I was one of maybe two or three black students in my classes. I did not have any classes with my friends except for Chapel but that was something that everybody had to attend. There

Super Senior

was no way for me to sit near any of my friends because we were all seated by alphabetical order. I only had two classes that day so my day was over at half past noon. Because of the previous night's event's I went straight to my room after lunch and took a nap until it was time for dinner. When I woke up and ate dinner, the rest of the night was spent playing video games with the fellas.

6
Simply Red

Friday came and ended my first week as a college student. I only had two days of class but it felt like a full week. I tried to hook up with Red after lunch but she had to work out with the softball team. I figured she'd be tired afterwards so I decided to let her call me if she wanted to chill. Even though we'd just arrived that week, NGC became a ghost town by the afternoon. The dorms were empty with the exception of the people that didn't have cars, the ones that lived too far away and the football team.

After I ate lunch, I hopped in the car and rode into the nearby town of Traveler's Rest. That was the closet city to us that had restaurants and grocery stores without having to venture into the city of Greenville. You could tell it was a small town because it didn't even have a Wal-Mart yet. The only stores they had were Ingles, which was a grocery store, Burger King, KFC and McDonalds. I stopped into Burger King to put in an application and got hired on the spot because of my experience and reliable transportation. My area of experience was as a cook but they hired me to be a cashier. The manager wanted me to start that Saturday but I told her I had a prior engagement so we agreed on Monday afternoon. The job was cool because of the hours. They closed at ten Sunday through Thursday. Friday and Saturday they closed at eleven.

After all of my paperwork was completed and she gave me my uniform, I went across the street to a plaza to get some black socks from Family Dollar. While in that plaza, I spied a Mom and Pop seafood restaurant sitting in the middle of the plaza. I walked in to check it out and to look at the menu. If Red was the country girl like I thought she was, she'd love it.

That Friday evening, the cafeteria made the campus seem like there were more black students than there really were because we seemed to be the only ones left. I shot the breeze with my roommate and my neighbors as we ate. After dinner, we all went back to my room to do what college guys did—play video games. I was in the middle of a close football game with Reese when the argument began.

"La'vell," Kevin began as he lowered the magazine he was reading. "I was just thinkin' about somethin. You and Reese were sitting at the table right beside me when I walked on the dance floor to confront old dude Wednesday night."

"Yeah…"

"When shit started gettin' hectic, why didn't you come out there? You saw that his boys were right there with him."

"To be honest with you, I don't involve myself in other people's business. That was between you and him.

Besides, security broke it up before it got outta hand anyway."

"So you sayin' if his boys had jumped in you had my back."

"Without question..."

"That's bullshit, La'vell and you know it," I laughed without turning my attention away from the game. "I came from all the way upstairs and by the time I got there, you and Reese were standing by the bar wit the white chicks."

"Oh word?" Kevin expressed with surprise. "Woooow... At least I know now who got my back. My room dog is a soldier."

"I was even in the middle of somethin' wit Red and stopped to see about my boy. Y'all Myrtle Beach niggaz is wack."

"We can sit here and what if all night," Reese interrupted. "What it all boils down to is that we don't get involved in other people's affairs."

"Spoken like a true white boy," I laughed. Reese put the controller down and walked outta the room with an attitude. "For real...? In the middle of a game...? You mad now?"

"On the real fellas," La'vell began to explain. "Reese is real sensitive about being called a white boy. People have been callin' him that all his life."

"Then he should be used to it," I laughed.

"It's a little deeper than I can't explain. Just chill out on that…please? The shit don't bother me. I can take it. Reese is just a little different."

"Aight then. I'll chill out on that...but y'all Myrtle Beach niggaz is still whack."

"Go to hell. I'll be right back. Let me go check on Reese." Ten minutes later, La'vell came back without Reese and got into a game of basketball with Kevin. As soon as the game started the phone rang.

"Who dis'?" I answered.
"Is that how your mother taught you to answer the phone?" Red laughed.

"My bad. What's up?"
"I need a favor."

"What do I get out of doing this favor for you?"
"Why you gotta get something out of it? Why can't you just be nice and do it?"

"I was just playin with you. What you need?"

"Can you take me to get something to eat? I got tied up after practice and missed the caf and the grill."

"Just you?"

"Yeah."

"Alright. Put something on and call me when you're ready."

"Put something on like what?"

" Something presentable."

"Why? You takin me on a date?"

"Maybe. Lemme ask you a question first. You eat seafood?"

"I love seafood."

"Alright. Get dressed and call me when you're ready."

"Okay." I hung up the phone.

"Look at'em?" Kevin laughed. "Roommate tryna get all romantical and shit."

Like JJ from Good times, "Well you know…What can I say?" The three of us shared a laugh as I pulled something out to wear. Twenty minutes later, I picked up Red and we headed to Traveler's Rest.

Red and I pulled up at the restaurant and went in. It wasn't busy at all for a Friday night. We were greeted with a smile and taken to a booth in the corner of the establishment. Like most seafood restaurants, it had the same motif. There were pictures of fish everywhere, fishing poles and nets. They even had a large aquarium in the middle of the restaurant. The pleasant aromas of authentic seafood danced throughout the place. We looked over the menu for about five minutes then our waitress came to take our order. After our order was taken, we engaged in small talk.

"This is cozy," Red began as she looked around the restaurant. "I like it."

"This is my kinda spot. I'm not big on fancy, overpriced restaurants. The food costs too much and you're never satisfied when you leave. I was raised on Grandma's cookin'. A brother likes to get full."

"I know that's right," Red laughed. "I'm not a hard girl to please. I don't like for guys to make a big fuss over me. As long as you treat me like a lady at all times, you can take me to McDonald's and I'm cool."

"I think that's the problem with relationships now. People get too caught up in the material things and forget that it's the little things that matter the most."

"I can agree with you on that but in the same breathe; it's nice to do something special from time to time."

"If you're with the right man, every day you're with him should be special." A huge smile spread across Red's face revealing those dimples. "I love it when you smile."

"Stop it," Red blushed. "I'm too light to be blushing."

In no time, our waitress returned with our food. We continued to talk as we enjoyed a delicious meal of fried flounder, fried shrimp, hushpuppies, French fries and coleslaw.

The more I spent time with and talked to Red, the more I learned about her. She was a very interesting person and had a mature mentality for an eighteen-year-old girl. Red was originally from Texas but moved to Florence when she was nine. Her father's grandmother passed away and left them her house so he packed up his wife and two children, at the time, and moved to South Carolina. When she was twelve, she learned that she had Dyslexia. Her parents knew that she was a smart girl but she was having trouble with her grades. For the remainder of her school years, she struggled with it. When she got to middle school, she started playing softball and became pretty good at it. Red received offers from several Division 1 schools to play softball. Because of her grades, and SAT scores, she couldn't get in. That's how she wound up being the heavily recruited, freshman phenomenon at New Grove College. Her plan was to play at NGC for two years while she got her grades up then transfer to a big school.

"I know it's a long shot," she said then sipped her drink. "But I want to play in the Olympics one day."

"Wow…that's hot. That's the first time I've heard someone say they wanted to compete in the Olympics."

"I just gotta make the grades so I can transfer in two years."

"I'm not the smartest kid in the class but if you need help in English or Spanish, just let me know."

"That's good to know because writing is not one of my strong points. I can already see that you're gonna have to help me get through freshman composition."

"I got you."

Time continued to pass and before long we were headed back to school. Because it was a nice night, we let the windows down and I opened the sunroof of my Hyundai Excel. The roads on the way back to NGC were dark and hardly any cars passed us by. We listened to the smooth R&B songs of a mixtape that Twist put together for me. I leaned on the armrest to be closer to Red. She put her head on my shoulder and sang along with EnVouge.

It was still early for a Friday night when we got back on campus. Curfew wasn't until one so we could chill together out on campus. In front of the cafeteria was a swing big enough for two people. After I parked the car, we went there to sit and talk some more. When Red sat down, I laid on my back, put my head in her lap and hung one leg over of the arm of the swing as the other brushed the ground as we swung.

"I don't know what it is about you, Dré." Red repeatedly ran her hand against the grain of my hair.
"What do you mean?"

"You don't act like other guys our age. Most eighteen year old boys are immature and silly."

"My grandparents held me to a high standard growing up. I wasn't allowed to act like my friends. When I turned sixteen, they pushed me to get a job. They taught me responsibility early. I guess that's why I act the way that I do."

"But it's not just that. I listen to you talk and the things you say don't sound like they she be coming from an eighteen year old. You talk like you're twenty-five."

"Age makes no difference," I laughed. "I know guys well in their thirties that still act like teenagers."

"Then what is about you that makes you so different?"

Super Senior

"I really don't know. It may have a lot to do with me growing up around a lot of women like my aunts and older cousins. I used to listen to them talk about what they wanted from guys and the things they liked and didn't like. I guess some of it stuck. One thing that stands out in my mind was when I was about twelve. I was at my other grandmother's house. I was in the room playing Nintendo when my one of my older female cousins came in a laid across the bed and started crying. She was about nineteen at the time. When I asked her what was wrong, she told me about how her boyfriend mistreated her. I got angry and wanted to do something but what could a twelve-year-old boy do to a twenty one year old man? She told me to never do those types of things that he did to any girl, to always be respectful, and treat a woman with love and respect. She also said that if I do, she'll love me back. I remember that day like it was yesterday."

"All I can say is keep on being who you are. From what I've seen of you so far, you're a good guy. You're going to make some lucky girl very happy for a long time."

"Are you that lucky girl?"

"I seriously doubt it. I'll only be here for two years at the most then I don't know where I'll be. I wouldn't want us to get deeply involved and then have to break up."

"I can feel you on that but you never know what life has in store for us as individuals or as a potential couple."

"That's true. We'll have to see what happens."

"How about this…? Let's try not to look too far into the future and enjoy the moments that we have together while we're here. How does that sound?"

"I can work with that. I just need you to promise me something."

"What's that?"
"Don't ever stop being you."
"I promise."

Red leaned down and kissed me on my forehead. We continued to talk about a host of different things until it was time for us to go our separate ways. I walked her to her dorm then went back to mine. Kevin was on the phone when I got there. I dapped him up then stretched out across the bed to watch TV. Before long, I was asleep.

At every college or university that had a football team, Saturday was always Game Day—even at NGC. The football team shared the same field as a local area high school. Funny thing about it, the high school team was better than us. As a former high school football player, I'd been to a few college games. The NGC games where nothing like any I'd ever been to. Because the school was a Southern Baptist college, there was no tailgating. How could you have college football without it?

We got to the game right before kick-off. We all knew that our team was destined to get murdered but we had a ball anyway. In one section on the home side, all of the Black students gathered—all twenty-five of us. Me, Red, Tanieka, Kevin and La'vell sat down front cracking jokes and coaching from the sidelines. Reese was still mad at me from the night before so he decided not to sit with us. At every school there is that one person that has more mouth than everybody and liked to be seen and heard. I liked to talk a lot and be the center of attention but this dude had me beat. His name was Mike Sanders but he went by Swift. Swift was a freshman just like us. He was dark skinned with a big nose and a small, curly Afro. Being an ex-high school football player like a few of us that attended, he swore he knew everything about the game. Swift had a certain cockiness about him because he was originally from New York but spent his last year in high school in South Carolina. When he talked, that New York accent showed.

"Son," he began as he pounded his fist in his hand. "I'm tellin' you. Coach need to pull the white boy and let the black man play QB."

"You know that ain't happenin'," I laughed.
"That's why we losin'. How you got a quarterback that can't even see over his offensive line?"

"I played ball and I can tell you that if the backup was better, he'd be startin'."

"Come on man. Look where we at. We at a school that only have 300 students and there are barely fifty blacks. Shit...half of'em on the football team and they still can't win."

"Swift talkin all that shit," one of his homeboys began to comment. "And look where he at...coachin' from the sidelines instead of bein' on the field. To hear you tell it, you was Randall Cunningham in school."

"I spent one year down here in school. The scouts wasn't lookin for me; they already knew who they wanted. Then the ones that did check me out weren't comin wit' no scholarships. So yeah I'm on the sidelines...just like you, Mr. All State wide receiver." The crowd gave that ever popular 'Ooooooooh!'

"I got bad knees!" he defended.

"If you look at it, we damn near got a team up here. I'm the QB. My man, Shelton, can run the ball wit' Dré clearin' the way for'em at fullback. I think Kev said he was a DB in school."

"You know it!" Kevin interjected.

"Even the ladies can get involved. Tanieka play softball so I know she can catch. Thick as Red is, she could be tight-end, linebacker or somethin'."

"Watch ya mouth," I laughed.

"My bad, Dre. You know I'm just clownin'."

"Don't tell 'em nuttin'," Red jumped in. Swift was a stone cold fool. Even with us gettin' blown out, he kept us laughing the whole game. I guess sometimes it wasn't always about what was goin on out on the field. When it was all said and done, we got murdered by a score of 45 to 6.

After the game, Kevin, the girls and myself decided to check out the mall. It was packed when we got there. I must've driven around for twenty minutes trying to find a parking spot. Once I found one we went inside. Since I'd been in Greenville, I'd been looking for more black people. I found them that day. They were everywhere.

The four of us decided on a time and meeting place then went our separate ways. Red and I went in one direction while Kev and Tanekia went the opposite way. For the first half hour, Red and I went in and out of stores laughing and talking. I stopped in Foot Locker and bought a pair of shoes then got drug into the Express. What ever Red was looking for took her forever. I never minded shopping with a woman but Red took it to a whole new level. I sat in a black chair by the dressing room while Red tried on about ten different outfits. The last outfit she tried on took the cake. A form fitting, black dress stopped around mid-thigh. It hugged every curve of her body. She stood in front of the three-way mirror examining the dress from all angles.

"What do you think?" Red asked as she turned to face me.

"That's the one right there."

"You sure it don't make me look fat?"
"Not at all...it makes you look sexy. Once you throw the right pair of heels with it and get you're hair done just right, it'll be perfect. I might just have to take you out to see how you put it all together."

"If that's the case, I might just have to buy it." I sat and watched as Red walked around the store looking for the perfect accessories to wear with it. The way her ass moved up and down as she walked had me hypnotized. That dress made me notice exactly how flawless her body was. Red was a thick girl but she had no stomach. Her chest sat up nice and perky and her legs, hips and ass complimented the rest of her body perfectly.

Red's task of putting the perfect ensemble together ended. After she made the purchase we walked out of the store and ran into a familiar face. It was Fly but the girl that he was holding hands with wasn't Zoë. His eyes got big as plates when he saw me. He tried to hail me like we'd been friends forever.

"What's up, Dré?" he greeted.
"What's good?" I forced myself to reply.

"I'm chillin'. Just out here spendin' a little bit of money."

"Who's ya friend?"
"This is Nicole. Nicole, this is my man, Dré and his friend…"

"Tiffany," Red answered.
"Nice to meet you," Nicole smiled.

"I'm not gonna hold y'all up. I just wanted to speak. I'll see y'all back on the yard."

"Indeed you will." Fly and Nicole walked off as I laughed.

"What's so funny?" Red asked.
"Dude is a trip. He's out here with another chick and got cold busted."

"That's not his girl?"
"Nope... He go wit' Zoë."
"The cheerleader?"
"Yup..."

"Some guys ain't shit. Zoë's a nice girl. We take Biology together."

"Its dudes like him that make it hard for guys like me."

"No it doesn't. A real woman should be able to tell that you're a good guy just by talking to you or spending a little time with you."

"I guess you're right. I bet he's nervous as hell right now. He probably thinkin' that I'm going to go back on campus and tell Zoë."

"Are you?"

"She's a really nice girl but that's not my business. Besides, I don't really know her like that. We spoke a couple of times but that was about it. What goes on in the dark will eventually come into the light. He's not too smart anyway. Why would you bring a girl that's not your girl to the mall on the weekend?"

"I think I might have to tell her."
"Don't do that. If you tell her, he's going to assume that it was me that told her and then we got problems. We've already had one run in. I'm tryna keep a low profile."

"Okay. I'll try but I can't make any promises. You know how us girls are."

"You can't hold water wit a bucket," I laughed.
"No, Sir…we look out for each other."

Super Senior

"And for that reason right there, I tell my boys that women have eyes everywhere." The time came for us to meet up with Kevin and Tanekia at the designated spot. They were already there when we arrived. Looking at the two of them then, one would almost forget what happened earlier in the week. They looked like they'd been together for years. Off to the car we went to head back to school. The four of us laughed and talked all the way back to campus.

Later that night, Red and I hooked up to go to the student center to watch a movie. Some of the football players had the TV occupied with the late college game. Instead of the movie, we decided on pool. In the middle of our first game, Fly walked into the poolroom.

"I been looking for you," Fly began with a certain nervousness in his voice. "We need to talk."

"We ain't got nothing to talk about," I responded while setting up for my next shot.

"Yes we do. Can you excuse us for a minute, Tiffany?"

"She don't have to excuse us. I already know what this is about. Whatever you have to say to me, you can say in front of her."

"Its cool, Dré. I'ma walk upstairs and grab something to drink. You want anything?"

"A Pepsi would be nice if you don't mind." I reached in my pocket to give her some money.

"I got it. I'll be right back." Red walked out of the poolroom.

As I leaned on the side of the pool table, "She's gone now. What's up?"
"I just wanted to tell you that what you saw today wasn't what you thought you saw." I laughed in his face. "What's so funny?"

"So you're gonna stand there and call me stupid to my face? I was born at night, not last night. C'mon Fly, I'm a dude just like you. What I saw today was exactly what I thought it was or else we wouldn't be having this conversation right now. You think I'm that dude that was gonna come back here and tell Zoë I saw you with another girl. That's not my business nor is that my style. The other thing that's funny is how you talked all big and bad to ya girl the other day in the caf' but now you standin' here shook."

"What ever, Man. Just keep ya mouth shut and we won't have no problems."

"You threatening me now?"
"Call it what you wanna call it."

"Lemme tell you somethin', Bruh. You don't know me like that. You might have ya girl fooled but I don't give two shits about you. I could fuck ya whole world up. You don't wanna go to war with me. So I'ma tell you like this. I'm not the one you should be worried about cuz I wasn't the only one from here that was in the mall today. A few other people saw you. If Zoë does find out, don't bring that bullshit to me or my girl cuz you fucked up."

"And I'ma tell you that if she does find out, you'll be the first person I come lookin for."

"I ain't hard to find. You found me tonight, didn't you?" Red walked back in just as Fly was storming out of the room.

"Was that about what I think it was about?" Red asked as she handed me a cup.

"You know it. Dude so shook right now."
"That's what his ass gets."
"I told him, straight up, that if Zoë finds out, not to bring that bullshit to me or you."

"What'd he say then?"
"He talkin about if she do find out, I'll be the first person he comes lookin' for. I laughed in that dudes face."

"Don't even sweat him."
"Sweat who?"

"Exactly," Red laughed.

7
Holidaze

My freshmen year got off to a great start. I'd met a lot of cool people. Red and I were getting tighter as the days went by. NGC wasn't all that bad. Before I knew it, the semester was ending. Final exams started and everyone was ready to pack up shop for the Christmas holiday.

I took my last exam on a Wednesday morning. I could have left to go home after I finished but Red asked if she could ride home with me. Her last exam wasn't until the next day. I was so ready to go that all of my things were packed since Monday. All I had to do was load them in the car.

I thought that we would be able to get on the road right after Red finished her exam but we were detained. Tanekia's parents were supposed to come pick her up that afternoon but they hadn't arrived. Since she lived in our area, we waited around to make sure she had a ride home. They arrived around six o'clock that evening. I was hoping to get on the road before the sun went down because we had a four hour ride ahead of us. Red suggested that we wait until the morning but I was ready to go.

Once Tanekia was squared away, Red and I jumped on the road. I was so excited to be going home, I'd forgot that I didn't sleep much the night before and was up early that morning. An hour and a half into our trip, my eyes started to get heavy. Red was asleep but woke up when I swerved onto the shoulder.

"You okay, Baby?" Red asked with startled concern in her voice.

"I'm trying but I don't know if I'm gonna make it."
"How far are we from Columbia?"
"The last sign I saw said fifteen miles."

"You wanna stop there for the night and just make the rest of the trip tomorrow?"

"Won't your parents be worried about you?"
"I talked to them when we were waiting for Tanekia's parents. I told them that if they came too late, we were going to wait until tomorrow. If I don't show up tonight, they'll just figure that we waited 'til morning."

"I was just checkin'," I laughed as I took a sip of my Pepsi. "Your dad is the last person I want lookin' for me."

"My daddy is as gentle as they come."

"Gentle or not, he got arms like Hulk Hogan. I'd hate to have to run his ass over wit' Da Bean."

"You so silly," Red giggled. "As soon as we get in Columbia, we'll get a room."

Super Senior

"You okay with spending the night with me?"
"If I could, I would spend every night with you."
"Really…?"

"I hate it when you walk me to my dorm at night then go back to yours. Some nights I just want to lie beside you and hold on to you."

"Well," I exhaled. "Tonight your wish will come true. Just don't be feelin' all over my booty."

"I should be telling you that, Mr. Nasty Man."
"Who me…?"

We talked and laughed for the remaining miles to Columbia. When we got into the city, we found a decent hotel and checked in. I thought we were going to be sleepy and tired by the time we got settled in but we were wide awake. We turned on the television and found a movie. About halfway through the movie, I heard Red's stomach growl.
"Damn!" I laughed. "What was that?"

"That was my stomach. I haven't eaten since this morning. I thought we'd be home by now."

"I'll go get us something to eat. What you in the mood for?"

"I saw a sign for Applebee's as we were getting off the highway. It's back down the other way."

"Applebee's? You must think I'm rich or something."

"Since you paid for the room, I can at least buy you dinner."

"I was kinda expecting another form of payment but I guess dinner will do."

"You know what? Get out!"
"You can't put me out before you tell me what you want to eat."

"Oh yeah…that might help. I want Chicken and Broccoli Alfredo."

"Cool. I'll be back in a minute." I put my shoes on and headed for the door.

"You're forgetting the money."

"I'm good. I just wanted to see where ya head was at." I left Red sitting in the bed with a huge smile on her face. Five minutes later I was at Applebee's placing our order. The restaurant was packed for a Thursday night. It took almost thirty minutes to get our food. I hurried back to the hotel because I knew Red was probably starving.

"Sorry it took so…"

I was speechless when I walked in the room. Red had candles lit all over the room and soft music playing in the background. The air was filled with the aromas of a freshly taken shower mixed with the scent of my favorite fragrance, Country Apple by Victoria's Secret. Red was lying across the bed wearing a black, Satin robe that barley covered her backside. Her hair was hanging long and straight.

"What took you so long?" she lulled in a seductive tone.

"Applebee's," I tried to begin but my voice cracked. I cleared my throat and tried again. "The restaurant was packed."

I placed the bags on the table as Red stood up and walked toward me. She held the robe closed until she stopped about two feet in front of me then released. The robe opened up to reveal the feature presentation that I'd been dying to see since I first saw the preview that day she tried on the black dress in the mall.

Red stood in front of me wearing a red, lace panty and bra set. I opened the robe up a little wider to get a better view. As I examined her body, I noticed her erect nipples pushing through the bra. A warm sensation rushed through my body as well as my loins. Red draped her arms over my shoulders as I wrapped my arms around her waist under the satin of the robe.

"You like it?" she whispered as she kissed me on my neck just below my ear.

"I love it."

"I'm glad. I bought it just for you."

We engaged in a deep, passionate kiss as Red grabbed me by my shirt and pulled me toward the bed. With our lips still locked on each other, she helped me remove my clothes. She turned me around with my back to the bed and used her body to lay me down on the bed. Her warm skin was as smooth as silk when it touched mine. The more we kissed, the more her passionate sounds filled the room. I couldn't believe that after four months of patiently waiting, Red and I were boarding the train to ecstasy.

Red sat up and straddled my legs. She began to stroke my soldier which was already at full attention. With a devilish look in her eyes and a sly grin, Red locked her eyes on mine. The more she stroked me, the more she got turned on. I closed my eyes and moaned due to the excellent sensation I was feeling. At first her motion was slow. When I felt her begin to speed up, I knew I had to stop her before I exploded.

"Wait, wait," I pleaded. She would not stop. She continued until my first orgasm shot from my shaft into her hand and all over my stomach. She let out a soft giggle as she got up to wash her hands and get a towel. When she came back, she cleaned me off. Afterwards she climbed back on top of me.

"Now that you got that one out of the way," she whispered. "We can get down to business."

I rolled her over and looked down at her. The soft candlelight reflected off her creamy flesh. I placed another kiss on her lips then moved down to her neck. I'd found her spot. Red put her hand on the back of my head and pushed me into her neck. I ravished it as if I'd been starving and that was the only thing that could satisfy me. From her neck I moved to her perky, C-cups. I ran my tongue around her hard nipples. I'd found another spot. In a matter of moments, her breasts were covered with passion marks. Red grabbed my head with both hands and pulled my face out of her chest. "I want you...now!"

I sat up then reached down to the floor for my jeans. Back in those days, we kept a condom in our wallet. I removed the Lifestyle from my wallet and opened the package. Once equipped, I was ready for insertion.

"Are you sure you're ready for this?" I asked. She bit her bottom lip and shook her head yes. With my right hand, I grabbed my manhood and rubbed the head in a circular motion around the entrance to her pleasure zone. Red rolled her hips in the same motion. I could hear how wet she was. It was as if it was calling my name.

Due to how tight she was, there was some resistance. Red released a stuttered breath and tensed her body until I was all the way inside. Once inside, I stopped to make sure she was okay. Red confirmed that she was fine and it was off to the races. I moved at a steady pace that wasn't too fast or too slow. Judging by Red's reaction and sounds, it was just right. She wrapped her arms and legs around me and held onto me for dear life.

"Oh Dre!" She shouted in ecstasy. "Yes! Yes! Just like that! Right there!" There is definitely something about a female extremely vocal during sex. It fed the male ego. The more she sounded off, the more I made her sound off. I could feel her juices soaking my pelvic region.

Red was the thickest girl I'd had sex with to that point. I quickly learned how athletic she was. She used her body to roll me over onto the bed without coming out of her. Now she was on top and in control. She placed her hands, palms down, on my stomach and went for the ride of her life. Every time she came down, I pushed inside of her. I'd never been ridden like that before. She would go up, and then come down. When she came down she would wind it up before she went back up. I didn't know what to do. All I could do was enjoy the ride. For the next hour and a half we were all over the place. From the bed we moved to the chair. From there it was to the bathroom counter then back to the bed—so many places and so many different positions. As tired as we were on the road, I didn't know where we got the sexual energy from. When it was all said, and done, we were spent. For twenty minutes, we were side by side, breathing heavily and soaked with sweat.

"That was everything I hoped it would be," Red moaned as she laid her head on my chest. "You okay?"

"I'm good. I hit my knee on the counter by the sink but it'll be okay."

"Why didn't you stop?"

"I couldn't," I chuckled. "It was feeling too good."

"Are you sure you're only eighteen?"

"Yeah, I'm sure. Why?"

"You don't make love like an eighteen year old."

"How does an eighteen year old have sex?"

"It usually lasts only a few minutes then its over."

"Minutemen get talked about…viciously. I refuse for that to be me." After lying there for a few more minutes, we took a shower together then heated up our food that was ice cold by then. Once we ate, we tried to watch a movie that was on TV. The movie wound up watching us.

The next morning we got back on the road and headed to our destinations. I greeted Red's parents when we got to her house. The four of us sat and talked for about thirty minutes then I headed home. I was so happy to see my grandmother. She latched on to me like she hadn't seen me in years. I was just home for Thanksgiving. Once I got my things out of the car and got my laundry started, I headed to the high school to visit some of my teachers. While I was there, I got a page from Red. I called her back when I got home. I had just dropped her off but she was already trying to find out when she was going to see me again. We made plans to spend that Saturday together.

There must have been a look out for me. I had only been in town for a few hours and my pager was already blowing up. I must have made a dozen phone calls in less than an hour. The last person I talked to was Tommy Girl.

"How'd you know I was home already?" I asked.
"My cousin said she saw you up at the school. How long you home?"

"I'll be here until after the New Year. I'll probably leave out on the 4th or 5th."

"Can I see you Saturday night?"
"I already got plans for Saturday."
"With who?"
"Don't worry about with who. I got plans."

"My bad...must be wit one of ya lil skeezers."
"I don't deal with skeezers. You should know me better than that."

"You know I'm just playin with you. What you doin' Sunday after church?"
"The family's coming over for dinner."

"I'm not getting' ready to go through your entire schedule. When you get some free time call me. If I see you, I see you. If I don't I don't."

"Why you gotta act like that. You know my people haven't seen me in a minute. This is my first weekend home. I'll be here for a whole month. You know I'll make time for you."

"I hear you talkin'."
"You just be available. I gotta go."
"Call me later."
"I'll see what I can do."

"Never mind Dré... You ain't gotta do nothin you don't wanna do."

"I'll talk to you later cuz you trippin' right now."
"How am I trippin'? All I asked you to do was call me later."

"And I said I'll try. I don't know what I'll be doing later. I don't want to tell you I'ma call you and then you don't hear from me. At least I'm being honest with you. What else do you want?"

"I want you to stop acting like you don't know me!" Tommy Girl yelled in frustration.

"Excuse me?"
"Ever since you left to go to school, you've been acting like you don't know me...like you too good for me or somethin'. I wrote you letters that you never answered. I paged you and you never called back. Every time you came

home, I tried to see you but you could never make time for me. I thought we were better than that. You're making me feel like everything you told me last summer was a lie."

"A lot has changed since I've been gone."
"No, Dré. You've changed."

"How have I changed?"

"Just because you went off to college and I'm..." Tommy Girl paused. "Just forget about it... I gotta go. Bye."

Tommy Girl hung up the phone. I sat confused because I didn't know where all of that had come from. Tommy Girl had just confused the hell out of me. I hoped that I would have a chance to find out what she meant by all of that before I left to go back to school. Until that time came, I wasn't going to stress about it.

That Friday night, I went to church with my grandparents. My grandfather had to preach at a church in Florence. We got there just before service started. I took a seat on a pew on the far left side of the church. A couple of faces caught my eye when I looked around the church. As soon as I realized that one of the faces was Red's mother, someone tapped me on the shoulder.

"What are you doing here?" a familiar voice asked. I turned to look over my left shoulder. It was Red. I stood up and hugged her.

"My grandfather is preaching tonight." Red took a seat beside me.

"I didn't know Pastor Henderson was your grandfather. He's been here a couple of times and we've been to his church. Why didn't I meet you until we got to school?"

"I probably had to work those nights. It looks like we were destined to meet anyway."

"I guess so."

Service started with prayer then moved on to praise and worship. I sat with a smile on my face because Red was sitting right beside me. Once devotion service closed, Red's Pastor introduced my grandfather. My grandfather was a short, stout light-skinned man in his late forties. He stepped to the podium in the pulpit and greeted the congregation.

"Let the chuuch say Amen!" he commanded.
"Amen!" The congregation responded.

"Praise the Lord. It feels good to be back in the house of the God one mo' time. I always feel like I'm home when I come here. I know my choir is ready to sing tonight but I wanna switch it up a lil' bit. I going to ask my grandson to come up here and sing a song for me."

"Alright now!" my aunt shouted out.

"He just got back in town yesterday. He's my first born grandchild but me and my wife raised him. He's the first one of my churin' to go off to college. We're very proud of him."

"Excuse me for a minute, Pastor," Red's Pastor interrupted. "That young lady sittin' beside him is my niece. She's the first one from our congregation to go to college."

"Thank the Lord. Y'all go to the same college?"
"Yes sir," I answered.

"Ohhhhh...that's why he sittin' over there grinnin' like that." The congregation laughed. "Come on up here and sing these folks happy so I can deliver this word." I stood up and walked to the front of the church. As he handed me the microphone he requested his favorite song that he liked to hear me sing. I walked over to the organist and told him what song I was singing. He gave me the key and began to play the music to Douglas Miller's, *My Soul has Been Anchored*.

As the intro played, I looked out over the people. My grandmother sat on the front pew smiling at me. Red sat in anticipation because she'd heard me lead a song with the gospel choir but had never heard me sing solo. All of the members of my church stood up as I began to sing. That's how we supported each other. From first note to last note, I sang the song from the bottom of my heart and the depths of my soul. I sang that song like I'd never sung it before. The entire church was on its feet by the time I got to the middle of the song. I could here the shouts of encouragement and approval as I sang. By the end of the song, tears of joy were streaming down my face. That's what singing gospel always did to me. When I opened my eyes, my grandmother, other members in the congregation and Red were all wiping tears from their eyes as they stood among the standing ovation I received. My grandfather stepped down out of the pulpit and hugged me then stepped back to the podium.

"That boy sang that song from his soul! Give him another hand." The congregation gave me another thunderous round of applause as I walked back to my seat. Red greeted me with a big hug when I got there. "I don't know if that was God or whether he was showin' off for that pretty girl right there cuz that boy ain't nevah sung that song like that! You hear me?"

My grandfather went into his sermon. I sat and listened as he preached his heart out. After service was over, Red and I went outside to wait for our people to come out. The way my grandfather talked, we were going to be waiting for a while. The December night was cold so we decided to sit in my car and wait.

"I've heard you sing several times," Red began as she adjusted the vent on the dashboard. "But I've never heard you sing like that."

"I don't know. It's just something about singing in front of my grandparents. When they first learned that I could sing, they put me in the choir. I love singing R&B but it doesn't compare to singing gospel. It's a different feeling."

"I see." Where my car was parked, we could see the entrance to the church. Our parents were walking out together. "There goes my mom and dad. I better go. We still on for tomorrow?"

"You know it. Just give me a call when you ready for me to come scoop you up."

"I will. Me and my Mom are going to the salon in the morning so it probably won't be until late afternoon."

"That's cool. My boy came home tonight so I'ma go holla at him."

"Okay. Talk to you tomorrow." Red leaned over and gave me a kiss then got out of the car.

I know what you're probably thinking. How could I stand in front of the church and sing a song like the previous night's events between Red and I never happened. That's what sets me apart from the hypocrites at New Grove. I don't claim to be something that I'm not. I love the Lord and I love singing gospel. I'm a sinner and I know that. My grandfather taught me that: even though I may not live the life that God wants me to live, if I just take time out to acknowledge his presence in my life, give him some of my time and always remember to thank him for the things that He has done for me, I will continue to be blessed.

The next morning I awoke to one of my grandmother's famous breakfasts. She must've really been happy to have her baby home. She threw down that morning on the home fries with onions, thick-cut bacon, scrambled eggs, and homemade biscuits. Mom knew she could throw down in the kitchen. I was so full, I wanted to go right back to bed but somehow I knew it was a set up. Anytime my grandmother wanted me to do her a favor, she threw a good meal at me. That is how I wound up so damn thick growing up.

"What you got planned for today?" She asked as she sipped her coffee.

"Nothing really… Nick was supposed to come home last night so I was gonna stop by his house before I went to Florence to see Red."

"Who's Red?"

"I meant to say Tiffany. She's the girl that was sitting beside me last night at church."

"I declare," Mom laughed. "You and them high yella girls."

"Don't start, Mom. You know I'm not color struck."

"Ha! Every girlfriend you have ever had has looked the same. You like light skin, long hair, and light eyes. I know you."

"Okay...you got me but it's not on purpose. Those are just the ones who just so happen to like me back." We shared a laugh then she brought up a name I hadn't heard in a while.

"When was the last time you talked to Alicia?"

Alicia Burroughs was my best friend since the fourth grade. I'd gotten into a fight with a sixth grader because of her one day on the playground during recess. After that, we became inseparable until about a year before I moved to South Carolina. We had a falling out over another female. Alicia and I never dated but I felt that there was always something between us that I could not explain. It was as if we were always supposed to be together but fought against it as hard as we could.

"Wow," I exhaled. "I haven't talked to her since we moved."

"You've been back to Fayetteville a lot since you got your car. You didn't see her any when you went back?"

"Every time I went by her house, she was never home. Eventually I just stopped going by."

"You know that's the girl you're…"
"Supposed to marry," I answered finishing my grandmother's sentence. "I know. I just don't think that's gonna happen."
"Always remember that if you love something and you let it go, if it comes back, that shows you exactly how strong it was. You got that?"

"Yes, Ma'am…"
"Good. Now go take your aunt to the grocery store. I told her you'll be by at ten."
"It's 9:45."
"Then I guess you better get a move on."

Messing around with my aunt, I didn't finish with her until almost four o' clock that afternoon. Red paged me three times before I was finally able to call her back. I let her know that I would be on my way to Florence within the hour.

I took my aunt back home and helped her get the groceries in the house then went home to change. I threw on a pair of black jeans and my white hoodie with Red's name on the back because those were the only things that I didn't have to iron. Once I let my grandmother know where I was going, I headed to Florence. It was almost 5:30 when I got to Red's house. I laughed when she came to the door. Red had on her black jeans and her sweatshirt with my name on the back. We had plenty of time before the movie started so we decided to go to the mall to hang out for awhile. That was a big mistake on my part.

As always during the weekend, especially a Saturday afternoon, the mall was overflowing with people. We ran into a few of our friends from NGC that lived in the area. I heard my name called as we walked by Fine's. It was Twist.

"What up, Dog!" He greeted as we exchanged one love. "When you get home?"

"Yesterday morning."
"And you couldn't call nobody?"

"I didn't know you were home yet."
"I got home Tuesday."

"My bad... Twist this is Tiffany. Tiffany, this is one of my aces from high school."

"Nice to meet you, Twist."

"Nice to meet you… Any friend of my boy's is a friend of mine."

"That's good to know. Baby, I'm gonna walk in Lerner's for a minute."

"Okay. I'll catch up with you in a minute." Red walked away leaving me and Twist in front of Fine's.

"Baby? That's you?"

"You know how I roll."

"It's like that up in Greenville? I might need to transfer."

"Nah. You good at State. Trust me."

"You talk to ya boy?"

"I was supposed to go by the house earlier today but I got tied up wit my aunt until it was time for me to come meet her. You talked to'em?"

"I hit'em on the hip a few times but he never called me back. When I called the house this morning, Grandma said he hadn't come home yet."

"He was supposed to come in last night."

"I know but you know how ya boy is. He probably somewhere caked up. Anyway, I get off at 10. What you gettin' into tonight."

"Me and baby girl catchin' a movie. Then we might go shoot pool at that spot out by South Side."

"You talkin bout the same spot we found?"
"Yeah…the small spot across from the driving range."

"That's what's up. I'll hit you on the hip when I get off. Me and my girl might catch up wit y'all out there. She live out that way."

"Your girl?"
"Shhhhhh! Not so loud. That's how rumors get started."
"Boy, you a fool," I laughed. "Just hit me." I dapped Twist up then walked toward Lerner's to catch up with Red. Right before I got to the entrance, I saw Tommy Girl coming out with two other girls. I made a quick U-turn and walked back into Fine's with Twist. I figured that since that's where Red left me, she'd come back there when she was finished. I continued to talk to Twist. I thought Red would've come out before Tommy Girl but she didn't. Instead, Tommy Girl walked out of Lerner's and straight into Fine's. They went to the opposite side of the store. I tried to slide out but she turned around just as I got to the exit.

"Dre!" she called. I turned around and acted surprised to see her.

"What's up?" Tommy Girl excused herself from her friends and walked over to me. When she got there, I positioned myself so that I could see when Red walked out of Lerner's.

"How are you?" she asked as she hugged me.
"I'm good. I thought you would've been in school today."

"We get out at five. Me and a couple of my girls from school came out here to walk around for a minute. What you doin' here? You know you don't shop here."

"I stopped through to holla at Twist."
"Oh okay…you still busy tonight?"
"Yeah...me and Twist supposed to go shoot pool after he gets off."

"He probably don't get off until they close. You wanna go with us to get something to eat?"

"I appreciate it but I got something else to do." At the end of that statement, Red walked out of Lerner's. She saw me standing in the entrance of the store talking to Tommy Girl. "I'll hit you up later. I gotta go."

"Where you rushin' off to?"
"You ready, Baby?" Red asked as she approached. Tommy Girl gave me a serious look of disapproval.

"Yeah. Tiffany, this is Chelsea. We went to high school together. Chelsea, this is Tiffany. We go to NGC together."

"It's nice to meet you," Red greeted as she extended her hand to Tommy Girl. Tommy Girl sucked her teeth and walked away. "What was that all about?"

"I'll tell you about it later. Come on." I signaled to Twist that I was leaving. Red and I hung a right and walked towards the other end of the mall.

"Who was that?"
"That was Tommy Girl."
"I thought you said her name was Chelsea."
"It is but that's what we call her because of her Tommy Hilfiger addiction."

"What's the history between you two to make her act like that towards me?" I began to explain the connection between Tommy Girl and I. Red listened carefully without judgment."

"We spent a lot of time together over the summer before I left to come to school. She knew that I was leaving but I guess she let her feelings creep up on her."

"What did you expect? From what you just told me, you and she were supposed to be together before her and her ex. If you treated her the same way you treat me, I can't blame her."

"But I didn't say anything to make her believe that it was gonna be anything between us."

"You didn't have to. You're a dangerous man."
"What? How so?"

"I've been peepin' you since I met you. You have a way with women that most men don't have. You treat all women the same even if she's just a friend. You got a couple other girls at NGC open too."

"Who?"
"I think her name is Torrie. She's from Columbia."
"Torrie? She's just a girl that I sit next to in Old Testament. I don't really talk to her that much."

"You must've said something because I over heard her talking to her one of my teammates about you a couple weeks ago."

"Who's the other girl?"
"Zoë…"
"Zoë…?
"Yes. How many Zoë's go to school with us?"
"Fly's girlfriend Zoë?"
"Yes, Dré. Zoë ."
"Get outta here," I laughed.

"I told you we take Biology together. We sit at the same table so we talk sometimes."

"Y'all supposed to be dissecting frogs, not talkin' bout me. How'd my name come up anyway?"

"I guess she saw us together a few times and asked me were you my man. This was back in September. "What did you tell her?"

"I told'er that you and I were just friends cuz that's what we were at the time. Then she started talking about how sweet and nice you were and the fact that Fly hated when he saw her talking to you."

"I wonder why," I laughed.
"Women like a man that they can talk to and will talk back to them. That's how you are. That's one of the things I like about you."

"Well rest assure, you ain't gotta worry about Torrie or Zoë."

"I know that. They know you're my man now."
"Since when...?"
"Dré, you know you my man. Don't even act like that."

"But we never made official. I didn't send you my patented 'Will you Go with Me?' letter."

"You so silly," Red laughed. "I'm not the type of girl that needs to put a label on my relationship. I know I'm with you and you're with me."

"Those are the best kind of relationships. I think that those labels but unnecessary pressure on things sometimes."

"Exactly... We've had a good thing going since we met. Why ruin it?"

Red and I continued our conversation as we exited the mall. We still had an hour and a half to kill before we had to be at the theater. I knew all the restaurants in the area were going to be packed so we decided to stop by this little fish spot down the street from the theater called Orangeland. We knew we could catch a quick bite before we went to the movies.

As soon as we got to Orangeland, my pager started going off. It was Tommy Girl. I ignored it the first couple of times it went off but she was relentless. She knew that I was with Red. I felt that she was doing it out of spite. I was trying to keep from calling back and cussing her out but Red told me not to worry about it. She knew what was going on. I walked out to the car and placed my pager in the glove compartment. Red laughed at the frustration on my face when I returned. I was glad that Red understood the situation. Not many women would have been as understanding.

Time flew by and before long our evening ended. I pulled up at Red's house around a quarter past eleven. Someone peeked through the curtains to see who was outside. We sat in the car and talked for another half hour. As Red and I were engaged in our goodnight kiss, someone tapped on my window. It was her father. I rolled down the window.

"I'm on my way in right now, Daddy," Red assured.
"Its okay, Baby Girl, I just wanted to talk to André for a minute."

"I'll call you after church. Good night." Red exited the car and walked towards the house. I stepped out. Red's father leaned on the side of the car.

"Yes sir?"
"My wife tells me that you help Tiffany out at school."
"Yes sir. She told me she had trouble writing papers."

"She's been dealing with a learning disability for a while now."
"She told me."
"I appreciate you helping her out."
"It's not a problem."

"Listen, André. I'm not gonna beat around the bush. This is not the part of the conversation where I threaten you or try to scare you in any way just because you're with my daughter. I stood back and watched my baby go through a lot with that last boy she was with."

"I can assure you that I'm nothing like him."
"I know. You already okay with me because I know who your grandfather is and I know Pastor Henderson don't take no mess."

"None what so ever," I laughed.
"Tiffany's my only daughter and I love her. She's a young woman now so I know I can't interfere with her life. All I ask from you is that you do the right thing."

"Yes sir. I will." The next thing that came out of his mouth blew my mind because I was not expecting it.
"I know y'all young and y'all on your own up at school. If you and Tiffany are having sex, please protect yourself. You both have bright futures ahead of you. Don't throw it all away by having a baby. I've been there and I know how hard it is. Trust me. You don't wanna be parents at eighteen."

"No Sir."
"Alright. Lemme get in this house so I can lay it down. We got church in the morning."

"I'm on my way home to do the same thing. Dad always says that if you can go out on Saturday, you can get up for church on Sunday."

"I tell Tiffany the same thing," he laughed. "You be careful goin back to Hartsville."

"I will." He shook my hand then walked in the house as I got in the car. I backed out and cruised back to the big city of Hartsville.

Before long, Christmas came and went. Red and I spent most of the break together. I even spent time with her and her family on Christmas day. I didn't get around to hanging out with my boys or Tommy Girl. My boys understood because they knew we had the whole summer to kick it. Tommy Girl stopped speaking to me right before Christmas when I told her that Red and I were together. It bothered me a little because I thought our friendship was better than that but I didn't stress over it. The beginning of January came and Red and I went back to school.

8
Snapped

They say that some of the lessons people learn in life are learned the hard way. Sometimes we don't realize that some of the things that we say, even in joking, can have more of an impact on people's lives than we think. I was always a person that never thought before I said things. I just thought that people knew how I was and knew that I never meant any harm by the things I said. Most of the time, the things I said were just for a laugh. I will never forget the events that led up to the day that a few people, including myself, learned a valuable lesson—the hard way.

Everywhere you go there is one person that always seems to be the butt of everyone's jokes. Some can handle it but others don't take to it very well. At New Grove, Reese was that person because he was the whitest black person that anyone had ever met. I joked about it around La'vell and other people but Reese wasn't around when I did. For some reason, Swift just wouldn't let up. I remember the first day Swift pissed Reese off. La'vell, Reese, and I were sitting in the cafeteria with a couple other people when Swift came in and sat down.

"What up, e'rybody," Swift greeted as he sat down. "What's up, White Boy?"

"Chill out," La'vell urged to Swift.
"What? I was just speakin' to e'rybody."
"Yeah right."

"Anyway…who goin' to the club tonight?"

"I was thinkin' bout rollin' out tonight," I began as I sipped my drink. "I hadn't been out in a minute."

"That's cuz Red got you locked down," one of the other guys joked.

"I don't even blame you on that one," Swift laughed. "She could lock me down any day."

"Watch ya mouth."

"You know I'm just fuckin' around." Swift turned his attention to Reese. "So, Reese…when you gonna hook a brother up wit a snow bunny? I ain't never been wit one before."

"On the 31st of Neveraury," Reese replied without look up from his plate.

"What kinda white boy shit is that? As a matter of fact, you need to go sit over there cuz this table's reserved for brothas only."

"Whatever," Reese responded.

"I'm serious. Go sit over there." Reese paid Swift no mind until Swift got up, grabbed his tray and sat it on the table next to us.

"What the fuck is your problem?"

Super Senior

"You my problem. I'm sick of whitewashed ass niggas like you."

"Chill out, Swift," I interjected.

"Nah…fuck dat Dré. Every time I see this dude he all up these white people face then wanna hang around us like he down." Reese closed his eyes and took a deep breath.

"You know what?" Reese exhaled. "I gotta bounce. If I don't somebody's getting' hurt."

"Hurt by who? You? Boy stop!" Swift and a couple of the other guys sittin' at the table started laughing. Reese got up from the table and walked out of the cafeteria.

"You need to chill out," La'vell began. "Reese ain't never done nothin' to you for you to fuck with him like that."

"Reese know I just be messin' wit him."
"You keep it up," I chuckled. "Reese gone snap on your ass one day."

"Reese ain't gone do shit but stay white."

"You know it's them quiet ones you gotta look out for." That day seemed like it sparked a series of events between Reese and Swift. The comments and jokes were funny at first but pretty soon it got out of hand. Swift's actions became down right juvenile. He would do things like tape signs on his back that said things like: "Uncle Tom" or "Wish I was Black." The more Swift dug in, the more I could see the rage building up inside Reese.

The night that, I believe, pushed Reese over the edge was the night of his 19th birthday. Reese and La'vell had a couple of friends from high school that went to Furman University in Greenville. They let La'vell use their apartment to throw Reese a birthday party. We all went to help him celebrate. The party was going good until Swift showed up. You could see by the look in Reese's eyes that he wasn't happy that he was there. I had that feeling like Swift was up to something. I knew Swift didn't talk to white girls but I kept seeing him talk to this one particular white girl that night. A couple of times, I noticed him pointing Reese out to her. As Red and I sat on the couch, she noticed that my mood had changed a little. She grabbed my hand and led me outside to talk to me because the music was so loud in the apartment.

"What's wrong?" Red asked as she put her arms around my waist.

"I don't know. I keep having this strange feeling. Something's not right."

"Something's not right about what?"

"I'm tryna figure out why Swift is here. If I knew that a person didn't like me I wouldn't go to his birthday party. He's gotta be up to something."

"I think you're overreacting, Baby. Just relax and enjoy yourself."

"Maybe you're right."
"I'm a woman," she giggled. "I'm always right."
"Is that so?"
"Yup," Red paused for a moment. "Okay maybe I was wrong about one thing but I made up for it."

"I'm glad you cleared that up cuz you knew I was gettin' ready to go there."
"I know."

"Let's go back in. It's a little chilly out here." Red and I walked back into the apartment. Everybody was laughing, drinking, dancing, and having a good time. Even Reese wasn't letting Swift's presence ruin his night.

Twelve o'clock rolled around and the party was in full swing. The alcohol mixed with teenaged hormones was kicking in. People were making out everywhere. In the middle of it all, Swift stopped the music.

"Can I have everybody's attention?" Swift asked as people turned their attention towards him. "I know I fuck wit Reese a lot but he's really a cool dude. I pulled a few strings wit my people and got him a hellavah birthday present." Swift grabbed a chair and sat it in the middle of the living room. He motioned for Reese to have a seat in the chair. Reese was hesitant at first but gave in and took a seat. "From parts unknown, I give to you...Lexi!" The music started and the same white girl I saw Swift talking to earlier in the night emerged from the crowd and started to dance for Reese.

The fellas went crazy as the girls faces displayed utter disgust. Dollar bills rained down on her from the circle of guys that engulfed her as she began to come out of her clothes. I put my hand in my pocket to grab a few dollars but Red gave me one of the nastiest looks. Needless to say, I took my hand out of my pocket and left the money in it. I watched the show but as I scanned the crowd, I noticed that Swift had disappeared. I kept looking for him but I couldn't see him. Ten minutes later, he appeared holding a birthday cake. The dancer removed herself from Reese's lap.

"Happy Birthday, White Boy!" Swift shouted over the music as he smashed the cake into Reese's face. The entire room laughed with the exception of a few of us. By no means were Swift's actions funny.

In a fit of rage, Reese wiped the cake from his face and rushed at Swift. Swift was about 6'1" and weighed about 220 pounds. Reese was only 5'5" and barely weighed 130. Swift tossed Reese back and forth like a ragdoll.

La'vell and one of the guys that lived in the apartment pulled Reese out the back door to calm him down. The other guy that lived there asked Swift and the stripper to leave. That killed the mood of the party and everybody disbursed.

After that night, Reese was a different person. He withdrew from everybody. Every time I saw him, he was alone. People spoke to him as they passed but he did not respond. La'vell tried to reach out to his best friend but he pushed him away too. A week later, Reese withdrew from school. Nobody saw or heard from him until that day in April.

One morning in the middle of April, I woke up to a strange feeling. I didn't know what it was but it bothered me for most of the morning. The way my schedule was set up for that semester, I had one class in the morning and my next two classes didn't start until 12:30. Because Red and I were up late the night before working our project for Psychology, I decided to take a nap after my 8:30 class.

After I woke from my nap, I put my clothes back on to go eat before class. When I walked up the hill from my dorm, I noticed that there were many people gathered in front of the cafeteria. I put a little pep in my step to see what was going on. Police were on campus surrounding the main building, Davis Hall. The police had the area taped off and the students backed up to the cafeteria. Kevin saw me coming up the hill and motioned for me to come to him.

"What's all this about?" I asked my roommate.
"Ya' boy done snapped."
"Who…?"
"Reese. He is holding his class hostage at gunpoint. A few people said they heard a gun shot but they haven't said whether anybody's hurt or not."

"What? How long this been goin' on?"
"Right as the 10:30 classes started."

"Oh shit! Red might be in there! She said Reese was in her 10:30 class."

"Calm down."
"Calm down? Where's La'vell?"
"He's up there with one of the officers." I pushed my way through the crowd and made it to La'vell.

"La'vell!" I called as I approached. "What's goin' on, man?"

"Sir, you have to step back," one of the officers commanded.

"Officer you don't understand. My girlfriend might be in that classroom."

"I assure you that we're doing everything possible to make sure nobody gets hurt." La'vell ducked under the caution tape and walked me off to the side.

"I think this has something to do with what went down between him and Swift."

"Are you kidding me? He's puttin' other people's lives in danger cuz he got beef with Swift? My girl is in there, Man."

"I know. I've been tryna convince them to let me go inside to talk to him but they won't. I know I can talk him out of this."

"There's got to be another way in."

"They got the whole building surrounded. This shit is way to out of hand. I heard them say something about bringin' in SWAT." I released a large exhale and wiped down my face with both hands. I walked over to one of the benches and sat down. I couldn't believe what was going on. This was the type of thing that you only saw in the movies. A feeling of helplessness rushed through my body because I knew my girlfriend was in there and there wasn't anything I could do to help her.

The stand off went into its third hour. By this time, the reporters had arrived. They were walking around talking to the students. Every student that attended NGC was out there. New Grove's President canceled the rest of the day's classes. The entire time I sat on that bench I surveyed the entire situation and the surroundings. There had to be a way inside. I kept coming up empty. I couldn't bear to stay out there any longer. I walked over to the adjoining building where my radio broadcast class was held. It was in the lower level of the science building. When I got there, my professor was there.

"Mr. Marshall," he greeted. "What are you doing here? Class was canceled."

"I know. I was outside in the madness but I had to get away for a minute."

"Do you know any of the students involved?"

"Yes sir. The guy holding everyone hostage, used to live across the hall from me. I think my girlfriend is in there, too."

"Oh my."
"Tell me about it."
"I'm sure the police have everything under control."
"I hope so."

"Can you give me a hand? I need to move this old equipment so they can take it to the storage area. We just got a new soundboard."

"Sure." I grabbed one end of the old soundboard and helped my professor carry it through a door and into a small room that was attached to the class room. Once we got in there, I noticed a hallway. "Where does this go?"

"It runs under Davis Hall. That's where the main storage area is."

"Really?"

"Yes." After my professor told me that the hallway lead to Davis, the wheels in my head started to turn. "I'm getting ready to go outside to talk to some of my journalist friends. Don't lock the door if you leave before I get back."

"Okay." As soon as he left, I walked back into the dimly lit hallway. I walked until I found the storage area. It was over flowing with a bunch of everything. It was too dark for me to get a good look around the room. I searched for a light switch. There was one on the wall at the entrance to the hallway. When I flipped it, a few dim lights came on. Beside the light switch, I noticed another door. It was a stairwell. Because the storage area was under Davis, it had to lead upstairs.

I ran back to the broadcast room then outside. I calmed myself as not to look suspicious. Through the crowd, I went once again to find La'vell. He was still with the police when I found him. When he saw me approaching, I motioned for him to come to me. I didn't want to tell him anything around the police. He followed me back to the broadcast room.

"Follow me." We walked down the hallway and into the storage area.

"Where are we?"

"We're under Davis. This stairwell has to lead upstairs. Are there any cops on the third floor?"

"I don't think so. When they talked to Reese, he said that if any cops came on the third floor he was gonna shoot somebody."

"Do you believe him?"

"I've known Reese since junior high. I've seen him get pissed off but I didn't think he would ever do anything like this."

"If we go up there, are you sure you can talk him out of this?"

"Reese has always listened to me. I pretty sure I can talk some sense into'em."

"I don't need you to be pretty sure. I need you to be sure. People's lives are in danger."

"I'll do my best." We quietly opened the door and crept up the stairs. I had no idea where the stairs would lead us. Once we got to the first floor, I knew exactly were we were. On every floor, we peeked through the window. There were cops on the first and second floors but none when we got to the third. "What room are they in?"

"I think its 304," I whispered as I peeked into the hallway. "From where we are, it's the fifth door on the left."

"Do you see any cops?"

"It looks like the coast is clear. We need to get a look inside the room before we go in."
The two of us eased down the hallway. The way the classroom was designed, it had two doors—one on each end of it. We could see inside without being spotted. La'vell peeked into the room.

"What do you see?"
"Reese is sitting behind the professor's desk. He has the gun sitting on the desk and everybody's sitting on the floor."

"Do you see my girl?"
"I can't tell. Wait a minute. Is she wearing a red windbreaker?"

"Yeah..."
"I see'er...Oh shit."

"What?"
"He shot Swift."

"Is he dead?"

"No. He is sitting in the corner beside the desk. It looks like he shot him in the shoulder. I think we need to go get the police."

"Do you want them to kill him?"
"No."

"If we show them this vantage point, they'll take him out. No questions asked. You gotta go in."

"I don't know if I can."

"You said he will listen to you."

"I know but he doesn't look normal. He has a different look in his eyes."

"Alright…if you wanna turn back, we can. If we do, gotta get the cops. It's up to you."

"Okay but gimme a minute. I gotta get my head right." La'vall paused for a minute and took a couple of deep breaths. "Alright…Come on."

"I can't go in there. You know Reese don't like me."
"You cool. I told him I asked you to chill out and you did. He told me he ain't got no beef with you."

"You sure…?"

"Yes."

"Okay. Let's go but take it slow." La'vell placed his hand on the doorknob and turned it slowly.

"Reese," he called. "It's La'vell." Reese grabbed the gun, walked over to Swift, and put the gun to his neck.

La'vell slid into the room with his hands up.

"What are you doing here?" Reese answered back. "Are you by yourself?"

"No. I'm with Dre."
"Get in here," Reese commanded. I followed La'vell into the classroom.

"Baby...!" Red called when she saw me.

"Don't move, Tiffany. I'm serious. I don't wanna hurt you."

"Just be cool, Baby. Everything's gonna be okay."
"You gotta stop this Reese. This isn't the way to deal with it."

"I can't. I'm in too deep."
"It's not too late."
"Yes it is. This is the end of the road."

"Don't talk like that. This can be worked out."
"How…? By me going to jail? I can't go to jail."

"You gotta turn yourself in. If you don't they're gonna take you out by any means necessary."

"Not if I do it before they do." Reese took the gun from Swift's neck and pointed it at his head.

"Come on, Reese. That is not the answer. We all make mistakes. Think about it. It'll break your mother's heart."

"She's not my mother! She's just some white lady that raised me!"

"Nancy loves you. You know she does. C'mon man. Put the gun down."

Reese began to shake his head. The more he shook it, the more his facial expression changed. The look on his face turned from evil to sorrow. Tears started to roll down his face.

"I never meant for this to happen. All I wanted to do was come to college and play baseball. Everywhere I go, people gotta single me out because I'm different. They don't know my life. They don't know what I've been through."

"But I do. We have been friends for a long time. I love you like my brother. Just let me help you."

"It's too late. I'm beyond help." Reese pointed the gun at Swift and cocked the hammer of the revolver. "But I'm not going by myself." Swift cowered in the corner begging for his life.

"Don't do it, Reese. C'mon man. That's not the way out. He's not worth it."
"It's the only way out I see that doesn't involve me spending the rest of my life in jail."

"That won't happen. You've never been in any trouble before. They won't send you to jail for life."

"I'm not willing to take that chance." Reese pulled the trigger and fired a shot into Swift's forehead.

Red and the other females screamed as the shot rang out. After firing the shot that ended Swift's life, he pointed the gun to his head.

"See you on the other side, Homie." Reese squeezed another shot into his own head then fell to the floor.

"Reeeese…!" La'vell yelled. "Nooooo…!" La'vell ran over to his fallen friend and wept uncontrollably over his body.

Red ran into my arms and cried. I stood there and held on to her. I could not believe what I had just witnessed. The cops rushed into the room with guns drawn. The professor let the police know that the shooter was dead. They put their weapons down and escorted everyone out of the building. Once outside, I sat down on the ground and held onto Red as she cried. Once the chaos was over, they took me and La'vell downtown for questioning because we entered the building without authorization. Three hours later, we were back on campus.

I sat in the room with La'vell as he cried. He told me the history between him and Reese. Along with that, he told me that Reese had been bullied all his life for being different. His foster parents raised him as a white child. He wasn't allowed to associate with any other Blacks besides La'vell because they thought that La'vell was just as white as him. A similar situation happened to him in high school like the one that happened on his birthday. Some black guys from the football team stripped him of his clothes and tied him up. They wrote 'white boy' on his forehead and put him on the stage in the gym before a pep rally. When the gym filled up, they opened the curtains. I sat in shock as La'vell told me the story. After an hour, La'vell said that he was going to bed. I walked back to my room. Kevin informed me that Red called while I was out. I picked up the phone to call her back.

"Hello," Red answered with a hoarse tone in her voice.

"You okay?"

"No. I need you. Every time I close my eyes, all I can see is what happened today. I just need to be in your arms right now."

"Meet me in front of the student center."

"Okay."

I hung up the phone and walked toward the student center. There was an eerie silence on campus that night.

I saw Red from a distance; she was sitting on the steps holding herself. When I got there she rushed into my arms and cried. Once I calmed her down enough to walk, we went downstairs into the TV lounge. No one was there. I sat on the couch. Red crawled in my lap and held onto me like a frightened child.

"I've never experienced anything like that before in my life," Red explained between sniffles. "I was so scared."

"I was about to lose my mind knowing you were in there and there was nothing I could do about it. I felt so helpless."

"When you came through that door, I knew I was going to be okay."

"You're the only reason why I looked for a way in. I don't know what I woulda done if something would've happened to you."

"I love you so much, Dré."
"I love you, too."

We sat for a while in silence then turned on the television to try to take our minds off everything that happened. Before long, it was time for the student center to close. Red did not want me to leave her so we decided to go down the hill and get a room at the little motel. We went to our rooms to grab a couple of things then left campus.

When we arrived on campus the next morning, NGC seemed like a ghost town. Classes were cancelled for the remainder of the week. I never thought that I would ever experience anything like that in my lifetime but it taught me a valuable lesson. I learned that just because someone was a little different from you, they were still a person and should be treated as such. My heart went out to La'vell. I couldn't imagine what was going on in his head. Reese was like a brother to him. After I dropped Red off and returned to my dorm, I saw a man and a woman carrying things from the second floor. They came out of the door that led to Swift's room. Looking closer, I noticed that the lady had Swift's letterman jacket draped over her arm. I spoke and gave them my condolence when they came down the stairs. They thanked me and walked away. I didn't know how she was holding up so well having just lost a son.

Super Senior

I couldn't fathom the thought of losing either of my grandparents. I'd probably go insane.

9
Just in Time

In the aftermath of that dreadful day, life still had to go on. It was a lot to have to deal with at the end of the semester. The first few days following the incident were rough for me. I couldn't completely deal with it because I had to keep my girl straight. She and I spent an entire week at the Cricket Inn because of the nightmares she was having. It bothered me a bit but I'd seen some crazy things in my short lifetime. The school urged us to seek psychological help but for most black people that wasn't an option. People like me chose to give it to God and let him work it out.

Before long, things were back to normal—or as normal as they could be. The semester's end crept up on us and finals were on the horizon. You could tell the students that partied too much over the semester because they were the ones walking around looking like stressed out zombies. I partied but I managed to keep my grades up. My grandparents weren't having that and neither was Red. Classes were light leading up to finals week. Most of the classes were used for review and preparation for the forthcoming exams. I helped Red bang out her last composition while I prepared for my finals. The weekend before finals, we decided to party like rock stars. They held an end of the year bash at Images on Friday. During the day on Saturday, we planned a cookout for La'vell's birthday

Super Senior

and we planned to go to a party in Spartanburg that night. Sunday was set aside for Red and I to spend some quality time together because that was going to be our last time to spend together before we went home.

After a long night of partying on Friday, we all woke up around noon on Saturday. Red and I went to the store to pick up a few last minute items for the barbecue then came back to campus. Throughout the semester I'd made quite an impression on the lady that ran the grill in the student center. Because of that, she allowed us to use the kitchen to prepare most of the food for the day's event. I loved that one thing about southern girls. They knew how to throw down in the kitchen. Once we got everything ready to go, I went out to the patio downstairs from the student center and fired up the grill. Once the smoke signals started going up in the air, the people started to gather.

It was a good start to a great day. The weather was beautiful and the people came to have a good time. We went all out for La'vell. It was more than a birthday party for him. The party was also our way of showing him that we had his back in his time of need. Around 1:30, the guest of honor arrived. I told him we were going to do a little something for him for his birthday so he wasn't expecting the bash that we had set up. He thanked me as everybody dug in to the spread that Red, Tanekia, and I prepared. As people ate, they engaged in heated games of Spades, and

Monopoly. We even had the Sega Genesis setup in the TV lounge.

"Hey man," La'vell began as he approached me at the grill. "I don't know what to say. I really appreciate this."

"It's all good man. After what we've been through, we needed this. Enjoy it."

"I wish Reese woulda been here for this. He loves barbeque."

"I didn't really get a chance to know Reese but I know you. If he was as cool as you, then he was a cool ass dude."

"He was a good person. He'd just been through a lot. I appreciate you havin' my back through it all."

"It's not that many of us here so we gotta stick together. It always seems that bad shit always happens to good people. Let's not dwell on that though. It is your 19th birthday. Let's celebrate."

"True indeed…" La'vell gave me a brotherly hug as my girl walked up.

"I knew you was cheatin' on me," Red laughed.
"Damn man, she caught us."

"I was just over here thanking Dre for everything. Thank you, too."

"You're welcome."

"Now if you'll excuse me, I'm gettin' ready for Round two on the fizood!"

"Don't hurt yourself!" I turned my attention to my girl. "What's up, Boo? What you need?"

"Let me know when you get ready to take that chicken off. I want to take Mrs. Cathy a plate. That's the least I can do since she let us use the kitchen."

"It'll be ready in about 20 minutes."

Everyone had a great time helping La'vell celebrate his birthday. Around 4 o'clock, we straightened up and took the remainder of the food and drinks to the softball field for the kickball game we had planned. For an hour and a half we ran around like big kids. After the game a few others and me went back to the student center to finish cleaning up. Once we finished. I went back to the room to take a nap before the party that night.

At 9:30, we left for O'Malley's in Spartanburg about nine cars deep with La'vell leading the way. O'Malley's was a club that La'vell and Reese turned us on to. All the college kids liked it because they served drinks to everybody—even if you were underage. The club was cool. It had a mixed crowd. The thing that set it off was the Irish theme. Because of that, the dance floor was a huge shamrock cut into the floor. One of the people in our caravan had a blow out so we didn't get to the club until 11:30. Once NGC and the kids from Spartanburg Methodist fell in the groove, we got the party started. I'd been to O'Malley's several times but that night was the most fun I'd ever had.

Red and I had already decided to stay in Spartanburg for the night because we planned to go to Gaffney to the outlets. The next morning we had breakfast at IHOP then headed to Gaffney. We got there a little before 1:00. To stretch the day out, we planned on going in every store regardless of what they sold. The two of us had a ball that day. We left the outlets around five and headed back to Greenville.

"So," Red began as she turned down the radio. "What's your plan for the summer?"

"I don't know. I saved a lot of money this year so I would not have to work this summer. I was thinking about taking a trip up north to see my family. I hadn't been up there in awhile."

"Really? Where at...?"
"Philly and Jersey."
"I got family in Philly. They're all in Germantown."

"That's where my family's at. You wanna go?"

"I don't know if my parents will let me go all the way to Philly with my boyfriend."

"You never know until you ask."

"That's true."

"What about you? What's on your agenda for the summer?"

"I have three softball tournaments in June."

"Are they all in South Carolina?"

"One is. The others are in Florida and Georgia."

"I might have to check you out."

"Are you going to St. Louis to see your dad?"

"I don't know yet. He said he was coming on this side in July. If he doesn't I'll probably go out there right before school starts back."

"I'm so glad we live in the same area. I've gotten so used to being with you everyday, I don't know what I'd do if couldn't see you this summer."

"I was thinkin' about that too."

"I know ya' girl ain't gonna be too happy with that though."

"Who...?"

"The girl you went to school with."

"Tommy Girl? Please. She'll get over it. I ain't payin' her no attention."

"She's a pretty girl. I'm sure she has a man by now." We continued to laugh and talk the rest of the way back to Greenville. Once we got back, we chilled out for a minute on campus then headed right back out.

The first stop was dinner. Red had been hinting about seafood so we went back to our little spot in Traveler's Rest. After dinner, we went to the movies. *Friday* had just hit the theaters. From there, we went to Frankie's Fun Park to play laser tag and mini golf, ride go-carts, and play video games. That was the thing that I loved the most about Red was the fact that she stayed true to her word. On our first date at the seafood spot she told me that it didn't matter what we did as long as we were together, she was happy. The little things kept our relationship going strong.

After a long day and a long night, it ended at the Comfort Inn. That night was going to be the last night we could spend together for a while. I was sure that we would have a chance to get together once we got back home and settled but any excuse for us to spend the night together was always a good one. The night started with conversation, moved on to sensual massages and ended in the aftermath of a three-hour session of lovemaking.

Super Senior

There were no classes that Monday due to the start of exams on Tuesday. We arrived on campus exhausted from the previous night's feature presentation and the early morning's sequel. I dropped Red of at her dorm and went back to mine to rest before I finished my studying for my exams that started Wednesday. I only had three exams that semester then I could begin my summer. Red and I both had our last exam on Thursday morning. We made plans to leave that afternoon.

Thursday came before we knew it and our first year at NGC had come to a close. We said our goodbyes and jumped on the road right before the sun started to go down. A few hours later, we arrived at Red's house. I helped her get her things in the house, spoke with her parents for a while then headed home. My grandmother greeted me with open arms. My grandfather was in the middle of a meeting at the church.

"I'm so glad to see my baby," my grandmother smiled as I sat down at the kitchen table. "Your room is just how you left it."

"It feels do good to be home."
"How'd your exams go?"
"I think I did pretty good on them."
"What about math?"
"It was a struggle but I think I passed that one too."

"Well that's good. As long as you tried, that's all that matters. You hungry…? There are some leftover pork chops and collard greens from dinner. I'll fix you a plate."

"I got it, Mom. I need to get this stuff out the car first."

"You go do that and I'll fix your food." I got up from the table and kissed my grandmother on the cheek.

"You're the greatest."
"I know."

I pulled my car from around back to the front so I wouldn't have to walk a long way. It took me about fifteen minutes to get everything in my room. Once everything was in, I went back into the kitchen. Mom was just putting my food on the table. "Here you go, Baby."

"Thank you." I bowed my head and said grace.
"So tell me, what are your plans for the summer?"
"I was thinking about taking a trip to Philly to see Granny and everybody else. It's been a while."

"That would be nice. They would love to see you. As a matter of fact, Mom asked me about you when I talked to her the other day."

"How's she doing?"
"She's doing better since she moved in with my sister. She was sick for a little while."

"That's good that she's doing better."

"What else you got planned? Are you going to St. Louis to see your Dad?"

"I don't know yet. He's supposed to be coming home in July. If he does, I'll just meet him in Fayetteville. If not, I'll probably go out right before school starts."

"What about work? Are you going back to the Sonic this summer?"

"Nope. I saved money all year so I wouldn't have to work this summer. I plan to relax and enjoy it."

"You still with that yella girl?"
"You mean Tiffany?"
"What other yella girl is there?" Mom laughed.
"Yes. I dropped her off before I came here."

"Chelsea came to church Sunday. She asked about you."

"I'm surprised. She hasn't had too much to say to me since Christmas."

"I couldn't tell. Not by the way she started grinning when I told her you were coming home this week." My grandmother and I continued to talk as I finished my food. Just as I finished, my grandfather came in and joined the conversation. We must've laughed and talked for a good two hours. Around 10 o'clock, I got a page from Red. I excused myself and went back into my room to call her back. She and I talked as I put my things away and straightened my room up.

"When do I get to see you?" Red asked.
"I just dropped you off."
"And...?"

"That means I don't want to see you for at least a week."
"What!"

"I'm just jokin', baby. We can get together this weekend."

"I was getting ready to cuss you out."
"I know."

"Has your girl sniffed you out yet?"
"Nah," I laughed.

"Give her time. As small as Hartsville is, she'll spot you or somebody she knows will see you. Then she'll be hot on the trial."

"Watch ya mouth talkin' about my city."
"I thought Fayetteville was your city, Dré Smoove aka Mr. North Carolina."

"You just full of jokes tonight, ain't you?"

"You know I gotta mess with you. I miss yo' bighead already."

"Which one?"
"Stop bein' nasty…"
We finished making plans for the weekend and ended our conversation. I went back out into the den and watched TV with my grandparents. As we watched television, they asked me about the day that everything went down with Reese. It was a hard subject to talk about but I managed to get it out. Before long, they turned in for the night and I went back into my room. I turned on my television and stretched out on the couch that was in my room. Talking about what happened with Reese got my mind going. I remembered hearing people say that death always came in three. There was no news of anybody passing away after Swift and Reese. I wondered who the third would be. The next morning I was pulled out of my slumber by a knock on my door.

"Andre," my grandmother called. "Wake up. I need you to go to the store for me." I rolled over and looked at my grandmother. She didn't look to good.

"What's wrong?" I asked as I sat up in the bed.
"I don't know. I think I ate something that didn't agree with me. It's probably just gas or indigestion. Run to the store and get me an Alka-Seltzer."

"Okay." I jumped out of the bed and threw on the clothes I had on yesterday and hurried to the store. By the time I got back, things had already taken a turn for the worst. When I walked back into the house, my grandmother was on her knees slumped over her bed. At first I thought she was praying until I noticed she was clutching her chest.

"Call an ambulance," she grunted. I ran into the kitchen, called 911 then went back to tend to my grandmother.

"The ambulance is on the way. Just hold on." I knelt down beside her and put my arms around her.

"I love you, Andre."
"I love you, too."
"If I don't make it, promise me you'll take care of your grandfather and finish school."

"Don't talk like that. You're gonna make it." Tears began to fall from my eyes. All my life my grandmother has been the stronghold that has held our family together. She has always been there for everybody. I didn't know what I would do if she didn't pull through.

"Just promise me that."
"I promise."
"Do me a favor. Pray for me." She grabbed my hand and placed it on her heart.

"Heavenly Father, we need you right now. One of your children is in need of healing right now. Lord we ask that whatever it is, you move it. Take away all the pain. We ask for a healing right now, Dear God. You said that where there were two or three touching and agreeing, you'd be in the midst. We need you to be in the midst right now…" My prayer was interrupted by the EMTs at the front door. I propped my grandmother up against the bed and ran to let them in.

When I returned to the room, she has slid down to the floor and was having a seizure. My grandmother wasn't an extremely large woman but she wasn't small either. I got pissed off because they sent two of the scrawniest EMTs they had. They couldn't get her on the gurney. I had to help them. When we finally got her on and strapped in, I had to search for her purse. I was going to ride in the ambulance with her but by the time I found her purse they had her in and were already backing out of the driveway in route to the hospital that was less than two minutes up the road. I hopped in my car and followed the ambulance.

Just as I was getting ready to make the right turn on the street that the hospital was on, I saw my grandfather's truck turning onto the same street that I was on. I pulled through the intersection and stopped him. When he saw the expression on my face he knew I something was wrong.

"Something's wrong with Mom. She's in that ambulance."

"Oh my God..! Come on." My grandfather sped off and almost sideswiped a car that was coming across the intersection. I jumped back in my car and made a u-turn to follow him.

When we got to the emergency room, they'd already taken her into the back. They wouldn't let my grandfather go back there with her. Instead, they escorted us to the trauma room to wait. I paced back and forth as we waited for any news concerning my grandmother. Thirty minutes passed and the doctor walked into the room.

"Mr. Henderson," he called.
"That's me. How's my wife?"

"Your wife lost consciousness while in the ambulance. They tried all they could do while she was in there and we tried all that we could when we got her in the back. She had a massive heart attack. I'm sorry, Mr. Henderson. Your wife didn't make it."

Each one of those five words pierced my soul as they came out of the doctor's mouth. It felt like all the air left my body at one time. With a stunned expression on my face, I looked at my grandfather. He shook his head in disbelief as tears rolled down his face. Other than in church, that was the first time I'd ever seen my grandfather cry. He looked at me then looked back at the doctor.

"Can we see her?"

"Give us about ten minutes then you can see her."

"Okay."

"I just want to say again that we did everything that we could possibly do."

"I know you did. Thank you."

My grandfather sat down in a chair and leaned back looking towards Heaven. He didn't say anything aloud but I watched as he silently mouthed words. I was still in shock. My heart was aching but it was hurting more for him than it was for me. My grandmother was my grandfather's world. She meant everything to him. They had been together for 25 years.

Ten minutes passed and the nurse came out to take us to see my grandmother. My grandfather told me that I didn't have to go back if I didn't want to but I had to. The nurse led us down a hall and into a room. The room was dimly lit and my grandmother was lying lifeless on the bed. My grandfather grabbed her hand and began to talk to her.

"When I left the house this mo'nin," he began as he wiped tears from his eyes. "I didn't realize that when I kissed you goodbye, that was the last time I would see you alive. You are in God's hands now. Just know that I will always love you and you will always be in my heart." I watched as he removed her wedding ring and the rest of her jewelry. He gave her one final kiss on her forehead and walked over to me. "Go say goodbye to your grandmother." I walked over to her and grabbed her hand. It was cold to the touch.

"I'm gonna miss you so much. You were my everything. You were always there for me and you had my back no matter what. I promise that I will take care of Dad. I also promise you that I will finish school and get my degree no matter what. I will always love you and you will always be in my heart." I leaned in and kissed my grandmother on the cheek one last time.

We finished with the miscellaneous items at the hospital then returned home. My grandfather made a few phone calls and in no time the house was swarming with family and church members. Everybody grieves in their own way. I felt that other than my grandfather, I was closest to her because it was always just her and me since day one. I grew weary of everybody asking me if I was alright. I appreciated the concern but it was getting a bit redundant. When my aunts came in hoopin' and hollering, I knew it was time for me to ride out. I told my grandfather that I was taking a ride and I would be back later. He walked me outside.

"You okay?" he asked as I unlocked my car door.
"I'm as good as I can be right now. I just need to get away for awhile."

"Alright but you be careful."
"I will."

I backed out of the driveway, turned left and kept driving. Twenty-five minutes later, I was pulling in Red's driveway. I saw her peek out the window then come running out of the house with a huge smile on her face. Her expression changed when she saw my face as I got out of the car. When she got to me, I put my arms around her and let it all out.

"What's wrong, Dré?" Red asked with genuine concern in her voice. "What happened?" I couldn't speak at the moment. "It's okay. Just let it out. Whatever it is, just let it go." For ten minutes, I cried like a baby in Red's arms. Her parents pulled up.

"What's going on?" Red's mother asked.
"I don't know yet. He just got here about ten minutes ago and hasn't been able to tell me."

"Bring him in the house, Tiffany." I continued to sob as Red put her arm around my waist, led me into the house, and sat me on the couch in the living room. I finally managed to calm myself enough to talk.

"My grandmother passed away this morning," I sniffed.

"Oh my goodness," Red's mother gasped.
"Dré, I'm so sorry."

"She wasn't sick or anything. We were all just laughing and talking last night when I got home. She woke me up this morning telling me she wasn't feeling too good and to go to the store for her. By the time I came back, she asked me to call the ambulance. I don't think she made it to the hospital."

"How's Pastor Henderson?" Red's father inquired.
"He's a soldier. Right now he's home surrounded by friends and family. I couldn't take it anymore so I had to get out of there."

"I think I'll go call our pastor to let him know then give him a call. You be strong, Dré. You know your grandfather's a tough man but he's gonna need you."

"I will. Thank you." Red's father walked out of the living room.

"If you need anything, don't you hesitate to ask. We're here for you."

"Thank you, Ma'am. I really appreciate it."

"I'm gonna leave you two alone. I'll be in the other room if you need me."

"Okay, Mom."

I sat back on the couch and released a deep exhale.

Super Senior

"You alright?"

"I'm okay for now. I'm glad you were here."

"I'm glad that you're letting me be here for you."

Red put her arms around me and rocked me back and forth like a mother rocking her child. We sat in silence for a while. Her mother and father checked on us periodically. I stayed at Red's for a couple of hours then felt it was time for me to get back to my grandfather. I said my goodbyes to her parents and thanked them then Red and I walked outside.

"I love you, Andre," Red assured me as she wrapped her arms around me. "I'm here for you when you need me. Just call me."

"Thank you, Baby. I really appreciate it."

"Call me when you get home to let me know that you got there safely."

"I will." I got in my car and rolled down the window. Red leaned in the window and gave me a kiss.

"God doesn't make mistakes. She's with him now."

"I know…Call you when I get home."

We exchanged lips once again then I pulled off. Twenty-five minutes later, I was home. By the time I got home, everyone had cleared out with the exception of a couple of people. I greeted everyone then walked into the kitchen to fix myself something to drink. My grandfather excused himself from his conversation and walked into the kitchen.

"You okay?" he asked.
"I'm as good as I can be right now."

"I know she meant just as much to you as she did to me. Keep ya head up. We gone be alright."
"I know we will."

"I know I got my other chur'en but right now, it's just me and you. I got yo back and I know you got mine."
"You know it."
"I know I don't say it much but I just want you to know that I love you."
"I love you too, Dad."

"The man from the funeral home comin' by in the mo'nin'. I need you to be here."
"I will."

"Alright. Lemme get back in here. You go get some rest."
"Okay."

I took my glass of iced tea and walked back into my room. As soon as I sat down, my pager went off. I didn't recognize the number so I paid it no mind. I wasn't in the mood to talk to anyone. I sat in silence watching the ceiling fan slowly spin around and around. Every time I closed my eyes, all I could see was my grandmother's face asking me to promise her that I would take care of my grandfather and finish school. While I was sitting, I heard the doorbell ring. I figured it was someone coming by to see my grandfather so I didn't bother to move. A minute later someone knocked on my door. When I opened it, Tommy Girl was standing on the other side.

"Hey," she greeted. "Would you like some company?"

"Come on in." I moved my laundry off the couch. "Have a seat."

"How you doing?"
"I'm okay."
"I'm sorry for your loss."
"Thank you. How'd you find out?"
"You know my mother works at the hospital. She was there when they brought your grandmother in."
"Oh okay."

"Listen, Dré. I know you're going through a lot right now. I just wanted to apologize for how I've been acting. Regardless of who you're with, you and I are still friends. I guess I was a little jealous because I felt it shoulda been me. Now I know how you felt when me and Mike hooked up."

"It's all good. I guess I should apologize to you too."

"What do you need to apologize for?"

"I know I said some things over the summer that might have led you to believe that there was going to be something between us. I guess I got so caught up in finally having you to myself, I didn't think about how things were going to be once I left for school."

"Neither of us did but that's all in the past now. I know you probably still with ya' girl but I just wanted to know if I could at least have my friend back."

"I never stopped being your friend." Tommy Girl leaned over and wrapped her arms around me.

"I missed you."
"I missed you, too." Tommy Girl and I talked for about an hour before she had to leave.

"If you need anything, I'm here for you. Just call me."
"I will. Thanks."

"Make sure you let me know when the funeral is. I know your girl's gonna be there with you but I just want to be there for moral support. I'll behave. I promise."

"As soon as I find out, I'll let you know." I walked Tommy Girl to her car. We exchanged hugs again then she got in and drove off.

Four days later, we had my grandmother's funeral. It was beautiful. The church was standing room only. Our Head Bishop delivered a great eulogy. I didn't realize how many lives my grandmother had touched. Many of my friends from high school came along with the numerous family and church members. It felt good to know that in my time of need, I had people in my life that were right there for me.

10
Keep it Moving

What do you do when you grow up as Grandma's baby boy then all of a sudden Grandma is no longer around? Losing my grandmother had a huge impact on my life. When she left, she took a piece of me with her. I still had my mother but it just wasn't the same because she was never there for me. In my mind, my mother was gone. For the first three weeks after she passed, I was a mess. I couldn't sleep, I couldn't eat and I didn't go anywhere. I ignored all calls from everyone except for one. The only person I talked to during that time was Red. She helped me keep from losing what little bit of mind I had left.

I was raised to believe that we didn't question God's will but after experiencing what I had in those two consecutive months, I started to doubt my faith. A lyric to one of my favorite gospel songs said: He may not come when you want him but he's always on time. I felt like I'd been slapped in the face because the prayer that I prayed for my grandmother that morning went unanswered. I didn't ask God for much but the one thing that I really needed from him, he didn't come through for me. That made it hard to believe that it was all in his will. My grandmother was the sweetest woman on earth. She never made an enemy and everyone loved her. Why did God choose to take her away from us?

Super Senior

At the end of the third week, my boys felt that enough was enough. They came to the house and strong armed me. I was lying on my couch in the dark when Nick and Twist rushed into the room.

"Come on man," Nick fussed as he removed the blankets I had over the windows to block out the sunlight. "Enough is enough."

"That's right, Dré," Twist agreed. "We've been as patient as we can be. It's time for you to move on with your life. We miss Mom just as much as you do but its time for you to get up and get outta' this house."

"Go away," I commanded from under a pillow that was over my face.

"We're not leaving without you." Nick snatched the pillow from my face. I had to squint because I had not seen the light of day in three weeks. "Get up!" I sat up and allowed my eyes to adjust.

"Why should I? The one thing that I loved more than anything in this world is gone."

"Do you hear yourself talking right now?" Twist asked. "Do you really think Mom would approve of this? You can't wallow in the misery of her death. What did your Bishop say at the funeral? He said that you have to celebrate the life that she lived."

"What if I'm not ready to celebrate yet?"

"It don't matter if your ready or not. You're getting out of this house…today."

The entire time I was being harassed by my boys, I didn't know that my grandfather was leaning in the doorway.

"They're right Dré," my grandfather interrupted. "I've let you grieve. I haven't bothered you cuz e'rybody deal with death in they own way but its time for you to get up and get back on ya feet."

"But Dad…"
"But nothing… You don't think I'm still hurting? I just lost my wife of twenty-five years. Not only was she my wife but she was my best friend. It hurts but I still have to live my life and so do you. You don't see me walkin' 'round here wit my head down do you?"

"No Sir."
"Alright then. I know she meant the world to you but you know she wouldn't want to see you like this. Get up and get out the house wit ya friends. You'll feel better."

"Okay." I peeled myself off the couch and sifted through the clothes in my closet. I pulled out a pair of jean shorts and a shirt. Nick ironed the outfit while I was in the shower. Twenty minutes later I was dressed and we headed out. "Where we goin'?"

"To the arcade to shoot some pool and grab a bite to eat," Nick answered.

"We need to take this nigga to the barbershop," Twist joked. "You look like who done it and why."

"And I still look better than yo' ugly ass."

When we got to the arcade there were a few familiar faces there. They gave me their condolences as I walked in. I thanked them and kept it moving. We ordered out food then went into the poolroom. Over a few games of pool and one of the arcade's famous double chili cheeseburgers, my boys managed to cheer me up.

"Eight ball, side pocket…"

"I see you ain't to down to whoop ass on the pool table," Nick laughed. "I thought I could take advantage of the situation."

"Now that you up and at'em again, what's ya next move?" Twist inquired.

"I had planned to go to Philly to see my family but all of'em came down for the funeral."

"True dat. What about school?"

"I don't think I'm goin' back next semester. I've been through too much in the past couple of months. I need time to get my head straight. Besides, I can't leave my grandfather right now."

"Why don't you transfer to FMU," Nick suggested. "That way you can go to school and still be close by your Pops."

"That don't sound like a bad idea. What's the scene like?"

"It's off the hook, Bruh. I'm talkin' bout mad honeys everywhere. The ratio is a good 7 to 1."

"Damn," Twist laughed. "Sounds like I need to transfer, too."

"What about classes?"

"Its not a cake walk. The people who've been there for a while have a saying: They'll let anybody in but you gotta work to get out."

"What was your GPA for the year?"

"I didn't do too bad. I finished with a 2.9. That ain't bad considering how much I partied."

"I partied too and finished with a 3.7."

"Everybody ain't got brains like you, Bruh. I'm a lover not a scholar."

"What about the Greeks? Who run the yard?"

"The Que's of course...Them and the Deltas... The Alphas and the Sigma's are pretty cool. As a matter of fact, my suitemate just went over Sigma right before school let out."

"What the AKA's look like?"
"Fine as hell..."

"You can always come to State with me," Twist interjected.

"That's a negative;" I laughed "I'm allergic to too many black people in one place at one time."

"But on the real, you should think about it. Its way cheaper than NGC and you don't have all those rules to deal with."

"I'll think about it."

The three of us continued to shoot pool for a couple more hours. By the time we finished up, the sun was going down. We dropped the top on the Mustang and hit the main drag.

In a small city, like Hartsville, Saturday night was one of the funniest things you ever wanted to see. There wasn't much to do so people drove up and down the street for hours. People would drive from the Sonic Drive In to Hardees, turn around, and come back to the Sonic. I worked at Sonic while I was in high school. To draw more business my manager had batting cages put in so on the weekends, the place was packed. We made a couple of rounds then decided to head to Florence. Before we left, I called Red to see what she was doing for the night. She said she was chilling with her girls. The three of them decided to meet the three of us at Applebee's. When we got to Applebee's, the place was packed. Lucky for us, the girls already had a table. We joined the three ladies.

"Hey Baby!" Red squealed as she greeted me with a big hug and a kiss. "These are my girls, Davita and Antoinette."

It was true what they say: Birds of a feather flocked together. I knew my girl was a knock out. Her girls looked just as good. Davita was short with a dark brown complexion. She had the same type of athletic build that Red had. Antoinette was what we described back then as the fine Amazon. She was about six feet tall with a killer body. Her green eyes complimented her light skin. Her hair was long and curly. I knew she was right up Twist's alley.

"This is my baby, Dré and these are his friends."

Super Senior

"What's up ladies," Nick greeted with his mack daddy voice. "I'm Nick. Pleasure to meet you..."

"I'm Felix but everybody calls me Twist."
"I wonder why?" Antoinette pondered with a grin on her face.

"I can't tell you. I have to show you...but we gotta be layin' down."

"You lay down with me; you might not get back up."

"All righty then...!" I interrupted. We took our seats with the girls and engaged in small talk. "Did y'all graduate from South Side too?"

"Yes," Davita answered. We all played softball together."

"What position did you play, Antoinette?" Twist asked with a devilish grin on his face.

"Catcher..."
"My favorite position..."

"Will you two get a room?" Red laughed.
"I'm down if she's down."

"Anyway," Nick interrupted. "What about you, Davita? What position did you play?"

"Third base... I didn't have to do too much when my girl, Red, was on the mound."

"That's what's up? Y'all playin' at the collegiate level?"

"I play for Coastal Carolina," Davita answered.

"I'm at USC," Antoinette replied sipping her water. Where y'all go to school?"

"State," Twist replied.

"I'm right down the street at FMU."

"Yeah," I interjected. "He was supposed to go to NGC wit me but he turned his back on me."

"You know it ain't like that, Homie. I gotta look out for Grandma."

"And that's the only reason why I forgive you."

Davita began while reaching for a menu, "Red told us your grandmother just passed away. I'm sorry to hear that."

"Thanks. That's why I look like this. It's been rough for me these past few weeks but thanks to my girl, I was able to keep from going crazy."

"You know I got ya back, Baby." Red leaned over and kissed me on my cheek.

"Today's the first day I've been out the house since the funeral thanks to my boys."

"We gave him his space," Nick started. "But we felt it was time to go in and get'em."

"Well thank you two for bringin' my baby to see me. I missed him so much."

The server came and took our orders. We continued to talk while we waited on the food. As we waited we decided to go to the movies to see *Tales from the Hood* after we ate. Once the food came, we dug in then headed up the street to the theater. Just as I suspected, Twist and Antoinette hit it off. Nick was odd man out because Davita had a boyfriend. When we got to the movie theater, they were the only two actually watching the movie. Once the movie was over, we said our goodbyes and headed back to our side. I thanked my boys for making me get out of the house. I enjoyed myself that day. I got a chance to spend time with my homies and my girl. What more could a man ask for?

The summer rolled in and I was enjoying it. I was still undecided about returning to school that fall but I did know that if I did, I wasn't returning to NGC. I hadn't broken the news to Red. I wanted to tell her every time we were together but I just couldn't bring myself to do it. She was always so happy when she was with me, I didn't want to ruin her mood. In not telling Red, I hadn't told my grandfather either. I broke the news to him the day before I left to go to Fayetteville to see my Dad. I was standing in the kitchen fixing a sandwich when my grandfather called me into the den.

"Come 'round here for a minute," my grandfather called from his recliner. "I wanna talk to you for a minute."

"Okay." I grabbed my sandwich and my drink and sat down on the couch.

"How you doin'?"

"I'm doing better. Keepin' busy helps keep my mind occupied."

"That's good. You goin' back to school?"
"I am but probably not this year. I think I'ma take a year off. College is tough. I have to make sure I'm focused."

"I can understand that but don't be like the rest of'em. They started, took time off and never went back."

"I won't be like that. I made a promise to Mom that I intend to keep. When I do go back, I'm not goin' back to Greenville though."

"Where you goin?"

"I'm planning to transfer to Franklin Memorial in Florence. That way I'll be close to home if you need me. Besides, FMU is a better school and it's cheaper."

"Well, what ever you decide to do, you know I'm behind you."

"Thanks."

"You told ya girlfriend yet?"

"Not yet. I've been trying to but I just can't bring myself to do it."

"The sooner you tell'er, the better..."

"I know. I'll tell her when I get back."

"Them people love you to death."

"Who...?"

"Brother and Sister Alexander. E'ery time I seem'em, you all they talk about."

"I like them, too. They're good people."

"What's that girl name that go to Pastor Roger's church?"

"You talkin about Chelsea."

"That's Mother Johnson's granddaughter, right?"
"Yeah…"

"She asked about you the other day. She saw me at the bank."

"Oh okay. She and I are still cool. She acted up when she first found out I was with Tiffany but then she came to her senses."
"I don't know what you be doin to these lil' girls," my grandfather laughed. "They be round here goin' crazy. What time you leavin' tomorrow?"

"Probably some time after I wake up."
"Shoot…that won't be 'til tomorrow night."

"Nah," I laughed. "I'm hopin' to get on the road at least by twelve."

"Bishop gone be in Fayetteville this weekend you should try to get by to see him while you up there."

"I'll go by the house Saturday." We finished our conversation and my grandfather left. I retired to my room to relax for a while. I watched a couple of movies then went fell asleep.

The summer continued to move along and before I knew it, July was coming to an end. In three weeks, Red would be leaving to go back to school. It was time for me to break the news to her. I didn't know how I was going to do it but I knew I had to. She and I spent a wonderful Saturday together. At the end of the night, I broke the news to her.

"I need to talk to you about something," I began as I shifted the car into park and turned it off.

"What's up, Baby?"
"I've been trying to figure out when was the best time or the best way to tell you this but…"

"You're not going back to school."
"How did you know?"

"When you told me the promise that you made to your grandmother to take care of your grandfather, I figured it out then."

"Why didn't you say anything?"
"I figured you'd tell me when you were ready."
"I'm sorry, Baby."
"Don't be sorry. Family comes first. I know you would understand if the shoe was on the other foot."

"So what now…?"

"We went into this relationship knowing that we weren't going to be together forever. I just didn't think it would end this soon. We got three more weeks then I go back to school. Wow."

"Can I see you when you come home?"

"Of course you can…as long as you're single; we can kick it like we kick it. If you're with somebody, I'll have to understand."

"Now I see why I love you so much." I leaned in and kissed Red on the lips.
"Just promise me one thing."
"What's that?"

"Promise me that after this year, you will go back to school."
"I promise."

"Do you have any idea where you might go?"
"I think I'm transferring to FMU."
"Really?"
"Yeah. It's close to home and I got friends there."

"Have you decided where you're going after you leave NGC?"

"I met with the coaches from Coastal and the coaches from NC State. Coastal is closer to home but NC State has a better team."

Super Senior

"You gotta go where you think you'll have the best chance to get to the Olympics." Red's eyes lit up and a huge smile spread across her face.

"You remembered."

"How could I forget? You told me that on our first date. I remember everything you told me about you."

"That's so sweet. I'm gonna miss you so much, Dré. I don't know how I'm gonna make it at NGC without you."
"You know with me out the way, the niggas gone be on you."

"I know, Baby. They know I'm not havin' it."

When we parted ways that evening, I did not feel as bad as I thought I would have felt thanks to Red. She took the news better than I thought she would take it. I guess that just had a lot to do with the type of relationship that we had. Red was a great girl and she was good for me. I hated to let her go but I didn't want to hold her back. I knew if I told her that I was willing to do a long distance relationship, she would have been all for it. It would not have been fair to her or me. Who knew what the future held for either of us. Maybe our paths would cross again—maybe they wouldn't.

Three weeks flew by faster than I thought they would. Red and I spent our last night together and made it a night to remember. She told her parents that she was sleeping over at Davita's so that we could spend the night together. When I got my hands on Red that night, I turned her every way but loose. Deep down inside, I knew that that was probably going to be the last time Red and I would be together like that. For the first time in my young life, I made love to a girl all night long—literally. Despite the previous night's event's it was so hard for us to part ways. She had held it in for so long but she finally had to let it go. The way she held me on the day my grandmother passed away was the same way I held her. When Davita picked her up from the motel that morning, I felt that I had said goodbye to my Sexy Red for the last time.

By the end of August, my summer funds were almost depleted. It was time for me to jump back into the work force. I could have gone back to the Sonic but I was tired of fast food. After a couple weeks of job hunting, I took a job as a sales associate at Foot Locker in the mall. It was a good job. The only thing I had to do was be careful because of my sneaker addiction. I was on the job for about a month before she walked into the store. I was stocking hats, so I had my back turned when she came in.

"Excuse me," she began. "Can I try this on in a size five?"

"Yes Ma'am," I replied without turning around. "Give me one second." After placing the last hat on the rack, I turned around and looked into the beautiful, light brown eyes of Tommy Girl.

"What's up?"
"Hey. How you been?"
"I'm good and you?"
"I'm doin' alright."

I took the shoe from Tommy Girl. "I'll be right back." I walked into the back to get the shoes for her then came back out to the floor. "You need me to help you try these on?"

"If it's not too much trouble."
"No trouble at all."

I followed Tommy Girl over to one of the benches. Her fragrance danced in my nose as I walked behind her. When she sat down, I noticed that she wasn't wearing any socks. "Let me go get a pair of socks. I'll be right back."

"I have a pair in my bag." Tommy girl reached in her bag and handed me a pair of pink footies that were rolled together then slid her foot out of her shoe.

"I see you still got the cutest feet I've ever seen." I slid the sock onto her foot.

"I try to keep'em up."

"How's school going?"

"I finished school back in February. I got my license in March and started working in a shop in April."

"You didn't waste no time."
"I told you. I gotta get this money."
"What shop you in?"
"I'm at Unique Designs on Evans."
"That's over by the Barber School, right?"

"About a block up. You should stop in sometime and let me wash your hair or give you a manicure or something. I mean if that's alright wit ya girl."
"We broke up a few weeks ago."
"What a minute," Tommy Girl paused and looked at me with a confused look on her face. "School started back in August, What are you doing here?"

"I decided to take a year off from school to get my head right. I'm going to FMU next Fall."

"Really?" Tommy Girl's eyes lit up.
"Yeah. I couldn't see leaving my grandfather right now."

"I feel you on that. Listen, I know we've had some rough times and I know you just broke up with your girl but I was wondering if I could call you some times. Maybe we could hang out. You know…like we used to."

Looking up at her, "I'd like that. I could use a friend right now."

"What time you get off?"

"We close at nine. I should be outta here by 9:45."

"Come by the shop when you get off. I should just be finishing up my last client."

"Okay, I'll do that. How does that fit?"
"I like'em. I'll take'em."

"I'll get'em with my discount and bring'em with me tonight. You can give me the money then. Cool?"

"That's cool. See you tonight." Tommy Girl pulled the sock off and slid her foot back into her sandal. I watched as that sexy 4'11" frame walked out of the store. Time moved on and before long, I was leaving the mall headed to meet Tommy Girl at the shop. When I got there, two other stylists were there besides Tommy Girl. One was an older black lady that looked to be in her mid-forties and a dark skinned sister that was about in her mid to late twenties.

"Hey ladies," I greeted as I handed Tommy Girl the bag with her shoes in it.

"I didn't know Foot Locker delivered," the oldest of the three stylists laughed. "We can't let you go no where."

"You so crazy, Mrs. Doris," Tommy Girl replied. "This is my friend, Dré. We went to high school together."

"So this is the infamous Dré," the other stylist interrupted. "It's so nice to finally meet you. We've heard so much about you."

"All good I hope..."
"Most of it..."
"So Dre," Mrs. Doris began.
"Mrs. Doris don't start," Tommy Girl pleaded.
"Hush, lil girl. I just wanna talk to the man. Is that okay with you, Miss Thing? Have a seat, Dre." I took a seat. "You got a girlfriend?"

"No, ma'am. We broke up a few weeks ago."
"Was this the girl from the beach or was this the girl from school?" The other stylist interjected.

"This was the one from school."
"Uh huh," Mrs. Doris replied as she continued to sweep around her station. "So she's the reason you and Chelsea aren't together."

"Mrs. Doris! You don't have to answer that, Dré."
"It's cool," I laughed. "Not entirely. Chelsea and I have known each other since I first moved to South

Super Senior

Carolina. I took too long to tell her how I felt when we were in school and another guy stepped in before I did."

"We know all that. Get to the part I wanna know."
"When I found out they weren't together, it was almost time for me to leave for school."

"What's that got to do with anything?"

"I didn't want to do a long distance relationship. When I got to school I met my ex. When Chelsea found out, she cussed me out and that was it."

"I did not cuss you out."
"Why you didn't want to do the long distance relationship is what I want to know."

"Because I respected her too much...I know how I am. I like to be in the company and presence of whomever I'm with. Instead of us getting together and then breaking up shortly after because someone that was physically there with me caught my eye, I decided to be honest with her and myself and not even attempt it."

"Okay, I can understand that. What about now? She's single. You're single. Make it happen."

"I just need a friend right. I've been through a lot."
"Yes, Mrs. Nosey...He just lost his grandmother back in May and him and his girl just broke up. I can't

expect him to jump right into a relationship with me or anybody else."

"We've both changed a lot since high school. We need to take time to get reacquainted with each other. Then we can take it from there."

"Just don't take too long like you did the last time," the other stylist mumbled under her breath."

"Don't worry. I won't." Tommy Girl finished her last client as I continued to be interrogated by Mrs. Doris. Once she was finished, we left.

"I'm so sorry about that, Dré."
"It's all good. I've spent some time with my grandmother in the salon. I know how women get in there. That's the sister to sister inner sanctuary."

"It's not that bad," Tommy Girl laughed.
"You hungry?"
"I little bit."
"Let's go to Angelo's. I hadn't been there since I've been home."

"Sounds good to me..." Twenty minutes later, Tommy Girl and I were at one of my favorite seafood spots. We went in, ordered our food, and took a seat. "What's your next move?"

"Well," I began. "The plan, as of now is to chill out this summer then start at FMU in the fall. What about you?"

"I've been saving money so that I can open my own shop in the next couple of years. My Dad said that if I can come up with half of the money, he put in the other half."

"That's what's up. What you gonna call it?"
"I'm torn between Chelsea's and Diva Style."

"I like Diva Style. It has flair and attitude...just like you."
"Excuse me? I do not have attitude."
"You're kidding me, right?"
"Okay...maybe I have a little. Have you talked to your ex lately?"

"I talked to her a couple of times. She was telling me how all my so-called boys are tryna get at her since I'm not there."

"I tell you, some niggas ain't worth a damn."
"Tell me about it. It's all good though. I can't be mad at'em. She's a good girl."

"This may sound odd but I'm glad she made you happy. It may not've seemed like it the way I acted but as a friend, all I ever want is for you to be happy even if it wasn't with me."

"That's how I felt when you started goin' with Mike. You seemed happy so I let you be."

"To be honest with you, Mike was one of the worst mistakes I ever made. I changed who I was just to be with him."

"What do you mean?"

"He had me doing stupid stuff. I was lying to my parents, sneaking out of the house and to top it all off, I was giving him the money. I was so stupid."

"Like my father always tells me, you live and you learn. I'm sure that situation taught you a lot."

"I learned that if a man can't accept me for who I am, then I don't need to be with him."

"That is so true." Before long, our food came. Tommy Girl and I continued to talk as we enjoyed our meal and each other's company.

Over the next few months, Tommy Girl and I spent a lot of time together as the communication between Red and I dwindled. She really helped me cope with what I was going through. Some days, my grandmother's death would just sneak up on me. Tommy Girl was there through it all. She held me when I cried, and she helped calm me down when I was angry. Tommy Girl hadn't changed a bit when it came to me. I was still her number one guy.

Super Senior

Months continued to go by and Tommy Girl and I became inseparable. We finally ventured into the relationship that should've happened back in '93. My family loved her, my boys were cool with her but most of all, I was happy again. Around June, Tommy Girl got tired of driving back and forth from Hartsville to Florence everyday and got an apartment in Florence. From the time she moved in, until it was time for me to go back to school, Tommy Girl's place was where I spent most of my nights. She tried to convince me to move in but I wasn't ready to take that step in the relationship yet. Deep down inside, I was happy to be with her but I didn't know what the future was going to hold once I went back to school. It was real easy to get caught up in campus life. It was like being in a whole new world.

11
Conspiracy Theory

By late July, I had everything in order for me to start my sophomore year at Franklin Memorial University. It wasn't an easy task to get everything done but I managed. Things were good with Tommy Girl and me up until two weeks before I was to move on campus. She and I were sitting on the couch in my room one Monday evening when she decided to lay all of her cards on the table.

"Baby," she began as she stopped the movie we were watching. "We need to talk."

"About what...?" I asked while sitting up.

"You're getting ready to go back to school in a couple weeks. I can't help but to think about how things were when you left the first time."

"When I left the first time, I went all the way across the state. This time I'm right here. You can be to me, and me to you, in less than 10 minutes."

"I'm more worried about the people you'll be surrounded by. You'll be hanging out with educated people, especially women that, in a few years, are going to be doctors, lawyers and teachers. I'm just a hair stylist. How can I compete with that?"

"You're not just a hair stylist. In a couple of years, you'll own your own business. Education doesn't make a person. Look at Nick's brother. He's smart as hell but still dumb as shit. You and I have a history that I'll never have with those people. You've been there for me through the good and the bad. They can't compete with that."

"Just promise me one thing."
"What's that?"

"If you feel that things aren't going to work between us, you'll tell me. I know how you are and I know that your personality attracts people to you...mostly female. Just keep it real with me if you decide that you want to move on to someone else. I'm not saying that I'll be cool with it but I'll have to respect it. I just don't want to be cheated on again. I've been down that road already."

After pausing for a brief moment, "I promise but you have to make the same promise to me. Being a student is rough. It takes discipline and it's time consuming. We spend a lot of time together because I'm just working. Things are going to be different once I go back. I'll be working and going to school. If you ever feel that I'm not giving you the time that you need and you feel that you need to move on, you keep it real with me as well."

"I will."

During the movie, I got bored and started pulling things out of my closet. Among the things that I pulled out was my photo album that had all of my pictures in it from my years in North Carolina. As soon as I tossed it on the bed, Tommy Girl spied it, walked over, and picked it up. She flipped through the pages as I sifted through a box of miscellaneous things.

"Who's this girl?" she asked flipping through the pages of the album.

"What girl?" I replied without looking up from my task.

"The girl in almost every picture in here..."
"That's Alicia. We were best friends growing up."
"Is she the same girl you used to talk about all the time when you first moved?"
"That's her."

"She's pretty. Did you two ever go together?"
"Me and Alicia were just cool like that."
"Like brother and sister."

"Sorta but it was a little more complicated than that." I sat down on the couch beside Tommy Girl and looked through the pictures with her. "I met Alicia in the 4th grade. I beat up a bully that was pickin' on her during recess one day. We were tight every since."

"What's the complicated part?"

"Even though we never pursued a relationship, it was like we were a couple and didn't know it."

"How can two people be a couple and not know it?"

"I told you it was complicated," I laughed. "It all started when we got to junior high. The only people I really hung with were my two best friends, Eric and Ty, Alicia and her two girls, Monica and Danielle."

"So it was three couples."

"That's what everybody thought but we were just a group of friends."

"Let me ask you something. Who did you have your first real kiss with?"

"Alicia."

"First slow dance?"

"Alicia."

"Who was the first girl to dedicate a song to you on the radio and what was the song?"

"Alicia and the song was *Your Sweetness* by the Good Girls."

"I hate to tell you this Dré, but she was your girlfriend."

"She was not my girlfriend."

"If you say so... When's the last time you seen or talked to her?"

"I haven't seen her since I moved here."
"That explains everything."

"What are you talking about?"

"Now I know why you and I didn't get together back then. You were still hung up on her. I woulda just been your rebound girl."

"Is that what you really think?"

"It's true Dré. You had just got out of a five and a half year relationship."

"You are wrong on so many levels. Alicia and I were in relationships with other people when I moved."

I proceeded to tell Tommy Girl about the events that led up to my relationship with the girl I was dating right before I moved. She kept insisting that Alicia and I were just taking some time apart from each other and would have eventually gotten back together had I not moved.

"You can say what ever you want but I know better than that."

Super Senior

Tommy Girl handed me the photo album then put her shoes on. After shoes were on, she reached into her bag for her car keys. "One last question before I go."

"Okay."

"If she came back into your life, would you leave me for her?" I never understood why women asked questions that they didn't really want to know the answer to.

"I wouldn't have to leave you for her. Alicia was my best friend. I don't see why I would have to choose between the two of you."

"Trust me; you'd eventually have to choose. No matter what any woman says, she's never comfortable with a man having an attractive female for a best friend."

"So you're saying that if by chance she came back into my life, I'd have to choose between the two of you."

"I don't make the rules, I just live by them."
"Well those are some pretty f'ed up rules," I laughed. I walked my girl to her car.

"You know I'm just messing with you. I would never ask you to choose between her and me. Y'all got too much history for me to compete with. If you say that she was your best friend, I believe you. I'd just have to treat her like I treat Nick."

"What about Twist?"

"I like Twist."

"That's cold."

"It is what it is." I put my arms around Tommy Girl and pulled her close to me.

"Well, you don't have to worry about dealing with that because the odds of her coming back into my life are slim to none."

"I know, Baby. I got you all to myself."

"Yes you do." I leaned in and press my lips against Tommy Girl's. We engaged in a passionate kiss. From her lips I moved to her neck. She giggled as she pulled away from me.

"Stop now. You gettin' ready to get somethin' started. I gotta go to work in the morning."

"Come back in the house for a minute."

"I will not. Your grandfather ain't about to catch me butt naked in his house and rebuke me in the name of Jesus."

"Come on. It'll only take a minute."

"We've been together for a while now. A minute man you are not."

"Then I'll come to your place."

"No, Dré. You will not have me up all night and tired in the morning."

"You suck."

"Yes I do. Just like you like it."

"Why you playin' wit me...?"

"Bye, Dré." Tommy Girl kissed me on my cheek then got in her car.

July came and went as did the first two weeks of August. It was time for school to start. During the two weeks before it was time for me to move on campus, Tommy Girl was relentless in her attempts to get me to move in with her. When she saw that I wasn't budging on the issue, she gave up. Despite the fact that we were going to be in the same city, she still had some reservations about me going back to school. I tried my best to convince her that everything would be all right. The thing about it was: I couldn't figure out if I was really trying to convince her or convince myself.

The third Monday in August found me rolling on the campus of Franklin Memorial University. The campus was beautiful. All of the landscaping was perfect. Flowers were in full bloom and the grass was as green as can be.

When you drove on campus through the main gate, the administration building was on your left. Once you made a right turn, that put the buildings that hosted the Schools of Business, Education, Liberal Arts, and Social Sciences on your right. They were two separate buildings connected by a large breezeway. After you drive down a piece you come to a round-a-bout. If you go straight, the road will end at a parking lot in front of the University Center after passing a large pond on the right. Going left around it then straight will put you on the road that leads to the dorms and on campus apartments. Before you get there, you pass the science and math buildings on the right. The Fine Arts Center was on the left, across the quad from the first buildings you passed.

Through the trees, I could see the apartments on my left and the dorms on my right. I came to a small intersection. I made a right turn and headed towards the dorms. There were six dorms broken into sets of three divided by the cafeteria which sat in the middle. Each building was three stories. The buildings were connected by walkways on the 2nd and third floor. Based on what Nick told me, the first dorms I passed were the older set. They were known as the *Ghetto*. The newer dorms were where I would be residing. They were known as the *High Rize*. He also told me that if I got confused, there was a way to tell them apart. In the Ghetto was a large concrete slab, three steps high in the shape of a triangle. It was situated directly in the center of the set of dorms that curved in a U shape. The High Rize was exactly the same as far as the way the dorms were situated. The difference was that instead of a triangle, there was an octagon—which only had six sides but we still called it the Octagon.

I found a parking spot in front of the housing office, which was in front of the High Rize. There were people of all races, shapes and sizes everywhere. When I got out of the car, I stood for a second and watched the people that were going in and coming out of the housing office. While I was standing there, a green Toyota Camry with tinted windows pulled into the empty space beside me. After the car turned off, a gorgeous being stepped out. She was about 5'1" with a high yellow complexion and coffee brown eyes. Her straight, black hair brushed the tops of her shoulders.

"Hi," She greeted as she closed the door.
"How you doin'?"
"You new here?"
"Yeah. I transferred from New Grove College up in Greenville."

"I know NGC. I'm from Easley."
"That's what's up."
"Were you there when the guy shot the guy then killed himself?"
"Unfortunately, I was in the room when it happened."

"Are you serious?"
"Yeah… It's a crazy story."

"Maybe you can tell me about it one day. That's if it's not too much to ask."

"It's easier for me to talk about now. Just let me know when."

"We'll see each other around. My name is Katrina."

"Nice to meet you, Katrina. My name is André but you can call me Dré."

"Nice to meet you, Dré. Well, I better get in here and get my keys. I got a lot of stuff to unpack."

"That's where I'm headed."

Once Katrina stepped into full view, I saw that the green shirt she had on bared the letters of Alpha Kappa Alpha spread across a nice, perky chest. According to her sleeve, she had just crossed the semester prior. On the back was a number 1 with the name "AKAnikulas" above it both in pink letters. Katrina and I continued to engage in idle chatter about Greenville as we walked into the housing office. There were quite a few people in there. We stood in line for a good thirty minutes before we finally got to the counter.

"Hello," the young lady behind the counter greeted. "Welcome to FMU. What's your name?"

"André Marshall…"

"Marshall, Marshall, Marshall….ah, here it is. Mr. Marshall we had a problem and had to move you."

"Move me?"

"Apparently, we had a record number of freshmen enroll this semester. Since you transferred as a sophomore, we moved you into the apartments. Is that okay?"

"No problem at all."

"Great," she replied as she handed me a form to sign. After I signed the form, she handed me large brown envelope and a smaller one containing my keys. Katrina finished up as I stood there looking for my apartment number.

"Where you at?" she asked as she pulled her car keys out of her pocket.

"I'm still looking for it."
"Lemme see." I handed her the paper. "You're in apartment G-6, room D."

"Room D?"

"There are four rooms in each apartment. The first room is A and the last is D. You got lucky too. Room D is the biggest room."

"Well, alright."

"If you want to, you can follow me. I'm in H-8. The buildings are right beside each other."

"Cool...I'm right behind you." We got in our cars and I followed Katrina to the apartments. She pulled through this narrow gate and parked in front of her building. After she parked, she pointed to my building. I backed in and turned the car off.

"You're right there on the second floor."
"Thanks a lot. I really appreciate it."

"No problem. Welcome to FMU. If you need anything, I'm right here. Stop by anytime." I watched as she walked up the stairs to unlock her apartment door. I popped the hatch and started taking things out.

When you walked into the apartment, there was a living area attached to a kitchen. In the living area was a couch. Behind the couch was a kitchen table with four chairs. On the counter was a microwave. On the far left was the stove. On the other end of the wall was the refrigerator. The sink, a counter, and cabinets separated the two. Beside the fridge was a door. Behind the door was a trash can inside of a small storage room. Also on that wall was the door that led to the bedrooms. On the right were the first two rooms. After you turn the corner to the left, the bathroom was on the left. There were two sinks, a separate shower area and a separate toilet area. Across from the bathroom door was the door of the third bedroom and to the left as you exit the bathroom was the door to my room.

In my room, to my immediate left on the same wall the door was on was a wardrobe with two drawers at the bottom of it. On the adjacent wall was the bed pushed against a narrow window. The base of the bed was a wooden box with two more drawers under the bed. On the wall directly in front of the door was a desk with a chair that sat under three shelves that stretched about five feet across in the middle of the wall. After further investigation, I noticed that the shelves could be easily removed or collapsed. I tossed my keys on the desk and headed back outside to take my things in. Fifteen minutes later, I had all my things in my apartment. While I was moving some things around, I heard Katrina call to me from the living room.

"What's up?" I inquired as I walked in the living room.

"Could you do me a huge favor?"
"What you need?"
"Can you help me with a couple of heavy things?"
"Okay, now I see. You buttered me up with conversation so you could use me later."

"You caught me red handed," Katrina laughed. I followed her out to her car to take her footlocker and her television into her apartment.

"Damn girl," I grunted as I lifted the trunk. "You smugglin' dead bodies?"

"That's just clothes and shoes."
"You only have two feet and one body."
"Excuse me? If I'm not mistaken, I counted ten Nike shoe boxes stacked up beside your car."
"This ain't about me, though." We laughed as she guided me up the steps and into her room. "I see you got room C."

"Yeah…its' not as big as D but it's a little bigger than A and B. I'm a little person. I don't require much room anyway." I took a quick breather then walked back downstairs to get her TV. "Thank you so much, Dré. I really appreciate it."

"No problem at all." I turned to walk away.
"I'm going grocery shopping in a little while. When I get back, a couple of my sorors and I are having dinner. You're more than welcome to join us."

"I appreciate the invite but I have to go to work for a few hours."
"Where you work?"

"I work in the mall at Foot Locker."
"That explains all the shoes," Katrina giggled. "What time you get off?"

"Probably around eight..."

"There'll be plenty of food left over and we'll still be chillin'. Stop through when you get off."

"Okay. I'll do that. I'll see you later." I walked out of Katrina's apartment and back to mine. When I got there, I started unpacking and putting things away so I wouldn't have to deal with it after work. Once everything was put away and in order, I threw on my stripes and headed to work.

After work, I stopped by the shop to see Tommy Girl for a minute then went back on campus. Upon arrival to my apartment, I saw the light from Room A on from outside. I walked in to the apartment to meet one of my roommates standing in the kitchen. He was a round my height with a similar complexion. He was slimmer than I was with a low fade.

"What's up, Roommate?" I greeted as I pulled my key out the door and walked over to him and extended my hand. "I'm Dré."

"I'm Theodore but everybody calls me Teddy."

"True dat. Where you from?"

"Fayetteville."

"I didn't know they had a Fayetteville in South Carolina."

"If they do, I don't know about it. Ain't but one Fayetteville in my eyes and that's in North Kak."

"You bullshittin'. I'm from the 'Nam."
"What school?"
"I was supposed to graduate from Oak Forest in '94 but I moved down here in the middle of my tenth grade year. What about you?"

"I graduated from 71st in '94."
"You know Maria White?"
"That's my homegirl."
"That's my cousin."
"Word? Shit…then you already good people."
"I was thinkin' the same thing."
"Maria is the only female that I know that loves hip hop as much as I do."

"That's why me and her so tight."
"This is a small ass world."
"Our other two roommates here yet?"
"Not yet. One of'em is my boy, Murph. We were suitemates in the dorms last year. He cool people. He'll be here tomorrow. I don't know the other one. Murph's roommate was supposed to be the fourth man but he transferred to Claflin."

"My boy from high school go to State. He supposed to keep me updated on what's good up that way."

"Just let me know. I'm always down for a road trip."

"That's what's up. Well, lemme hop in the shower. I'm supposed to go next door and kick it wit some AKA's."
"Who?"
"The only one I know is Katrina. I met her earlier today."
"Short, light skinned, fine ass Katrina?"
"Yeah."
"You don't waste no time, do you?"
"Nah. It ain't like that. I got a girl."
"She go here?"
"Nah but she live in Florence."
"All I can say is good luck."
"Judging by what I've seen so far, I'm gonna need a lil bit more than luck."

"It's serious here. I don't think this is a normal school. It goes down. I had a girl back in the Ville when I first got here last year. That lasted every bit of two months."

"Damn. It's like that?"

"Worse. All I can say is do you." I thought about what Teddy said and the conversation me and Tommy Girl had before a few weeks ago as I got in the shower. This was exactly what we were both afraid of. I knew how the girls were at NGC and it seemed like nothing judging by what Nick told me and Teddy confirmed. All I could do was live life for me and if it came to it, be open and honest with my girl.

After I got out of the shower, I threw on a pair of light blue denim shorts, a black Carolina Panthers jersey and pair of black Air Force Ones. I was rockin' Air Force Ones way before Nelly hit the scene. I splashed on a dab of Polo cologne and headed next door. When I got there and knocked on the door, I was greeted by another fly female. This one was chocolate brown with medium length hair and dark brown almond shaped eyes. She was a couple inches shorter than I was with a slim build.

"Is Katrina here?"
"You must be Dré. Come on in." I walked in to find Katrina sitting on one end of the couch. Sitting at the table behind the couch were two more females. The one that sat on the end closest to the refrigerator was an Indian girl—an India Indian. She had long, silky, black hair and dark brown eyes. She was thicker than any Indian I'd ever met. Sitting beside her was another light complexioned girl with short hair.

"Hey Dre!" Katrina got off the couch and greeted me with a hug." "You smell good. Is that Polo?"
"Yeah."

"Ain't nothing like a man that smells good," The light skinned girl sitting at the table commented."

"Okay!" the Indian consigned giving her a high five.
"You hungry? We got plenty of food left."
"Sure. Just point me in the direction of the plates."
"I'll fix it for you. You have a seat." As she fixed my plate, she introduced me to the other females in attendance. "These are my lovely LSs. The one that opened the door is Julie. The one with her face in the plate is Melissa."

"Shut up," Melissa laughed as she continued to eat her chicken wings.

"And the foreigner right there is Ghandi's granddaughter."

"Pay her no mind. She went to the little school behind the big school. I'm Priyah."

"It's a pleasure to be in the presence of such beauty."

"He can't be from around here," Julie laughed. "Not saying stuff like that. Where you from?"

"I graduated from Hargrove but I'm from Fayetteville, North Carolina."

"That's where my Baby's from!" Priyah squealed.

"There you go," Katrina laughed.

"Do you know Teddy?"

"I just met him for the first time tonight. He's one of my roommates."

"Ya'll didn't go to the same high school?"

"Fayetteville's not a big city but it is big enough to have more than one high school. As a matter of fact, we got eight."

"That's right," Melissa interjected. "Not every place is small like Sleasly."

"Watch ya mouth talkin' bout my city," Katrina joshed. "That's how people get cut."

"Wait a minute," Priyah interrupted. "Did you say that Teddy's your roommate?"

"Yeah."

"Where you stay?"

"Right next door in G-6."

"Is he there?"

"He was when I left."

"I'll be back. I gotta go see my baby." Priyah grabbed her glass of wine and left.

"Just so you know," Katrina chuckled. "You may be seeing a lot of Priyah. Her and Teddy been goin back and forth since last year."

Super Senior

While walking to the refrigerator Julie added, "Those two get on my nerves. One minute they love each other then the next minute they can't stand each other. I don't know why she let him do her like that."

"Hold up now," I defended. "You said they been going back and forth since last year. A woman won't let a man do to her what she doesn't want to have done. She allows herself to stay in the situation so you can't put it all on Teddy. I don't know him like that but that's just fact."

"He's right," Melissa agreed. "Everything she's been through with him, she lets it happen."

"Teddy must got that good wood," Julia laughed.
"I mean no disrespect to the guys down here but we do things a little bit different in NC. I've noticed that since I've lived here for the past three years."

"What do you mean?" Melissa asked with curiosity in her voice.

"From what I've noticed of the guys that I've met since I've been here is that they don't have a handle on the needs, wants, and desires of a woman. I'm not saying that all guys here are like that because I haven't met them all but judging by the ones I have met, that's my observation."

"Can you elaborate on that?"

"In order to keep a girl happy, you have to know what she needs and what she wants. It takes time to gather that type of information. It's no secret because a girl will tell you everything if you just take the time to listen. From what I've observed of guys here, the satisfaction is in getting the girl but not keeping the girl. It's the opposite for me. I can get the girl with no problem, keeping her is the hardest task but the most satisfying." As I talked, the three ladies had their eyes locked on me. They hung on my every word.

"How do you keep her?"
"For me, it's all about remembering what I did to get her. The things I did to make her interested in me are the things I do to keep her interested in me. In addition to that, I have to keep the lines of communication open. She has to know that I'm her man and she's my woman. The guys down here don't do that. They get'em and that's it. Then they wonder why she doesn't stay around long."

"Do you have a girlfriend?"
"Yes I do."
"Does she know you're here?"
"Yes she does."
"And she's cool with that."

"My girl knows that she's number one in my life. There are some reservations about me living on campus and being back in school but that has a lot to do with the history between us. I promised her that if my feelings changed then I would be open and honest with her. I'm not going to have her thinking that every thing is all good and I'm here running around with other females. That's not my style."

"Can you teach a class?" Julia laughed.
"I'm serious," Katrina added. "I know a whole gang of dudes that need to take it."

"One thing you'll learn about me as you get to know me is that I don't follow the crowd. I'm my own person and I don't care what people say or think about me. As long as I'm happy with me, that's all that matters."
The three ladies and I continued to chat about relationships and dealings between men and women. Judging by the questions they asked, they seemed to be those that they always wanted to ask a man but never felt that they would get a straight up, unbiased answer. The thing that really set me off as a good man, in their eyes, was when Tommy Girl paged me and I called her back while I was sitting in the room with them.

Time went by as we talked and one by one the ladies went back to their apartments. I thanked Katrina for the warm welcome as she expressed her gratitude for the insight that I provided her and her girls with. The thing I did notice about the three women was that one of them was into what I was saying more than the other three. As I talked, Melissa never took her eyes off of me. It also seemed that the questions she asked were more than general questions but more along the lines of seeing what type a man I was. By the time I got back to my apartment, Teddy and Priyah were locked in his room with R&B music playing. I heard her giggle as I walked past the door and into my room.

12
Reunited

I've often heard people say that if you speak things into the Universe, it will come to past. I never really bought into that because I believed in faith. Sayings like that usually fell on deaf ears when it came to me. That's just how I was. When I woke up the next morning, I felt great. It was that feeling of knowing that that day was just going to be a good day. I didn't have to work that night so I had time to really enjoy myself and explore campus. As I looked in my wardrobe to pull out an outfit for the day, I heard a lot of bumping in the hallway. I opened it and saw an average height, brown skinned male with a khaki polo hat pulled down to his eyes fighting with a trunk.

"You need a hand, Bruh?"
"I think I got." When he stood up and face me, I noticed that his shirt said Kingstree High on it.

"You must be Murph."
"The one and only. Kingstree's most wanted. Nobody does it better."

"I'm Dré. Teddy told me about you." We exchanged dap then he pulled his trunk into Room C.

"Where you from?"

"I graduated from Hargrove but I'm from Fayetteville."

"You must be Nick's homeboy. I ran into him in the mall a couple weeks ago. He told me his ace was transferring here."

"That's me."
"He back on the yard yet?"

"I don't know what's up wit that dude. I ain't talked to him in about two weeks."

"Knowin' him he somewhere tryna take over the world."

"That's that nigga, Nick." I walked outside with Murph to help him bring in the rest of his things. As we were walking back up the stairs, Priyah was coming out of the apartment.

"Hey Murph," she greeted. "Hey Dré."
"What's up, Priyah?" I responded.
"And the saga continues," Murph laughed as Priyah passed him on the stairs.

"Go to hell, Murph."
"I love you, too." Teddy was coming out of the bathroom as we were putting Murph's things in his room.

"You a rude ass nigga, Murph. How you come in this time of the mornin' makin all that noise?"

"Nigga please. You know we don't sleep around here until classes start."

After pausing for a minute, "True dat. What's the deal, my nigga?" Teddy greeted Murph with one love.

"You know me. It's hard to stay Kinda Fly."
"True indeed. Speakin' of Kinda Fly, did she make it back this semester?"

"I almost traded her in for a newer model but I changed my mind. I ain't tryna work hard this year."

"Who's Kinda Fly?" I asked with confusion.
"My bad. That's my car. The plate on the front says: Kinda Fly."

"Oh okay. I was lost for a minute."
"So what's the 411? Who throwin the first party?"
"The Alphas throwin a party in the UC on Friday and the Ques got the Sweat Box on Saturday."
"Sweat Box?" I pondered once again.
"You know that American Legion right down the road?" Murph asked.
"Yeah."
"That's the Sweat Box." Murph and Teddy replied at the same time.

"That's were it goes down," Murph continued. "You take every black student on the yard and pack them into that little ass building. We call it the Sweat Box cuz that's all you do when you in there. You don't even have to be dancin'."

"That sounds like a party to me."

"If you don't pull a girl out the Sweat Box, you're either a geek or you gay. But back to this nigga over here… please tell me you and Priyah are not gettin' ready to do the same thing you did last year."

"That girl's like a virus. I can't get rid of her ass. As soon as Dré left last night to go over to Katrina's she popped up."

"That's my bad, Dog. I told her you were here."

"Ain't no love lost. You didn't know. She woulda found me sooner or later. I was just hopin' for later. But on the real, I told her last night that we wasn't doin the same thing we did last year."

"You told her this before or after you fucked her?" Murph asked while putting his suitcase on his bed.

"Before. And your point being?"

"All that shit went in one ear and right out the other. I'm tellin' you...if she's here like she was last year in the dorms, we splittin the light bill five ways."

"Whatever, Nigga. So what's on the agenda for today?"

"Two words: Change Check!"
"Change checks come today?"

"If all ya shit was in order it should be in Cashier's office."

"That's what's up," I expressed. "I need that too. The new Air Max come out today."

"How you know?" Murph asked.
"I work at Foot Locker."
"You get a discount?"
"Of course...Thirty percent."
"I'm really getting ready to be broke now."
"Just let me know what you want and I'll get it."
"That's what's good. What time we hittin' the mall?"

"I was getting ready to walk over to the dorms to see what it look like over there," Teddy answered.

"That sound like a plan, too." We chopped it up for a few more minutes then I jumped in the shower. Me and Murph talked more while Teddy took his. Once Teddy got out, we got dressed then walked towards the dorms. I could tell that Murph and Teddy were pretty popular by the way they were being hailed as we walked through the apartments. As soon as we got to the Ghetto, we were drafted by this girl's mother to help carry some of her daughter's things to the third floor. Once we finished, she complimented us on being good young men then gave us each a peppermint and sent us on our way. We took a seat on the Triangle to observe the scene. As we talked, Murph pulled out a Black & Mild and fired it up.

Every type of female you could imagine either passed by us or stopped and talked to us as we chilled out on the Triangle. As the freshmen moved about, the sharks started to circle. Dudes came out of the woodworks to see what the freshmen class of fall '96 had to offer. When it started to get too crowded at the Triangle, we moved to the Octagon. Murph and Teddy sat on the Octagon as I positioned myself on a bench. That's when I saw her. She was a towering five feet even. Her curly, brown hair was pulled back into a ponytail and pulled through the back of a khaki cap like the one Murph had on. The sun beamed off of her brownish bronze complexion as she struggled with a suitcase that was too heavy for her.

"I'll be right back," I told the fellas as I walked over to help her. "Let me get that for you." I took the suitcase from her.

Super Senior

"Thank you so much," she replied as she exhaled. "I don't think I would've made it to the third floor. Do you mind if I run to my car and grab something else? I don't want to go up empty handed."

"Sure." I waited for about three minutes as she went to her car and grabbed another bag. She came back and I followed her upstairs. "What's you're name?"

"Alexandria but everybody calls me Alex."
"I'm Dré. Nice to meet you."
"Is that short for André?"
"Yeah."
"Okay. We're cool. Nice to meet you."
"What was that about?" I chuckled.
"My ex-boyfriend went by Dré but his was short for Deondre."

"How did any man let a pretty girl like you get away?"

"By being a boy instead of a man. I told myself I was going to stop dating guys my age. They're stupid and immature."

"How old are you?"
"I turn eighteen tomorrow."

"Well let me be the first to wish you a happy birthday."

"Thank you," Alex expressed as she opened the door to her room. "Here we are. You can put that on the bed. Thank you so much for helping me."

"Do you need help with anything else?"
"The rest of the stuff is light. I think I can handle it."

"Okay. I guess I'll see you around, Alexandria." I walked to the door.

"I told you, everybody calls me Alex."

"I'm not everybody." A huge smile spread across her face as I winked and walked out of the room. Murph and Teddy were surrounded by a crew of four girls when I got back downstairs. They introduced me to them and informed me that we would be hosting some pre-party festivities on Friday and Saturday. The seven of us talked for a few minutes longer but the heat drove us back towards our apartment. Murph suggested that we go pick up our change checks while we were out so we bypassed our apartment and walked to the administration building. The Cashier's Office was packed when we got there. We stood in line for about an hour before we got our money. We were at the door of the apartment when I realized that I needed to go back to the Registrar's office and pick up a copy of my schedule. I told the fellas I would be right back so we could head to the bank and to the mall then walked back to the administration building. On my way back, I bumped into Melissa in the parking lot behind the apartments.

"Well hello pretty lady," I greeted.
"Hey Dré," Melissa obliged. "How are you?"
"I'm good. What you up to?"
"I just picked up my change check. I'm getting ready to go put it in the bank then go to the mall to pick up a couple of outfits for this weekend."

"Now why do I believe that in your room is a wardrobe full of clothes. Among those clothes, there are probably a few items that still have tags on them."

"I'll have you know that I'm not that kind of girl," she giggled. "All the clothes in my wardrobe have been worn. Thank you very much, Mr. Smartie. I worked hard this summer to save up money so I wouldn't have to work a lot this semester. I deserve to treat myself to a couple of new outfits."

"I respect that. I withdraw my previous comments."
"Thank you. What are you up to?"
"I'm on my way to the Registrar's office to pick up a copy of my schedule then me, Murph and Teddy are headed to the mall."

"Sounds like fun. Maybe I'll see you there."
"Maybe you will. I'll talk to you later. Enjoy your shopping."

"I will." Melissa called to me moments after I walked off. "Dré." I turned around. "I enjoyed the conversation last night. It was refreshing to have a decent conversation with a guy that thinks with the right head."

"I'm glad you enjoyed it. Maybe we can do it again sometime."

"Didn't you say you had a girlfriend?"

"What's that got to do with anything? All I suggested was conversation."

"That you did. I'll see you around." I watched as Melissa climbed into her SUV then continued on my way.

When the administration building came into sight, I noticed a light complexioned female walking toward the same building. She looked as if she was coming from the Fine Arts Center. As I watched her, I noticed that her walk looked familiar. The closer we got to each other, the more I felt as if I knew her. She kept looking my way as she walked. Maybe she was experiencing the same feeling I was. Once we got close enough to each other for me to see her face, I stopped in my tracks. I couldn't believe it. The angel that I thought I'd lost forever had returned. The young lady noticed that I'd stopped and smiled at me as she looked my way. Then she did a double take. On the second look she stopped with her eyes widened and her mouth open.

"Andre!" she screamed as she dropped her backpack and ran into my arms.

Over three years had passed and Alicia Burroughs had not changed a bit; except for a noticeable scar on the right side of her face that started at the middle of her ear and extended to directly under her eye. That blemish still couldn't hinder the natural beauty that she had. Once again I was face to face with my favorite girl in the world. When she smiled at me and I saw her dimples and those beautiful white teeth peek from behind those full and sexy lips, which were a shade of natural brown that day, my mind told me that I could never be apart from her again. I could feel her body trembling as she held on to me. She asked as we were still hugging, "Oh my God, what are you doing here?"

"I transferred from junior college. What about you?"

"I changed my major to marketing and came here from A&T because the program's better."

"This is a trip. I thought I'd never see you again and here you are. You never cease to amaze me."

"What are you getting ready to do?"

"I just need to run in and pick up a copy of my schedule. Me and my roommates were going to the mall but all that can wait. What's up with you?"

"I'm going to drop something off in the Financial Aid office. Then I'm free."

"Okay. Meet me back out here when you're done. Then we can walk to my place."
"That sounds good to me. I'm so anxious to catch up."

"I won't be long."
"I'll be waiting right here."
"You promise?"

"I've waited this long for you. A few more minutes won't kill me."

I walked into the Registrar's office in disbelief. I wondered how time had affected our friendship. Granted Alicia and I weren't on the best of terms when I left, I believed that what we built in the years that led up to my departure was still there. When I returned to the front entrance, I could see Alicia looking at herself in her compact mirror. I stopped and basked in the moment of being in the presence of my best friend. She noticed me standing there looking at her.

"You ready?" Alicia asked with a huge smile on her face.

"Willing and able." I grabbed her backpack and hoisted it over my shoulder as we walked toward the apartments.

"I see you're still quite the gentleman."

"I guess I'm still used to carrying your books," I laughed.

"So how you been?"

"I'm doing better now that I'm back in school."

"Back in school?"

"Yeah. I sat out last year after Mom passed away." Alicia stopped in her tracks and covered her mouth with her hand.

"You're grandmother died? Oh my goodness, Dré, I am so sorry."

"I'm cool. I'm just glad she lived to see me graduate high school and start college. Now I have to finish because I promised her I would."

"That is so sweet. You were always grandma's baby boy."

"And I still do everything as if she was still here." As we neared my apartment, the question came that I knew was coming.

"So who's the lucky lady?"
"Her name is Chelsea but everybody calls her Tommy Girl."

"Is she black?"
"What kinda question is that?"

"I know you and you don't discriminate. Besides, how many black girls do you know named Chelsea?" We laughed as we entered the apartment. Murph and Teddy were sitting on the couch playing football on the Sega Genesis. I introduced them to Alicia and told them that I wouldn't be leaving for the mall just yet and that they could go ahead if they wanted to. They said they were cool and that they'd wait. I escorted Alicia to my room.

"Where they got you staying at?" I asked as I moved some clothes off of the chair so she could sit down.

"I'm in A-1 now answer my question. Is she black?"

"Yes she's black."
"She's light skinned, ain't she?"
"Do you know her?"
"No but I see you're still color struck."

"I am not."

"Negro please. Every girl you ever went with since I've known you has been light. If not light, she was white."

"Can I please continue?"
"My bad...please continue."
"Tommy Girl was the first girl I met when I moved to South Carolina. We got close but I waited too long to tell her how I felt and somebody else stepped up. We chilled together for the summer then I went off to school."

"You didn't wanna do the long distance thing?"
"We both agreed that it wouldn't work. She came back in the picture after my grandmother passed away."

"That's interesting. She caught you while you were vulnerable and reeled you in."

"It wasn't like that. I was with somebody at the time. She and I didn't get together until after me and Red broke up because I decided to transfer to be close to home for my grandfather. Now stop being judgmental."

"I am not a judgmental person."
"Yes you are or at least you are when it comes to the women I date."

"Cuz all the girls you date are skeezers."
"Excuse me?"

"Nothing has changed, Dré. When it comes to you, no girl is ever going to be good enough for you."

"Then why were you never my girl?"
"You never asked. Did you?"

I paused for a minute and gazed into Alicia's eyes then laughed, "Just promise me you'll never leave my side again."

"You left me, remember?"
"You know I had no choice."
"I know. I'm just messin' with you but you gotta promise me the same thing."
"I promise to never let anything come in between us ever again."

"Not even another girl or distance?"
"Nothing."
"Andre Marcellus Marshall, I've always been there for you and I always will."
"Promise?"
"I promise."

Never in a million years did I think that I would reunite with my best friend at a school in South Carolina. Life was just funny that way. Alicia and I continued to catch up on old times. Pretty soon, the money started burning holes in the pockets of my roommates. They informed me that we needed to go before the banks closed.

The four of us loaded up in Kinda Fly and headed into town. The way Alicia fell into the groove and cracked jokes with me, Murph and Teddy, I knew it was going to be like the UE Crew all over again. After the mall, we dropped Alicia off at her apartment and headed to ours. When we got there, we found that our final roommate had arrived. As we talked to him we knew that that he wasn't going to be a part of the click. He was too quiet. We put all of the shoes and clothes in the rooms and gathered back in the living room to break open the Playstation.

"That's right," Murph began as I plugged the game console into the television. "Break open that Tekken so I can get up in dat ass."

"Yeah right," Teddy laughed. "I'm the king of fightin' games. I couldn't be touched in Street Fighter or Mortal Kombat. Ain't nuttin changin."

"Fightin' games are cool but I'm that dude when it comes to football and basketball," I interjected. "That's why I made sure to pick up that Madden and that College."

"I gets down on dat, too. Lemme whoop Murph's ass a few times in this Tekken then we can get down on that Madden." Once everything was hooked up, Murph and Teddy jumped head first into Tekken. I sat and laughed as Murph wore Teddy's ass out.

"On the real though, Dré," Murph started without taking his eyes off the TV. "Ya girl is cool as hell. What's up wit'er."

"I'm getting' this out in the open now. Out of all the girls on campus, Alicia's off limits."

"It's like that?"
"Y'all my boys but me and her go way back. I'm not sayin y'all bad dudes or nothing but I don't want nothing to come between us as homies. Feel me?"

"I can respect that."
"Its all good," Teddy assured. "A fine female like that is bound to run wit a crew just as bad. She'll be our man on the inside."
"I'm tellin' you. Alicia don't roll wit nothing less than silver dollars. Wait until her girls Monica and Danielle come to visit."

"That's what's really good."

Later on that night, the fellas and I were still glued to the television engaged in heated battles and barn burners. Alicia came back over and chilled out with us. She and I sat at the kitchen table while she filled me in on the things that I missed after I left. Our conversation was interrupted by heavy trash talk and loud displays of victory. It got too loud so we moved our conversation to my room. Alicia slid her feet out of her sandals and curled up on my bed.

"This really feels like old times," Alicia commented as she rubbed her feet together and got comfortable in my bed. "Murph and Teddy remind me a lot of Ty and Eric."

"I said the same thing. All we need is two more females and we'll have the UE Crew part 2."

"There'll never be another UE Crew," Alicia laughed.

"I know right. We had so much fun together."
"Did you ever see Vickie again after you left?"

"Nope. I met a girl at the beach after graduation that graduated from Smith with her. You and her have a lot in common."
"Who? Me and Vickie? I think not."

"I'm talkin' about Lena, the girl I met at the beach. She can't stand her either. She said that Vickie wouldn't stay away from her boyfriend."

"She did have a way of coming in between people but enough about her." We continued to talk until something popped in my head. I got up and searched through the VHS tapes that were sitting on the shelf above the television. I pulled one from the collection and popped it into the VCR. "What is that?"

"School Daze."

"You really takin it back now. I remember the first time we watched this. We were at your aunt's house out in Scottsdale."

"Yup," I laughed as I turned the TV on. "We used to watch all the movies we didn't have no business watchin out there."

"I missed hangin out with your family. They were so cool."

"They still ask about you to this day...especially my grandma."

"How is Grandma?"
"She ain't changed a bit. Now the kids up under us are feelin' the wrath of the Filipino Ninja."

"Grandma didn't play no games."

"And she still don't." The movie came on and we laughed like old times at one of our all time favorites. As time moved on and the night went into it's later hours, Alicia and I fell asleep side by side. I felt that if I died that night, I would've died the happiest man in the world.

13
Beginning of the End

At nine o'clock in the morning, the August temperature started to rise. There wasn't a cloud in the sky. Since Alicia and I didn't have class until 9:55. She cooked breakfast for me and the fellas at my place. Once we ate, we headed to class. Murph, Alicia, and I walked across the perfectly manicured lawn on our way to Fisher Hall. Since she and I were both new, we got a lot of looks from the resident old heads and upper classmen. Murph introduced us to a couple he knew before he made his way to the science building. Katrina was standing in front of Fisher Hall with Priyah and Julia when we got there. I stopped to say hello and to introduce Alicia to them. Through conversation, Alicia found that she had her first class with Katrina and Priyah. She walked to class with them. Julia and I had different classes in the same building. She and I laughed and talked on the way to class.

"My girl has been talking about you nonstop since Monday," Julia began as I opened the door for her.

"Who?"

"Melissa. You really peaked her interest. Too bad you got a girl though. I think y'all woulda been good together."

"What makes you think so?"

"Don't tell her I told you this but Melissa has been through a lot with guys. They come out the gate talking a good talk but never back up what they say. She's talked about you more in two days than she's talked about any guy she's known or dated."

"Really?"

"Yes. She told me that she thinks you're different and she wouldn't mind hanging out with you as a friend but she doesn't want to cause any confusion between you and your girlfriend."

"I don't have a problem with she and I being friends and hangin' out."

"I'm sure you wouldn't but you're girl might."

"My girl's cool. She knows that besides my two homeboys from high school, most of my closest friends have been females. I seem to get along better with females."

"If it's like that you should talk to her. She'd really like that."

"I will. Thanks a lot, Julia. I appreciate it." After I walked Julia to her class, I went upstairs to mine. Since the day was nothing more than introductions to the courses it went by rather fast. Once classes were over I went to the bookstore to buy my books then went back to the apartment. I chilled out for awhile after I ate then went to work. Tommy Girl was sitting on a bench in front of the store. The look on her face showed that she was not happy at all. I tried to hug her but she pulled away from me.

"Why haven't I talked to you in two days?" Tommy Girl demanded to know.

"Baby, I just moved on campus and I was trying to get settled in."

"Settled into who?"
"What? You trippin'."
"How am I trippin'? You just got to school and you're already ignoring me."

"Tommy Girl…we don't talk every day and you know it. Last week we talked to each other twice and saw each other once. You already lettin' the fact that I'm back in school mess wit ya head. I told you. You don't have anything to worry about. We've already had this conversation." Tommy Girl's facial expression did not change one bit. As a matter of fact, it seemed like it got worse.

"How many females have you met?"
"I'm not getting into this with you right now. I gotta go to work."

"So now you blowin' me off?"

"I'm not blowing you off. I just refuse to have this conversation with you right now."

"If not now, when?"

"I'll come by your place when I get off. Okay? Besides I got something to talk to you about anyway."

"Why can't you tell me now? Why we gotta wait until tonight?"

"Because unlike you, I have to punch a time clock."

"What's that supposed to mean?"

"This conversation is going no where. I'll talk to you tonight."

"Okay. I'll drop it for now but you better come over as soon as you get off."

Looking at her with a confused face, "I better come by? Since when you start making demands?" I felt my anger levels rise. I didn't want to have an argument with her, especially in front of my job. "You know what? I'm going to work. I'll talk to you later." I left Tommy Girl standing in the entrance of Foot Locker. That was not how I wanted to start my evening. After I clocked in, I stayed in the stock room and straightened up the shelves to calm down before I went onto the floor. My manager knew that was out of character for me so she came to check on me. Kim was a light-brown complexioned Hispanic female in her early thirties. She had coffee brown eyes and long, curly black hair that she kept in a ponytail while at work. The ponytail extended to the small of her back. The thing I like the most about Kim was her accent and that cute mole that was right above her lip on the right side of her face.

"Jew okay, Papi?" Kim asked while poking her head in the stockroom door.

"I'm good, Kim."

"No jure not. Jew neber stay back 'ere. Jew always clock in and come straight to thee floor. Did chee upset jew?"

"Upset is putting it mildly."

"Come out here and talk to Mami. There are no customers." I put the last shoe box back on the shelf and walked onto the sales floor and immediately started straightening hats that were behind the register. "Papi stop. Talk to me. What's wrong?"

"It's my girl. I just went back to school and she's already buggin' out?"

"About wha?"

"She thinks that because I'm back in school, I'm going to forget about her. We've already had this conversation numerous times and at the end of every conversation she says she's cool but it manages to come back up."

"Does chee hab a reason to be insecure?"

"Not now but she probably will once I talk to her tonight?"

"I don't understand." I briefly filled Kim in about the history between Tommy Girl and I and the conversation she and I had at the beginning of July about Alicia.

"Now she's back in my life."
"Aye Dios Mios…this is no bueno, Papi."

"I know she is going to flip once I tell her. She's gonna swear up and down that I knew but was hiding it from her."

"Listen to me, Papi. All jew can do is be honest. If chee can't deal weth it, that's not jure problem. Jew just said that chee said that if your friend came back into jure life, chee would deal weth it. Now chee has to deal with it. If chee can't, that's her loss. Jew are too jung to be dealing with relatchonchip problems. Jew should be concentrating on getting your degree and libing jure life."

"I guess you're right."
"I know I'm right. Chee's just lucky I hab a man."

"Why?"
"Coz if I deedn't, chee would not hab jew. I would."

"You can't be tellin' me stuff like that right now," I laughed. "My mind ain't right."

"I'm just saying, Papi. I know jew are a good man and every real woman needs a good man. I just hope chee realizes what a good man chee already has."

"I hope so, too." A customer walked into the store.

"Now that we got that out of thee way, go make Mami some money." My mind raced with a million thoughts as I worked through my shift. I played every possible scenario in my mind of how I thought Tommy Girl would react to me telling her about Alicia. When there were no customers in the store, I tried to role play the situation with Kim but she wouldn't be serious. I never paid Kim any attention because she was my manager but after she told me what she did, the attractiveness that she already possessed intensified.

The nine o'clock closing hour found Kim and I wrapping up our last few customers. She counted the money while I straightened up the sales floor. Once she finished with the money and put it in the safe, she returned and started vacuuming the carpeted areas of floor. We finished around 9:30. I walked Kim to her car and thanked her once again for her advice. She gave me a hug and pressed her soft B cups against my chest. Before she let me go, Kim gazed into my eyes as the parking lot lights twinkled in hers. She kissed me on my cheek and told me to go talk to my girl.

I arrived at Tommy Girl's apartment at a quarter to ten. I'm glad I looked in the mirror before I went in because Kim had left a nice sized lipstick print on my left cheek. That really would've caused problems. Tommy Girl was sitting on the couch reading a book when I walked in. I tossed my keys on the coffee table and sat down on the other end of the couch. We sat and stared at each other for about five minutes before either one of us said anything.

"I'm sorry about earlier," Tommy Girl apologized as she eased to the end of the couch where I was. "You were right. I was trippin'."

"It's all good. I'm so happy to be back in school, I guess I got a little caught up. You have no idea how good it feels to be back around people like me. I was going insane not being in school last year. You're the only thing that kept me from going crazy." Tommy Girl crawled in my lap and put her arms around my neck.

"I'm just glad you let me be there for you." She started to kiss me on my lips. When she got to my neck she paused, looked at with confusion then removed herself from my lap.

"What's wrong?"
"Why do you smell like perfume?" I grabbed my shirt in the chest area and pulled it to my nose.

"That's probably from Kim."

"What was Kim doing that close to you to leave perfume on your shirt?"

"I was bothered by how things went down between us today so I talked to Kim about it while we were working. At the end of the night, she hugged me when I walked her to her car. It was nothing."

"I'm trying to trust you, Dré but you're not giving me much to work with. I can't just have you to myself. There's always another woman involved in your life some way."

"The hug between me and Kim was the same as the hugs you give people after church. It was nothing."

"Nothing, huh?" Tommy Girl flopped back down on the opposite end of the couch and folded her arms. "What do you need to talk to me about?" I took a deep breath then exhaled. I stood up.

"Remember the conversation we had about my best friend from back home back in July?"

"Yeah. What about it?"

After pausing briefly, "She goes to FMU now."
"Excuse me?"
"Alicia transferred to FMU from A&T."
"So that was the friend that you said you was going to chill wit on Monday."

"No, its not. That was Katrina. I didn't run into Alicia until the next day."

"Let me guess, you two have been catching up on old times since then."

"Well yeah. I haven't seen or talked to her in over three years." Tommy Girl sat looking at me and shaking her head. "Come on now. You said you would be cool with it if it ever happened."

"I said I would deal with it. I didn't say I would be cool with it. Besides, you said the chances of her coming back into your life were slim to none."

"I didn't know she was transferring there."

"I find that hard to believe. Right before you leave to go back to school, we have a conversation about her and now all of a sudden, she's back."

"Are you trying to say that I've been lying to you about her?"

"I'm not saying that but it sure looks like it."
"You know what? I don't need this shit. I'm going back on the yard."

"What do you want from me, Dré? First you come over here smelling like another woman and then you drop this on me. How am I supposed to act?"

"You could at least act like you're happy for me. Alicia has been my best friend since I was nine years old. A piece of my life came back to me and I'm not about to turn her away because you can't handle it. Since we've been together, I've never given you any reason to doubt me and my faithfulness to you. You looked me in my eyes and said that you would deal with if it ever came up. It's here. You can either deal with it or let me go. The choice is yours."

"I see what this is. She's back so now you don't need me."

"You said you would never make me choose and I'm not going to. She is my best friend and you are my girlfriend. If there is any way possible that I can have you both in my life, I'd love that to happen. If not, you just let me know and you'll never have to see me again. Think about it and let me know when you figure out your answer." I grabbed my keys and stormed out of the apartment. Tommy Girl ran out of the apartment as I started my car. I was so furious I acted like I didn't see her and drove off.

The ride back to campus was a silent one. I didn't know what to expect when I told Tommy Girl about Alicia but I didn't expect for her to act like that. As soon as I got back to my apartment I changed clothes, got a Black & Mild from Murph and took a walk. My path led me from the apartments to the University Center, which was already closed, then to the Octagon at the High Rize. It was only half past eleven but nobody was out. I sat and puffed away on the cigar trying to figure things out. From the parking lot, Alexandria emerged wearing a pair of short denim shorts and a white tank top. As I sat engulfed in smoke, she smiled when she got close enough to see that it was me.

"You know smoking kills people," Alexandria laughed as she approached.

"The way I feel right now, I would be better off dead." Alexandria sat down beside me on the Octagon.

"What's wrong?"

"I'm just going through some things right now. I'll be alright eventually."

"You want to talk about it?"

"I don't wanna bore you with my problems."

"I've been sitting in my room for the past hour and a half listening to my roommate talk about all her allergies and ailments. Please...bore me."

"I just had a huge fight with my girlfriend."

"About what?"

"My best friend."

"She's saying you spend too much time with him and not enough time with her."

"I really wish it was that simple. My best friend is a girl. We've been best friend since we were nine years old. I haven't seen or talked to her since I moved to South Carolina back in '92. She transferred here this semester."

"That's great."

"My girlfriend doesn't seem to think so."

"It's hard for some to understand that two people of the opposite sex can be best friends. My best friend is a guy. We've been best friends since kindergarten."

"How did your boyfriends deal with that?"

"The ones that were insecure, I let go. The ones that could handle it became friends with him."

"That's all I want. I want my best friend and my girlfriend to be friends. She won't take her head out of her ass long enough to meet her. Alicia is one of the coolest people you'd ever wanna meet. For me, hangin' out with Alicia has always been like hanging out with one of the fellas. She's just cool like that."

"Just give your girlfriend some time to come around. I'm sure she would rather deal with your friend than to lose out on good man."

"What makes you think I'm a good man? I could be crazy like the rest of'em."

"Trust me. I know you're a good guy. If you weren't, you wouldn't be out here stressin' about it."

"Now I see why you shouldn't date guys your age. They're not on your level."

"I've been saying that for a while now." Alexandria picked up her keys and stood up. "Everything will work out the way they're supposed to work out."

"Thanks." I remembered something as she walked off. I stood up and called to her. "Alexandria." She stopped and turned.

"What's up?" Alexandria responded.

"Me and my roommates are having some pre-party festivities on Friday and Saturday. You should come through."

"Can I bring my suitemates?"
"The more the merrier."
"What apartment you stay in?"
"I'm in H-6. We'll probably kick off about 8 o'clock on Friday night."

"Cool. If I don't see you before then, I'll see you Friday." I watched as her small but thick 5'0" frame walked up the stairs, across the breezeway and into her dorm. Talking to Alexandria made me feel a little better but the problem was still there. I just hoped that Tommy Girl would come around.

Loud voices leaked through the door and windows as I walked up the steps to my apartment. Alicia, Murph, Teddy and one of Murph's homeboys were involved in a heated game of Spades. On the couch was another guy that I hadn't met. With a dry voice, I greeted my friends and walked back to my room and threw myself on the bed. Minutes later, Alicia knocked on the door.

"Dré?" Alicia called through the door. "You okay, Baby?"

Without removing my face from the pillow I had over it, "Me and Tommy Girl got into a fight."

"I can't understand a word you just said." I rolled over to face Alicia.

"I said that me and Tommy Girl just got into a fight."

"About what?"

"Stupid shit." Alicia sat down at the foot of the bed as I rolled onto my side to make room for her. "Answer this question for me. Why do girls say one thing then change it up later on?"

"What are you talking about?"

"Me and Tommy Girl had a conversation about you back at the beginning of July. I told her all about our friendship. Then we got on the subject of how she would handle it if you ever came back into my life. She said that she'd be cool with it. I went over her place after work to tell her that you're here now, she all of a sudden flips the script."

"You know as well as I do that girls and guys will never understand the relationship we've always had. They can't fathom the idea of a guy and a girl being best friends. You shouldn't stress yourself over it. Everything will work out the way it's supposed to work out."

"You're right. It's not like this is anything new to me. I guess it's been so long since I've had to deal with it."

"Can I ask you a question?"
"Sure."
"When was the last time you were single?"
"Wow." I paused for a minute then answered. "I haven't been single since the beginning of '93. After I took too long to tell Tommy Girl how I felt about her back then and she started goin' wit Mike, I met Jocelyn. She broke up with me Graduation night."

"Now that's a hellavah graduation present," Alicia giggled.
"You tellin me. After we broke up, I was technically single but me and Tommy Girl spent the summer together. When I got to NGC, I met Red and we hooked up. We stayed together until I decided to sit out last year. After her, Tommy Girl came back around and we've been together almost a year."

"You're still the same old Dré. I figured you would've grown out of that. Every since you started dating, you've hopped from girl to girl. You never take time to be by yourself. Relationships weigh heavy on the mind and you need time to reboot after one fails. If you don't you just stack pain on top of grief on top of every thing that made each relationship fail. You can't have a successful relationship like that. On top of all that, you've added the death of your grandmother…"

"And the fact that I watched a friend kill someone and himself about a month prior to that."

"What?"
"That's a whole different story for a different story for another day."

"You've been through a lot. Your mind is exhausted. If you keep going like this, the smallest of things are going to start setting you off in relationships. Then you'll find yourself running through women like cars at a car wash."

"Are you saying that I should break up with Tommy Girl?"
"I'm not saying that. I would never tell you to break up with anybody." I looked at Alicia with that "yeah right" look. "Okay…I would never tell you to break up with anybody that wasn't Victoria."

"That's what I thought."

"You understand where I'm going with this, right?"

"Yeah…I need to stop falling victim to my need to be with someone and give my mental a break."

"Exactly." I sat up and positioned myself with my back against the wall at the head of my bed facing Alicia.

"I don't know how I've managed these past years without you."

"Me neither cuz you're a hot mess right now," Alicia laughed.

History had proved itself again. Alicia always knew how to cheer me up when I was down. We continued to talk until it was time for us to call it a night. She tried to leave but I suggested that she stay. Alicia put on one of my t-shirts then we talked until we fell asleep.

The first week of school had its ups and downs but ended on a good note. Me and my crew had a ball at the first two parties of the semester and ended the week with a cookout that Sunday afternoon. Judging by my course load and my professors, I knew there wouldn't be too many weekends like that. In addition to that, I also knew that Kim wouldn't be giving me two many weekends off with the holidays approaching.

14
Trouble in Kingstree

For two months straight, Tommy Girl and I went back and forth with each other. Our relationship never seemed to recover from the night that I told her Alicia had come to FMU. Things started getting petty and the relationship was getting on my nerves. The thing that pissed me off the most was the snide comments Tommy Girl would make about Alicia but would never take the time to meet her. Every time I tried to get the two of them together, there was always an excuse. After two months of it, I stopped trying. Our relationship hit its breaking point around the end of October.

It didn't take long for Me, Murph, Teddy and Alicia to receive the label of *Road Trip Crew*. We went everywhere together. If there was a party going on, we were there. After South Carolina State's Homecoming, I thought we were going to be still for awhile—at least that's what I told Tommy Girl. I actually thought I meant it until Murph came in the apartment one Wednesday afternoon with the news of a party that would change my relationship status. I was stretched out across my bed reading chapters in my Intro to Mass Communications book. Alicia was sitting at my desk working on a project for her Public Relations class. I heard Murph when he came in but I thought he went in his room, instead he stood in the doorway staring at us.

"Look at the good little students," Murph laughed.
"Hey Murph," Alicia greeted.

"What's good, homeboy?" I responded without taking my face out of my book.

"It's going down this Saturday night."

"What ever it is, I don't want no parts in it. I'm done for a minute."

"Come on, Dude. It's my boy's birthday and he doin it big in Kingstree. I'm talkin' about Moet, VIP status at the party and a limo."

"Can't do it. I told Tommy Girl I would spend the weekend with her."

"Did you not hear what I said? I said limo."
"He said limo," Alicia cosigned. "As in Limousine."

"You stay out of this Cyndi Lauper. Wit' yo girls just wanna have fun ass. I told you, I am spending the weekend with my girlfriend. Besides, I gotta work Saturday."

"According to the schedule you have posted on the fridge, you get off at four o'clock. That gives you plenty of time to get back here so we can get to Kingstree. My boy said he would pick us up from my crib around nine. To make it even sweeter, Pops is throwin' some ribs on the grill."

"Now you're not playin' fair. You know I'm weak when it comes to anything ya Pops throw on the grill."

"Then it's a done deal."

"What am I supposed to tell my girl?"
"Tell'er you have to go to the Ville to take care of some business."

"That won't work. She got spies all over."
"She don't have spies in the real 'Ville," Alicia instigated without looking up from her paper."

"I swear I asked you to stay out of this. You know my relationship is unstable as it is."

"I'm just sayin."

"Come on, Dude. You can't break up the crew."
"I'll think about it."

"Just so you know," Alicia indiscreetly whispered to Murph. "That means he's going."

"That means I'll think about it.
"And that further lets me know that he's going."

"Bet." Murph laughed as he walked into his room. Alicia and I continued what we were doing prior to being interrupted.

The next night, Tommy Girl and I were in bed at her place. We'd just finished a heated love making session. With the party being three days away, I felt that it was time for me to make my move and tell her what the deal was. I wanted to be honest but the way things were between us; I felt that a lie would work a little better.

"You sleep?" I asked as I rolled over to face Tommy Girl.

"No. What's up?"

"I know that we were supposed to spend this weekend together but something came up."

"What's going on?"

"I have to go to Fayetteville this weekend to take care of some family business."

"I thought you had to work this weekend."

"I did but I asked Kim if she could get my shifts covered for me."

"That's cool. We can get together next weekend. Family always comes first. Besides, Tonya asked me to ride to the beach with her Saturday night."

"Oh okay." After our conversation, I got out of bed to put my clothes back on.

"Where you going?"
"I'm going back on campus. I have class in the morning."

"I thought you were staying here tonight."
"I would but I have to give a presentation tomorrow. I need to make sure that I have everything together. I'll stay next time." Once I was dressed, I leaned over and kissed Tommy Girl on the lips then headed back to campus. Upon arrival, I let Murph and Teddy know that it was a done deal and called it a night.

Saturday came and it was party time. I was nervous the entire time I was at work because I didn't want Tommy Girl to come in the mall. When quitting time came, I darted through the mall and made my way back to campus. Alicia, Murph and Teddy were waiting for me. I tried to take a shower but Murph convinced me to wait until I got to his parent's house in Kingstree. I grabbed my overnight bag and we hit the road.

To hear Murph talk about Kingstree, one would think that it was a metropolitan city like the ATL or LA. I couldn't be mad at him though because everybody thinks that their city is the best in the world. I know that's how me, Alicia and Teddy felt about Fayetteville. The one thing I do remember him saying about Kingstree was: "All roads lead past McDonald's." That was the truest thing he could have ever said. We went a few different places before we went to his parent's house and we must've passed Mickey D's about five times.

    Around 6:30, we pulled up in Murph's front yard. The smell of good barbeque hit me in the face as soon as I stepped out of the car. Murph's little sister came running out of the house and jumped into Murph's arms. He introduced her to us then we went inside. We were greeted by his mother and father. His mother had the table all prepared for us. After we washed up, we sat down to eat. Murph's dad kept us laughing the entire time we ate telling us childhood stories about his son. I think Murph turned about three different shades of red from embarrassment. He knew we weren't going to let him live those stories down. Once dinner was over, we all got dressed and waited for the limo to arrive. Right on time, a black, stretched Mercedes limousine pulled into the front yard. From the sunroof, Murph's homeboy yelled for us. The four of us got in and we were off.

    We cruised around Kingstree for a while making odd stops and picking up more people. By the time we had everyone, there were about 10 of us inside. That's the one thing I loved about growing up in the South; the only person in the limo Teddy, Alicia, and I knew was Murph but because everybody else was cool with him, they were cool with us. Before we were anywhere close to the club, we had already started popping bottles of champagne. I wasn't much of a drinker until my mother passed. Many nights after her death, I found myself searching for the prize of comfort at the bottom of a bottle of Gin. As time passed and the wound started to heal I stopped drowning my sorrows with alcohol and became a social drinker.

Around half past eleven, we pulled up in front of a semi-packed club. The parking lot was starting to thicken. The driver opened the door for us and rolled out the red carpet. When I stepped out of the limousine, I stood in shock. The building that was before me didn't look like anybody should be inside of it. It was the most run down place I'd ever seen before in my life. The club was called the Hideout. The building looked like one of those old-style plantation houses that someone had turned into a club. It was two stories with a balcony on the second floor. Murph informed me that that was the VIP section of the club. Having gone to lavish clubs, Alicia, Teddy, and I all had the same look on our faces. We quickly found that you can never judge a book by its cover. The inside was amazing.

When you first walk in, there was a closed in lounge area by the counter where you pay before you get patted down and walk through the door that lead to the main area of the club. The first floor was completely gutted and wide open. As soon as you walked through the door, the bar was on the left and extended all the way to the far end of the club. To the right there were numerous tables, chairs and couches scattered about. The dance floor was on the far right directly across from the bar. On the far right wall was a stage where the DJ was set up. On the other end of the bar were the stairs that led to the VIP section. We mingled on the first floor for a minute as Murph introduced us to all his people. Alicia and I got in a couple dances then followed the rest of our crew upstairs.

The VIP section was immaculate. It had its own bar and a full buffet of assorted finger foods. There were tables in the middle and the outer walls were lined with booths of different sizes. Within the VIP area was an exclusive area close to the balcony. That area was reserved for us. The four of us settled into a booth and commenced the beginning of what was deemed to be the *Party of the Year*. At New Grove, people used to embellish the truth about how they were this and that in their hometown. Murph said that everybody in Kingstree knew him and he was 100% correct. Every time I looked up, someone different was coming over to talk to him.

"Why you sitting way over there?" I asked Alicia noticing that she was sitting on the edge of the booth and far away from me.

"Because I don't want anybody to think that we're together," laughed Alicia. "It's some fine ass guys in here."

"Anybody you want to know about," Murph began as he leaned toward Alicia. "Let me know." Alicia scanned the VIP section.

"Who's the guy in the khakis and polo shirt?"
"That's my man, Vaughn. He's on a full ride to play ball at UNC. That's his girl right there. They been together since ninth grade."

"Next!" I clowned.
"Yo!" Teddy interrupted. "Who is that light-skinned chick right there in the black dress? No disrespect, Alicia, but baby got the fattest rumpshaker."

"That's Gloria Lomax. We call her the Queen of Kingstree. She was Homecoming Queen, Prom Queen and Miss Boll Weevil."

"Boll weevil?"
"Stop trippin'. That's our mascot and you know it. Last I heard she was back on the market."

"Bet. I'll see y'all later." Teddy slid out of the booth and walked out on the balcony to talk to Gloria.

"What about you, Dré? Anybody caught your eye?"
"I'm good. I got a girl." Alicia continued to point out different guys as Murph gave her the lowdown on each one. Ten minutes into it, a tall, dark skinned brother walked up. He asked if either of us were Alicia's man. Once we

told him that we weren't he asked her to dance. The two of them walked downstairs leaving Murph and me sitting at the table. We continued to talk until Murph brought to my attention that someone was trying to get my attention.

"I think somebody's tryna get your attention." I looked to my right into the eyes of a fine, brown skinned young lady. She smiled at me. I smiled back and went back into my conversation.

"So like I was saying…"

"Here she comes." I looked over again to see that she was walking towards us. This girl was a show stopper. I noticed the looks on the guy's faces as she passed them. Judging by the way the black skirt she wore hugged her hips; I knew exactly what they were looking at. Who ever invented the halter top should be given the Nobel Prize for the greatest invention known to man—next to the thong. Her chest, which looked to be a large C or a small D, was leading the way. Because of her height, they were right in my face when she approached the table.

"Excuse me, she began. "Don't you work at Foot Locker?"

"Yes," I answered looking past her breasts into her eyes.

"I thought so. I was in there with my girl about two weeks ago. You helped her with some shoes."

"That's what's up."

"I'm Vita." She extended her hand.

"Nice to meet you, Vita. I'm Dré and this is my boy, Murph."

"Do you mind if I join you?"

"No problem at all," Murph responded as he stood up. "You can have this seat. I need to go check on something." Murph walked away leaving me alone with Vita.

"You look a lot different with regular clothes on."

"Thanks. Are you from Florence?"

"I work in Florence but I'm from Darlington."

"Mayo or St. John's?"

"Golden Bears all day, Baby."

"True dat. A few of my people graduated from Mayo."

"Really? Who?"

"Do you know Irvin Kendall, Ben Blackmon or Shandra Collins?"

"I know all of them. As a matter of fact, me and Shandra work together at Blue Cross Blue Shield."

"No doubt. It's a small world."

"And Darlington's even smaller," Vita laughed then sipped her drink. "So what do you do besides work at Foot Locker?"

"When I'm not being Sneaker Man, I'm a student at FMU. You in school?"

"I go to Tech right now. I'm thinking about transferring to FMU to finish my nursing degree."
"I hear the programs good but it's hard to get into."
"I'm already on the waiting list. Hopefully by the time I get my Associates from Tech, I'll have been accepted into the program." Vita and I continued to talk. One by one, Teddy, Murph and Alicia all returned accompanied by someone. The booth wasn't large enough to accommodate us all so we moved to one of the larger tables in the middle of the room. The eight of us sat and had a grand time. Periodically, we would go downstairs to dance.

As the night moved on, I began to learn a valuable lesson: never mix alcohol, a fine female and a relationship on the rocks together. By no means is that a concoction that will lead to anything good. The more I drank, the more I got into Vita. The combination of her looks and personality acted as a magnet that inched us closer and closer to one another until it pulled her out of the seat beside me and into my lap. I knew it was wrong but the alcohol made it feel so right.

A quarter 'til two found Vita and I on the dance floor surrounded by my crew and the other party people in attendance. The DJ had the dance floor rocking with Craig Mack's classic joint, *Flava in Ya Ear*. With Vita's ass pressed directly on my pelvic region, I threw my hands in the air and sang along with the song. We danced to hit after hit. After the DJ finished his Reggae set, he dropped the song that made every female in the building lose their ever loving minds. Ladies screamed at the first note of Ginuwine's *Pony*. Vita turned around to face me and wrapped her arms around my neck and commenced to moving her hips to the rhythm of the song. Normally that would have been cool but she had her hips pressed right up against mine and Lil Dré had a mind of his own. I managed to maintain composure until the end of the song then led Vita to the bar. I sat on a bar stool as Vita positioned herself between my legs facing me. I put my arms around her and locked my fingers in place right at the small of her back.

"It's been a minute since I've danced with somebody that could hang with me," Vita complimented.

"I do what I can," I laughed.
"I gotta tell you, Dré. Today had to be one of the worst days of my life. I almost didn't come out here tonight but I'm glad I did."

"I can feel you on that. My world has been kinda shaky here lately, too." As Vita continued to talk to me, something in my head told me to look up. When I did, I found Tommy Girl staring right at me with her girl standing right beside her. She had the same look on her face. If looks could kill, I would have been slain on the spot. As soon as my eyes met hers, she turned and rushed toward the exit. I moved Vita out of the way and headed out of the club behind her. When I finally caught up to her she was fuming.

"I thought Fayetteville was in North Carolina. Last time I checked this was Kingstree!"

"Can you please calm down and stop yelling?"

Looking across the car to her friend, "I just catch my man, who is supposed to be in another state, hugged up with another chick and he wants me to calm down." Her girl didn't say anything. She just shook her head with a scowl on her face. The she turned back to me. "Okay, Dré. I'm calm. Lie to me some more. Tell me that I didn't just see you up in some other chick face like you single." I couldn't say anything. "That's exactly what I thought. If you didn't want to spend the weekend with me you coulda just told me. You didn't have to lie to me."

"Baby, I'm sorry."

"Sorry won't fix this one, Dré. Not this time. I've had all I can take. I'm sick of sharing you with the world. It's never been just me and you. There has always been someone else. I can't do it no more. I'm done." To make things worse, at the close of that statement, Alicia came out of the club looking for me.

"Dré!" Alicia beckoned from about forty feet away. "Are you okay?"

"Are you serious? She's here, too?"

"I'm good," I yelled back to Alicia. "I'll be back inside in a second." Alicia turned back around and walked back in the club.
"You know...its funny how you said that you wouldn't choose between me and her. From the looks of things, I guess you've made your choice. Once again, I wasn't the one that was chosen." Tommy Girl took off the bracelet that I gave her for her birthday and put it in my hand. "You know, Dré...there will come a day when you're going to have to choose." I stood in silence as Tommy Girl climbed into her friend's SUV and drove away. I opened my hand, looked at the bracelet then turned to walk back inside the club.

When I got back inside the club, I ordered another drink and sat alone at a table. Within ten minutes, Alicia found me and sat down. I told her what happened. She apologized to me for pressuring me to break of the weekend with my girl and go to the party. I assured her that it was my own fault. While we were talking, Vita came to the table to tell me she was leaving and gave me her number. She hugged me then left the club. An hour later, the crew gathered up rolled out. I sat in silence the entire way back to Murph's house. The four of us crashed on the floor in the den. The next morning, Murph's mother cooked us breakfast. After we ate, we headed back to campus. I locked myself in my room and didn't come out until it was time for class the next day.

That next morning I awoke with the strangest mix of emotions running through me. I was mad but the only person I was mad at was me. I was hurt because I had hurt Tommy Girl but not by the fact that I'd lost her. I could've been like other guys and blamed the entire situation on somebody or something else to help ease my mind but the reality of it all was that there was no one to blame but myself. The entire day I went through the motions of being a student. I went to all of my classes but I had no recollection of anything that was said. Instead of going back to my apartment after classes were done, I walked to the track behind our University Center and walked around it. As I walked, I searched for answers. The answers eluded me because I had no idea what the questions were. When I couldn't walk any more, I laid down on the bleacher with my backpack fixed under my head as a pillow. I closed my eyes and tried to clear my head. Fifteen minutes in, my silence was interrupted.

"Hey," Alicia greeted. I opened my eyes to find Alicia standing over me looking down at me. "You okay?"

"I can think of a lot of words to describe how I feel right now. Okay isn't one of them." Alicia lifted my head and removed my book bag from under it then replaced it with her lap.

"I'm sorry, Dré. I should've never pushed you to go to the party."

"It wasn't you're fault. I'm a grown man and I made the decision to go."

"Me pushing you couldn't have helped." Alicia started to run her hand with the pattern of the waves in my hair. "It's just that I'm so happy to have you back in my life. I want to spend every day with you to try to make up for the time we've lost. I guess some old habits never die."

"Old habits? What are you talking about?"

"I wanted it to be like it used to be. Before Shawn or Victoria, we used to spend so much time together. I missed that and that's what I was hoping to get back since we've been back together. Selfish old me. I always have to have you to myself. I didn't stop to think that you had a life before I got here."

"You can't put the blame all on you. Since the day I saw you, everything else went out the window. I was the one that pushed everything in my life aside. I guess I finally get the break that you said I needed."

"I said you needed a break but I didn't want to be the cause of it."

"Everything happens for a reason."

"I guess they do."

"I do plan to take your advice though. I'm going to chill for a while before I attempt another relationship. I need to let my mind rest and start fresh later on down the road."

"Are you sure you don't wanna try and fix things with Tommy Girl?"

"Our relationship has been on the outs for a while. This weekend was just the breaking point. No matter how hard I tried, I just don't think Tommy Girl and I were ever meant to be."

"Well…it's your life and you have to live it the way you see fit. As always, I'm there for you."

"And I appreciate it."

That day marked a new beginning in our friendship as well as our lives. For the first time in three years I was free to enjoy life as a single man. Alicia took advantage of the fact that I was single though. She had me all to herself without having to worry about pissing off another female or causing any drama in my life. I also took advantage of the situation. No longer did I have to find time to fit anybody in. All I had to do was focus on school. In the process I enjoyed my life. People at FMU didn't know what to think about Alicia and I. Most of the time they saw us together then they would see us chilling with other people. I was enjoying living the single life but pretty soon those manly urges started to set in. That's when Alexandria came into the picture.

One evening in early December I was sitting in one of the small study rooms in the library working on my final paper for one of my English classes. I was bobbing my head to the songs of Outkast that played in my headphones as I highlighted things in my text book. Over the music I heard a tap on the window of the door. When I looked up, Alexandria was on the other side smiling at me. I motioned for her to come in.

"What ever you're listening to must be the bomb," Alexandria laughed as she sat down.

"Just listening to Outkast and working on this paper," I replied taking off my headphones.

"I just saw you in here and wanted to say hello. I'm getting ready to get some studying done."

"You can join me if you like."

"I don't want to be a bother." I moved some of the papers that I had spread over the table to the side to make room for her.

"No trouble at all. Have a seat." Alexandria sat down and pulled out her Biology book, a pen, a highlighter, and a brand new pack of index cards. Once she got out all her supplies, she jumped into the same study mode I was in. We sat in silence working on our individual tasks. As I sat, what ever fragrance Alexandria was wearing started dancing in my nostrils. "What is that you're wearing?"

"That's Sweet Pea."

"From Vickie Secret?"
"Yeah. How did you know?"

"I'm a big fan of their fragrances. I love a woman that smells good."

"What's your favorite?"

"I would have to say…Country Apple. It just does something to me."
"I wear that one two."
"Just be careful if you ever wear it around me. I might bite you."

"I might not mind as long as you don't bite too hard." The entire time we were talking, we weren't looking at each other. When she said that, I looked up from my book and she had a sly grin on her face but she wasn't looking at me.

"Stop being grown," I chuckled.

"I'm a grown woman. I can't help it." We shared a chuckle and a giggle and went back to our studies. Silenced filled the room once again and lasted for about an hour.

"Can I ask you something, Dré?"
"What's up?"
"Look at me." I paused from my writing and looked up at her. "The girl I see you with all the time, is that your girlfriend or the best friend you told me about?"

"That's my best friend. Her name is Alicia."
"Oh okay. I was just wondering because I always see you two together. Did your girlfriend finally adjust to it?"
"We broke up back in October."
"I guess she couldn't handle it."
"Not one bit."
"Are you seeing anybody else?"

"I decided to take a break for a while. I need some time to let my mind rest. I've been in one relationship after another over the past three years."

"I guess we're in the same boat then. I dated my ex, on and off, since freshman year. We broke up because he didn't want to do the long distance thing. I thought I was going to be hurt but I realized that he did me a favor."

"How so?"

Super Senior

"For one, I didn't have to worry about who he was running around with while I was gone, and two, I get the chance to enjoy the single life for awhile. I feel like I missed out on so much in high school because I had a boyfriend. I'm not saying that I wanted to wild out or anything like that. There were just limitations on what I could and couldn't do just to keep the peace."

"You are preachin' to the choir, my sista. I'ma be straight up with you. I ain't lookin' for a relationship right now but I would like to chill wit' ya sometimes. You know…hangout, chill, go to a movie or something."

"I'd like that. I'm not looking for a relationship either but I do miss chilling with a guy from time to time. Just give me a call anytime you wanna get together and do somethin'."

"I gotta give you fair warning now. I'm not like other guys. Even if we're just friends and chillin' together, I'll always treat you like a lady at all times. That's gotten me in trouble before because females don't know how to handle having a guy that's just a friend treat them like a boyfriend should. If it starts getting to be too much, let me know."

"Trust me. I'm cool. You just let me know if you start catching feelings. I'm a different kind of female. I take care of who I'm with even if we're just kickin' it."

"I'll keep that in mind."

With the semester coming to a close as fast as it was, Alexandria and I didn't get a chance to chill like we thought we would. The only thing we really managed were a few phone conversations on study breaks and an occasional drop in here and there. Despite the fact that we didn't get to spend that time, everything led up to the night of the last party of the semester. Where was it? The Sweat Box.

15
The Sweat Box

Reading Day, which was a day of no classes before exams started, fell on the second Monday in December that year. Despite the upcoming exams, the campus was buzzing about the final party of the semester. The Sigma's had the honor of hosting the final throw down. Because of inventory at the store, I didn't get off work until eleven o'clock that night. By the time I got home, Teddy, Murph, Alicia and a few of our other friends were already deeply engaged in the pre-game activities. To my surprise, Alexandria was in attendance at my apartment. A barrage of cheers rang out when I walked through the door. Murph greeted me with a cup, Alicia gave me a hug and Alexandria winked at me as I walked through the crowd to take a shower and get dressed.

Fresh out of a hot shower, I sat in a chair in my socks, boxers and wife beater applying baby lotion to my skin. Once that task was finished, I stood up to look in my wardrobe to pick out my outfit for the night. While standing deep in thought, someone knocked on my door.

"Come in," I commanded without turning away from the task at hand.

"Hey you," Alexandria greeted as she came in and closed the door behind her. "Really? Scooby Doo boxers? Aren't you a little too old for Underoos?"

"Don't sit there and act like you ain't got Strawberry Shortcake panties," I laughed as I pulled out a pair of dark blue, Tommy jeans, a navy blue long sleeved Tommy button down and a black Ecko wind suit and laid them on the bed side by side.

"For your information, I do not have Strawberry Shortcake panties…thank you very much. They're Hello Kitty."

"Which one should I wear?"

"You definitely don't wanna wear the wind suit. Once you start sweatin' it's gonna start stickin' to you."

"You right. I'll do the jeans and the shirt. Can you look over there and hand me the box with the black Air Force Ones in it? They should be in the second or third stack closest to the wall."

"This is just ridiculous," giggled Alexandria. "You are the only man I know with more shoes than the average female."

"Some guys collect baseball cards. I collect sneakers." By the time she sifted through the boxes and found the shoes, I had on my jeans and was in the process of buttoning up my shirt.

"Wait a minute." Alexandria walked over to me and unbuttoned my shirt. "Do you have a black t-shirt?"

"Yeah, why?"
"Put that on under the shirt and wear it open. That way, when you get too hot, you can just take the long sleeved shirt off."

"What about a hat?"
"No hat. You just got a fresh cut. Besides…I like looking at your eyes."

"Really?" Alexandria wrapped her arms around my neck as mine went around her waist and pulled her close to me.

"Yes. Your eyes are what I find most attractive about you."

I moved my face towards Alexandria. Right before our lips touched. Alicia knocked then barged in.

"Hey Dre! Murph said…my bad. I'll catch you when you come out front."

"It's cool. What's up?"
"Murph said he's ready whenever you are."

"Aiight. Oh yeah. Alicia, this is Alexandria. Alexandria, this is Alicia." We let each other go as Alex walked over to greet my best friend.

"I've seen you around and Dré talks about you all the time. It's nice to finally meet you."

"You too." The two ladies shook hands. "You rollin' wit us?"

"I was gonna drive but I can if it's not too much trouble."

"You driving, Dré?"

"Yeah cuz I'm not tryna be out all night messin' with you, Murph and Teddy. You and Alexandria can ride with me."

"Okay. I'll go let Murph know and I'll meet y'all outside." Alicia left the room and closed the door behind her.

"Sorry about that."

"It's cool. We better get goin' anyway. I'd hate for us to have to park all the way by the road. I can't do too much walkin' in these heels."

Super Senior

Alexandria and I exchanged a quick peck then joined my friends outside in front of the apartment. After a quick discussion about who was riding with who, we all loaded up and headed to the Sweat Box.

By this time in my collegiate career, I'd been to quite a few clubs across the state by none could hold a flame the Sweat Box. The Sweat Box was something special. It was like FMU's very own club. If the frats, sororities or a few of the old heads that graduated from FMU weren't having a party, it sat there empty. The building wasn't big and there was nothing special about it. Before I became a student at FMU, I'd driven by it a thousand times and never paid it any attention.

When we pulled into the parking lot, it was already packed. I drove around the back of the building and parked right beside the DJ's SUV. There was a small driveway that led into the driveway the ran beside the building. I was set to make a quick get away if I needed to. I looked like the man walking toward to building with two of FMU's sexiest females on each arm.

As usual, security was posted at the entrance. Once you were patted down, you approached a table that was set up right across the threshold to the building. The first area was separate from where the main party was. This was what we called the *Breathing Room.* There were long tables and chairs set up on the left side of the room. These tables were for people to sit and talk or for people coming out of the party to catch a break from the heat. On the right side of the room was the bar. Depending on who was throwing the party, sometimes there were drinks, sometimes there weren't. That night the bar was wide open. On the left, beside the bar were the bathrooms.

The only thing that separated the party from the Breathing Room was a set of double doors. Once you went through them, you were officially inside of the Sweat Box. After the doors closed behind you, the only light to lead your path was the lights coming from the stage where the DJ was. It was only fitting because you don't need light when you're gettin' ya grind on.

DJ B Lord, one of the Carolina's up and coming DJ's, had the Sweat Box rockin' when we got there. As soon as we walked through the double doors, he dropped *Only You* by 112 featuring the Notorious B.I.G. The crowd lost its mind. Alexandria grabbed my hand and pulled me onto the dance floor. After pushing through the crowd, we found a spot in the middle of the dance floor. Once in place, Alexandria turned around and pressed her soft ass right up against my pelvis and commenced to give Lil Dré a preview of what I hope would be the perfect ending to a good night.

We danced to hit after hit. The more we danced, the hotter it got—in more ways than one. Before long, I was surrounded my by entire crew. That's when we started to act like stone cold asses. I don't think anybody in the building was having more fun than us. Me and the fellas switched from girl to girl, caught a couple girls up in a sandwich and eventually we were all in a circle with the girls of our choice facing the middle throwing ass on us from Flo-town to Chucktown.

After an hour and a half of non-stop dancing, I had to take a breather. With my long sleeve shirt thrown over my left shoulder, I walked out of the Sweat Box and into the *Breathing Room* to get a drink and some cool air. Once I had my drink, I walked outside. The cold, December air caused steam to float from my body. A familiar voice made a joke about it.

"Damn!" the voice blurted. "This nigga's on fire tonight!" I turned to my left to see a short, bald brown-skinned guy with big sleepy eyes and a well-groomed beard. It was my boy, Snipes.

"What's up, Homeboy?"

"I'm doin' the same thing you doin'…tryna breathe."

"It's hot as hell in there. You rollin' solo tonight? I didn't see the rest of the Ques."

"Them niggaz went to a party at Morris and left me."

"That's messed up."

"Tell me about it," Snipes laughed. "Now I can't fight."

"That ain't never stopped you before."

"True dat. Oh yeah…before I forget, we're havin' an interest meeting when we get back next semester. We not puttin' it out there for everybody but I wanted to let you know cuz you my boy."

"That's what's up. I appreciate that."

"Just let me know if you wanna come check us out and I'll give you the rest of the info when we get back."

"I'll keep that in mind."

"Aiight man. I'm gettin' ready to get back up in here and get up on some more of this scattered ass in here. I'll holla at you."

"Peace."

Not too long after Snipes went in, the cold air started to get to me. I walked back inside. By this time, Murph and Teddy were sitting at a table talking to Alexandria and a couple of her friends. I joined them. The five of us sat there laughing and talking until Alicia came rushing out of the Sweat Box and into the bathroom. I ran in right behind her. When I got there she was on her knees vomiting into one of the toilets.

"I told you to stop acting like you grown," I laughed. "You gone learn about fuckin wit Murph and that Kingstree Kool-Aid."

"Shut up and pull my hair back." I bent over her and pulled her hair out of the path of what she was bringing back up. Alicia threw up for a good five minutes. When she finished, I flushed the toilet then put the lid down so she could sit. Alicia sat with her elbows on her knees and her face in her hands.

"You alright?"
"I'm good. Just gimme a minute."
"I can take you back on the yard if you want me to."
"That might be a good idea. I think I'm done for the night."

After sitting for a few minutes, I helped Alicia stand up. She leaned on me as I walked her out of the bathroom. I informed the crew that I was taking her home. Murph offered to give Alexandria a ride back on campus if she wanted to stay. She declined and left with me and Alicia. When we got to my car, Alicia crawled in and stretched out across the back seat. On the way back on campus I tried to hit as few bumps as I could.

Once on campus, Alexandria helped me get Alicia upstairs into her apartment and into her room. I gave Alexandria the keys to my car and asked her to park it and wait for me in my apartment while I got my best friend situated. As soon as Alexandria left, I helped Alicia out of her party clothes and into her night clothes. Once she was dressed she got into bed. I put a cold cloth on her head then slid the trashcan beside the bed in case she needed it in the middle of the night. In less than five minutes Alicia was passed out. I kissed my lush of a best friend on her cheek and made my way to my apartment.

Alexandria left the front door cracked for me to get in and was waiting in my room. Soft music met me as I walked around the corner. I opened the door and made my way to the bed by the light of one candle. When I got to the bed, I notice that the outfit that Alexandria had on that night was neatly folded and draped over the back of the chair that was parked at my desk. I kicked off my shoes and stripped down to my Scooby Doo's and undershirt. I blew out the candle and slid into bed. As soon as I was in, she rolled over to face me.

"Is Alicia okay?" she asked as the scent of spearmint gum and vodka hit me in the face.

"She's passed out."
"You're such a good friend. Not many people take the time to take care of their friends like that."

"I gotta look out for Alicia. Outside of my roommates and the few people that we've met since we've been here, all we have is each other."

"Well right now, you got me."

Alexandria pushed her lips against mine. When my mouth opened, her tongue came in searching for mine. I pulled her on top of me and repositioned myself in the middle of the bed. She paused and pulled my shirt over my head and tossed it to the floor. Her warm flesh felt so good pressed against mine. While she kissed me on my lips and neck, I reached around her back and unfastened her bra to unleash her soft, round breasts. My touch caused her nipples to become erect. I could feel them on my chest. With a soft touch, I ran my hands up and down her smooth, bare back to the ending point of her soft cheeks that were hanging out of a pair of lace bikinis. The motion sent chills through her body causing her sexual mood to escalate.

With Alexandria still on my chest I sat up. She continued to kiss me on my lips neck and chest as I reached for a condom. Once I was protected returned to my previous position with Alexandria on top of me. She reached behind her, grabbed my member and positioned it with the head pressing into her flesh. Her body tensed and she inhaled quickly as the head pushed into her tight, wet pleasure zone. She paused for a moment.

"You okay?" I asked.
"Yeah. I've only been with one guy and it's been a few months since my last time."

"Take your time. Whenever you're ready."

Alex rolled her hips and slid down on it until it was all the way inside of her. Right before she came all the way down, I hit her spot causing her body to jump. Once it was inside she paused again and sat straight up on it. Alexandria rolled her hips a little more then slowly slid up and down being cautious not to go down far enough for me to hit her spot again. After a minute of moving slow, she broke out of the gates like she was on the back of a bucking bronco.

"Whoa," I whispered. "Slow down. We got all night."

"My bad. I'm so used to having to hurry to mine."

"Those days are long gone. I'll make sure you get yours. Trust me."

I pulled out of Alexandria and rolled her off of me onto her back. She opened her legs to allow me to position myself in between them. On my knees, I leaned down and gently kissed and sucked her on her neck. From her neck, I went back up to her lips. It drove her crazy when I sucked on her bottom lip. The more we engaged in foreplay, the hotter and wetter she became. I felt her wetness on my stomach when it touched the zone. I let the lip go that I was sucking on and ran my tongue down her chin to her neck to betwixt her breasts. From nipple to nipple I sucked and nibbled on then. I could tell by her actions and reactions that her ex-boyfriend had never taken the time with her body the way that I was.

Once I felt that her breasts had receive the attention they deserved I moved further down south. My tongue slid down her slightly muscular stomach to just above the mouth of a river that was flowing. I kissed the inside of her left thigh as close to her little lady as I could. This drove her crazy. From the left thigh, I moved to the right thigh. Every time I got close to her southern hospitality she tensed up and released stuttered breaths. I took my fingers and spread her lips apart then lightly touched my tongue to her clit. Her hips began to move out of control. In a quick motion I took it into my mouth and sucked on it. Alexandria sat up and grabbed my head. It was dark but my eyes had adjusted with the light coming from the streetlight pressing against the blinds. She had a confused look on her face and was biting her bottom lip.

"Something wrong?" I asked with concern.
"Fuck me," Alexandria whispered. "Fuck me right now."

I crawled back up and pressed my lips to hers pushing her onto her back with that motion. Alexandria spread her legs to accept the feature presentation that she had just had a sneak preview of. I rose to my knees and readied my member for insertion. The entrance that I had just recently exited must've been made of elastic because it tightened right back up. Inch by inch I eased inside of Alexandria. Slow, deep strokes caused her body to jump every time I hit her spot. Anytime a man finds a woman's G-spot, his mission changes from *Operation Slow Grind* to

Destruction with No Remorse. I knew I had her right where I wanted her and was getting ready to give Alexandria the ride of her life. A voice inside my head told me to use caution but was overpowered by another voice telling me to make her remember me for the rest of her life.

As the session got more and more intense, the louder Alexandria got. I knew Murph and Teddy were still at the Sweat Box but I didn't know where my other roommate was. I kept trying to tell Alexandria to suppress her noise but it fell on deaf ears. She finally took both of the pillows and buried her face into them. It helped but not by much. The more noise she made, the more I wanted to make her make noise.

Against my better judgment, I took both of Alexandria's legs and put them over my shoulders. This position opened her up for me to explore deeper depths. She moved the pillow from over her face and looked at me with that confused look again. The sensation from this position started the process of my first orgasm. I slowed down because I felt her body begin to tremble signifying hers. The strokes were slow but they were deep. I played a crucial game of tag with her G-spot. I let her legs down and continued to slow stroke her.

"Dre!" she screamed through the pillow. "I'm comin'!"

Alexandria and I came to a dual orgasm. She wrapped her arms and legs around me and held on to me like I was trying to throw her over a cliff. Her body convulsed and the muscles of her lady parts tightened around my manhood. Because of the after orgasm sensitivity I told her to stop moving. For five minutes we were as still as statues. The only motion was caused by our heavy breathing. I grabbed the condom at the base and pulled out of Alexandria. I pulled the condom off, tossed in the trash and collapsed on the bed beside her. Alexandria was lying in a fetal position facing the wall. She was still experiencing aftershocks. I put my arms around and pulled her close to me.

"You good?" I asked pulling the sheet over our bodies. Alexandria rolled over and buried her face in my chest.

"That was amazing. I've never felt like this before."
"Like what?"
"Satisfied. My ex used to get him and quit."
"I told you. Those days are long gone."
"I hope so."

As we engaged in pillow talk I heard Teddy and Murph come in and go into their rooms. In a matter of moments I heard Jodeci and the giggles of a female through the wall that separated Murph's room and mine. I got up and turned up the volume on my stereo. Before long, Alexandria and I were out.

Lorenzo "El Gee" Gladden

By that Friday, exams were over and my first semester at Franklin Memorial had come to a close. If this semester was any reflection on what the rest of my time at FMU was going to be like, I needed to make sure that my mind stayed right. Alicia and I parted ways for the winter break. I assured her that I would be in the Ville over the holidays. I didn't have any specific plans for my break. Other than work, my holiday was open to whatever was going to happen. When Twist came home from State, he and I hung out a lot. We later found out that Nick got somebody pregnant and withdrew from school to move to Columbia to be with her.

16
Blue Splash '97

Christmas came and went. Before I knew it, the spring semester had begun and we were all back on campus. I made a couple of trips Camden to see Alexandria over the break. She and I had gotten pretty tight but weren't pursuing a relationship. That spring semester was pretty tame for the most part. Nothing out of the ordinary happened outside of classes and parties. The biggest event of the semester was the annual Blue Splash hosted by the Sigma's. Because of the line that the Zetas had, it turned out to be a hellavah weekend.

The Friday night before the pool party found the area in front of the entrance to our university center packed with students. Teddy, Murph, Alicia, and I were right down front. It was like we were all standing in front of a stage. The atmosphere was bananas. Sigma's and Zetas from all over South Carolina and North Carolina assembled at Franklin Memorial to welcome the newest members of Zeta Phi Beta. Though the Sigma's and Zetas were the smallest in numbers, they were always the hypest and always had the most support from other chapters. Having gone to New Grove, I hadn't experienced Greek life until I came to FMU. The only thing I knew about Greeks was what I saw on School Daze and A Different World—and to my knowledge, Gamma Phi Gamma and Kappa Lambda Nu didn't exist.

At 9:20, the probate began. One of our home girls and current member of Zeta Phi Beta introduced "The Octikal Illusion" to the students that were in attendance. Eight ladies walked into position and solidified their membership into the organization. From what Murph told me, this was the largest line of Zetas to cross at FMU to date. I sat and watched how the crowed reacted to them. People cheered, whistled and screamed for the ladies as they stepped and introduced themselves. I could only imagine what it would be like to be standing up there in front of everybody.

After the probate was over, the crew and I kicked off our Friday night in my apartment. Alicia's roommate, Alexandria and a couple of her friends and a few other people fell into the groove at *Club H-6*. Alexandria and Alicia battled Teddy and Priyah in a heated game of Spades as Murph and I played host to the event by serving drinks and making everyone feel welcome. After about an hour, Teddy and I stepped outside to catch some air. While we were talking, Tony Sherman and Brandon Rice, two members of Phi Beta Sigma, walked by.

"What's up, fellas?" Tony greeted as he approached. Tony was about 5'6" with brown complexion and a slim build. He had a khaki hat with the letters of Phi Beta Sigma on the front of it, pulled down to his eyes and a T-shirt that also displayed the fraternity's letters. Brandon was a little shorter than Tony with a bald head and about the same complexion. Brandon must've just come from work or something because he had on slacks and white button down shirt. "Y'all ain't comin' over to E-1?"

"We started to but people followed us here," I replied as I blew smoke into the air.

"Ya girls did they thing tonight," Teddy interjected.

"'Preciate that. This is just the beginning. After this pool party tomorrow, everybody gonna be tryna go blue."

"That's right," Brandon added after taking a puff from his cigarette. "We gettin' ready to blow up."

"That's what's up." I replied.
"If y'all get a minute, come on over to the spot. We got plenty of drinks."

"We might just do that."
"Alright, fellas. We'll holla at y'all later. Y'all comin to the pool party, right?"

"We been talkin about it since y'all first put up posters."

"Aight then…we'll get up." Tony and Brandon walked off leaving me and Teddy standing in front of our apartment.

"You thinkin' about pledgin'?" Teddy asked me as he passed me the Black & Mild.

"I was thinkin' about it but I don't know what I wanna pledge. What about you?"

"Everybody in my family is either a Kappa or a Que. Since I been here, I ain't been feelin' them. Know what I'm sayin?"

"I feel you on that. Ain't no Greeks in my family. I'm the first one to go to college."

"I've been checkin everybody out since I been here and truth be told, the Sigma's are the coolest on the yard."

"That's true."

"It's somethin' to think about." In the middle of our conversation, Alicia came outside to let us know we were up on the table. I extinguished the cigar as Teddy and I walked back upstairs.

As we enjoyed the rest of the night, a few Sigma's and Zetas came over after their get together was broken up by Public Safety. They had a few drinks and chilled out with us. Around 4:30am we shut down shop and I hit the sheets with Alexandria.

The next day, Alexandria was gone by the time I woke up. I didn't realized how trashed our place was until I walked into the kitchen to get something to drink. When

Super Senior

Teddy and Murph woke up we cleaned the apartment and started the pre-game for the pool party. Around two o'clock, Alicia and her girls came over to chill before we headed to the pool party. I was in my room when Alicia walked in. I had my back to the door because I was in my wardrobe looking for the t-shirt I'd plan to wear.

"What's up, Big Head?" she greeted.

"I know you ain't talkin' with that monster dome...," I became speechless when I turned around and saw what Alicia was wearing. She had on some super short white cut-off shorts and a yellow and white, floral print bikini top holding her light-skinned and fairly large breasts. "Ummm...where in the hell do you think you're going with that on?"

"To the pool Party."
"No the hell you ain't."
"Boy, stop playin," Alicia laughed.
"I am dead serious. Put a t-shirt on." Alicia noticed that I wasn't laughing.

"Are you serious?"
"As a heart attack." I reached into my closet and tossed her one of my t-shirts to put on.
"I can't swim in a t-shirt."
"You can take it off before you get in the water."

"I don't believe this," Alicia pouted as she sat down on my bed and pulled the shirt over her head. "Happy now?"

"Yes I am. Thank you."
"I swear, Dre. Sometimes I don't know if you're my best friend or my boyfriend."

"I'm just tryna look out for you."
"I feel you and I appreciate it."

"Look, Alicia. We go back. Like I told Alexandria, besides Murph, Teddy and a couple others, we all we got. I know how a lot of these dudes are around here and I don't know what I would do if something happened to you."

"We're not at Westchester anymore. I can handle these dudes. Contrary to what you think, I am a big girl."

"Yes you are and I apologize if I go overboard sometimes. Do ya thing. Just know that I got ya back." Alicia stood up, walked toward me and put her arms around me.

"I'm lucky to have had a friend like you in my life all these years. Thank you for just being you."

"You're welcome."

"Now can I take this shirt off?"

"Hell no."

"I can't stand you," Alicia laughed.

"I love you, too."

Around 4 o'clock we arrived to the pool party which was being held behind our University Center. The pool was indoors but the party was outside. People were everywhere and the DJ had the sounds blasting. I'd never seen so many Sigma's and Zetas at one time. It was blue and white as far as the eye could see. Once Alicia and her crew saw all the guys walking around with their shirts off, they got away from us like we were infected. Me, Teddy and Murph headed straight for the pool. Once inside it was like we stepped onto the set of a Sports Illustrated swimsuit issue photo shoot. There were so many beautiful black girls in bikinis. I surveyed the scene to check out the new faces. As the three of us were talking and commenting on the things we saw, a female standing within a group of females waved as us.

"Who is she waving at?" Teddy inquired.

"I have no idea," Murph relpied.

"Dre!" the female called.

"You know her?" Murph asked.

"Her face looks familiar but I can't tell from here."

"Then lets go over there and take a closer look."

The three of us made our way to the other side of the pool. As I got closer, I recognized who it was. It was one of the twins from a little group I was in back in junior high school called Smoove and Sweet. Tina and Tonya Whitehurst were two of the four dancers that were a part of the group.

"I can't believe it," she squealed as she hugged me. "It's been too long. How you been?"

"I'm good. Forgive me when I say this but I know who you are but I don't know which one you are."

"I'm Tina."

Tina was a towering 5'3" with a light brown complexion and light brown eyes. Her hair was in micro braids that were pulled back into a ponytail. The last time I saw Tina we were sophomores in high school and her body hadn't started to blossom. My how things changed over time. Tina was short but she was stacked. Her body was similar to Alexandria's only Tina had a slightly rounder ass and was probably one more cup size larger than Alexandria's C's.

"I'm glad you cleared that up for me," I laughed. "Time has been good to you. You look amazing."

"Ahem!" Teddy interrupted.

"My bad. These are my boys Teddy and Murph. As a matter of fact, Teddy is from the Ville, too."

"For real? What school."

"I'm a Falcon…tried and true."

"I won't hold that against you."

"Ahhhh…she got jokes. It's all good…you can't expect too much from somebody whose mascot is a condom."

"Watch ya mouth." Turning back to Tina, "So what brings you here?"

"I'm here to support my Blue and White family."

"Word? That's what's up. When you cross?"

"Last sememster. Those are my line sisters."
Tina pointed to three girls sitting on the edge of the pool.

"That's just three of them. It was seven of us. The others are around here somewhere."

"Where you in school?"

"I'm at UNC Pembroke. My sister stayed home and went to Fayetteville State. I couldn't do it. I know its right down the road but I had to get out of Fayetteville for a minute."

"I feel you. It was good seeing you. I'll catch up with you a little later. I just got here so I need to get my mingle on."

"That's what's up. I'm getting ready to chill in the pool for a while."

"No doubt. If I miss you, we're having an after party at my apartment on campus. H-6." Come through."

"Okay. I will."

When I turned around, Murph and Teddy were in the pool talking to Tina's line sisters as they sat on the side.

"I'm going outside."

Without looking at me Murph replied, "Aight, Kid. Do ya thing."

I laughed as I walked off. Teddy and Murph were two of the funniest dudes in the world when they got in front of females. I walked around the pool and out the side door. Alicia and her roommate were sitting at a table talking to two dudes. I threw her a peace sign and headed to the table where the food was.

While I was sitting there eating, I began to look around. It amazed me how so many strangers could come together as a family under the umbrella of two organizations. I watched as they laughed with each other. I listened as one person would start a chant or their call and the rest would join in. That was something that I could see myself being a part of. As I sat lost in thought, a familiar face sat down at the table with me.

"You behaving yourself out here with all this booty running around?" Melissa asked.

"Yes, Ma'am," I laughed as I covered my mouth to keep from spitting food out.

"I'd hate for your girl to come out here and show her ass."

"It's been a minute since we really had a chance to talk. She and I broke up back in October."

"I kinda thought you did because I kept seeing you with that lil' young girl."

"That's Alexandria. She's cool people. We hang out from time to time. What about you? You still dating that Kappa dude?"

"That's a negative. It's hard to date a man that thinks he's prettier than me."

"Wow. I guess its true what they say about them pretty boys," I laughed.

"You silly. Where ya other girl at? I know she out here somewhere."

"Last I saw her, she was up there talking to a couple guys with her roommate. Knowing her fast ass, she's probably in the pool by now."

Melissa and I sat and talked for a good while. As we talked, I noticed different things about her. The first thing I noticed was how pretty she was. There were a lot of pretty women at FMU but there was something different about her. She was that pretty that was natural. With the exception of lipstick or lip gloss, she didn't wear make-up unless she was going out—even then it wasn't excessive. She had that grade of hair that didn't need to be relaxed too often. I think I remember her saying she got one about once every six months.

Another thing I noticed about her is the way she paid attention to me when I talked to her. She always looked me in my eyes. That has always been important to me. That let me know she was interested in what I had to say. I also noticed that my conversations with her were a lot different with her than any other female. We talked about everything from sports to politics. Melissa stimulated my mind.

After about an hour of conversation, Melissa's sorors came and hauled her off. This was shortly after the DJ announced that the bikini and hard body contests were about to begin. Before long, Murph and Teddy found me. We went to try to get a good spot for the bikini contest but all the Sigma's had the area surrounded. We wound up

Super Senior

standing on one of the tables. It was crazy to see how the guys acted as the girls strutted out. They acted like they'd never seen a female in a bikini before. The contest was momentarily interrupted because some of the guys kept touching the girls. After they got everything calmed down they wrapped up the contest and the guys came out. All the guys disbursed and the females took their places.

Once the sun started going down, the DJ kicked it up a notch and the same area that hosted the bikini contest became a dance floor. While dancing with Alexandria, Tina found me. Teddy took over with Alexandria and I turned my attention toward Tina. We laughed and danced for a good hour before we sat down. Feeling that the party wasn't going to last too much longer, I gave Tina the apartment number once again and headed to the apartment to get set up for the after party.

After I took my shower and changed clothes, I took all the VHS tapes, the VCR and everything else that could be stolen or broken and put them in my room. Once everything was safe in my room, I turned on the music then proceeded to set the bar table up with the bottles and cups. While I was adding more liquor to Murph's signature *Kingstree Kool-Aid,* Alicia called my name through the open window.

"Open the door, Dre!" Alicia called.
I opened the door for her.
"Is the party over?"

"Yeah. Some Ques started acting a fool so they shut it down before a fight broke out."

"Was Snipes involved?"
"He was the main one," She laughed. "Murph and Teddy were rounding people up when I left so people should be coming soon."

"Cool."
"Can I ask you a question?"
"What's up?"
"Who was that girl you were dancing with?"
"That was Tina; one of the twins from the group."
"I thought she looked familiar."
"She's a Zeta from Pembroke."
"Oh okay."
"What?"
"Nothin'!"

"It's never nothing with you when there's a girl involved."

"What are you talking about?"
"Out of all the girls I danced with tonight, she was the only one you didn't know but its funny how I knew exactly who you were talkin' about."

"I was just curious cuz I didn't know who she was. That's all."

"Okay that's all. You just tryna keep tabs on me like you always do. Did I ask you about the buff dude I saw you talking to?"

"Shut up and give me a drink!"
"Just for that, you gotta bartend first."
"What!"

"You know the rules. Everybody in the crew has a job to do. I came to set up and Murph and Teddy are doing promotions. What are you doing other than standing here interrogating me?" I paused and waited for her to respond. "Exactly. The tip cup is right there. You can take my t-shirt off now. I need these niggas to dig in they pockets."

"You won't let me walk around the pool party in just my top but you'll let me stand here in it so you can get money? You are not going to exploit me, Andre Marcellus Marshall."

"Yes I am, Alicia Renee Burroughs because the refrigerator is empty and last time I checked you eat here too and ain't put in no snaps this month."
"I hate you so much right now," Alicia replied as she folded her arms and poked out her bottom lip.

I walked to her and wrapped my arms around her. "I love you, too. Now get Daddy's money."

Alicia moved her face as I tried to kiss her on the cheek. I let her go and smacked her on the ass then walked toward my room.

Our apartment filled up in no time. There were people inside as well as outside. It was still kind of early and our favorite Public Safety officers were on duty so it was cool. As I was mingling with my guests, over the music I heard a lot of commotion going outside. I made my way to the balcony. When I got there I saw a mob of Sigma's and Zetas walking down the small road in front of our apartment chanting and doing their calls as they made their way to the Sigma spot, E-1. I stood and watched but in my mind I wanted to be a part of it. When they got in front of my apartment they heard the music and started a party line down the road. The onlookers went crazy. From the street, Tina spotted me and waved as she walked by with her Sorority sisters from Pembroke. She motioned to me telling me she would be back. I gave her a nod and walked back into the apartment.

When I checked on Alicia, the tip jar was overflowing. I removed some of the money from the jar and the rest that she had in her back pocket and took it to my room. After I counted it and put it under my mattress, I laid back on the bed and stared up at the ceiling. As I gazed at the AC vent, I could hear Brandon saying, "After this pool party, everybody gonna be tryna pledge blue." I didn't know about anybody else but I knew I was going to the interest meeting next fall. As I lay there, my body reminded me how much the heat of the day had drained me. I dozed off. I was out for about thirty minutes when Alicia came in and woke me up.

"I know you not back here sleep while a party going on out there," Alicia said as she repeatedly hit me with a pillow.

"Girl," I groggily began. "If you don't stop hittin' me with that pillow…"
"What you gonna do? Nothing." As Alicia continued to assault me I heard Murph calling my name as he came down the hall.

"I know this nigga ain't in here sleep."
"Hell yeah…I came back here and he was knocked out."

"It's a short, brown skinned Zeta out here looking for you."

"Tell her I'll be right out."
"Bet."
"Oh…so you get up for some random chick but you wouldn't get up for me."

I sat up and straightened out my clothes.
"You're the reason why I'm up in the first place."
"I shoulda let you sleep."

Alicia threw the pillow in my face and turned to walk out. I threw the pillow and hit her in the back of the head.

"Take yo' high yella ass back out there and get my money!"

When I walked back out into the common area, Tina was sitting on the couch with two of her line sisters. Murph was entertaining them while they waited. I approached them and grabbed Tina's hand. With my peripheral vision, I saw Alicia watching me take her back to my room. Once inside my room, Tina sat on the bed and I sat in the chair at my desk. She slid off her sandals of and got comfortable.

"You don't mind do you?" Tina asked wrapping her arms around my pillow.

"Not at all…make yourself at home."
"It is so good to see you again after all these years."
"It's good to see you, too. How've you been?"

Tina began to tell me about everything that she had been through since she graduated. She told me about how she started stripping. Living that fast life led to heavy drug use.
"How'd you end up at Pembroke?"

"I almost overdosed one night at a party. I woke up in a hospital bed all by myself. I was really shook. As soon as I got out of the hospital, I was on the first bus back to the 'Ville. I chilled out for about a month then I started working at the mall. When I got my first paycheck I felt insulted considering the money I used to make. That's when I started dancing again. Low and behold, I found myself in the hospital again because of drugs. The difference this time was when I woke up, all my family was right there. When I looked into my Dad's eyes, I realized right then, it was time for me to get my life together before I destroyed myself. Two semesters ago I enrolled and now I'm here…a Dean's List student and a proud member of Z Phi B. My Sorors and LSs mean the world to me."

"Wow," I sighed in absolute astonishment. "You've been through it. I'm glad you came to your senses."
"So am I…but enough about me. When you pledging Sigma?"

"How did I know that was coming," I laughed. "The Sigmas are real cool here. To be honest, I could see myself pledging. I just don't know when."

"Well when you do, make sure you let me know. Me and my people will be down here to represent."

"When's the last time you talked to Victoria?"
"Fuck that bitch!" Tina uttered with a look of disgust on her face.

"She seems to have that same effect on a lot of people. I met a girl at the beach that felt the same way."

"Let me tell you, Dre. After you left, she went down. She couldn't keep her hands off of other people's men."

"That's the same thing Lena said."
"Lena Braxton?"
"Yeah…I met Lena during Senior Week."
"That's my girl. Lena goes to Pembroke, too."
"I thought she was supposed to go to Johnson C. Smith?"

"She went for a year and didn't like it. I caught up with her the summer before I started. Lena was the one that convinced me to go."

"This is really a small ass world."

Tina and I talked for a while longer than joined the rest of the party. For the remainder of the night we Teddy, Alicia, Tina and I reminisced about growing up in Fayetteville. It was a good night.

17
Burning Sands

A warm, September night found me, Murph and Teddy dressed in light blue jeans and white t-shirts in my car headed to an unknown destination. I don't know about the others but my heart was pounding and my mind was racing. I had no idea what to expect.

"Do you know where you're going?" Teddy nervously asked.

"Brandon said to come to the Apts," I answered.
"Y'all boys ready for this?" Murph inquired.
"I'll let you know the answer to that when we get back on the yard."

We found our destination. When we entered the apartment there were about eight Sigma's with evil grins on their faces. We were instructed to line up in the middle of the floor according to height. From left to right it was me, Teddy then Murph. I was nervous as hell. Brandon stood up and walked over to us.

"You mean to tell me," Brandon began. "Out of all the guys at the interest meeting, these three assholes were the best FMU had to offer?"

"These three are it," Tony answered.

"Well fellas…welcome to your worst nightmare. From this night forward you will be known as #1, #2 and #3. I'm Big Brother Superstar and your Dean of Pledges. When I call you, you come and the same goes for any of your big brothers. Anything that needs to be done, you will do it. You are not responsible for just yourself. You are also responsible for your line brothers. When one fucks up, you all fucked up. Learn everything we give you. Learn all of your Big Brothers past and present. From this night forward…No smoking, no drinking and no women. If we catch you, may God have mercy on you. If you don't believe me? Ask Big Brother Warlord what happens when you get caught with a female."

For three hours straight, the three of us stood in the midst of eight guys yelling and interrogating us. No matter what we said it was always wrong and there were consequences. I must've done about a thousand push-ups and sit-ups that night. After the third hour, our Big Brothers got bored with us and sent us back on campus. There was complete silence as we rode back on campus.

"Y'all good?" I asked as I shifted the car into park.
"I'm good," Murph replied.
"You straight, Teddy?"
"I'm straight."
"For some reason I think that tonight was the easiest night that we're ever going to have."

We drug ourselves into our apartment and into our rooms. My arms were so sore I could barely set my alarm clock. I tried to get myself together to take a shower but Murph beat me to it. The next thing I know, it was morning and my alarm was going off.

After I showered and got dressed, I left for class. I had to take the long way because we weren't allowed to walk on the grass. As I approached the quad, I saw a group of Sigma's and Zetas standing by the clock. I tried to pay them no mind and continue to my class but I was summoned by Big Brother Superstar. He walked away from the group and met me halfway.

"Greeting Big Brother Superstar."
"Cut that shit out. You don't have to greet me when we're in public. You okay?"
"Yeah, I'm good."
"What about your LBs?"
"Everybody's straight."
"Good. When you finish classes for the day, come to the SGA office. I need you to do something for me."

"Okay."
"Alright. I'll catch you later."

I continued on to class. By 12:30, my classes had ended for the day. I went back to the apartment, grabbed a bite to eat and headed to the SGA office in the University

Center. Brandon was already there when I arrived. I knocked then entered on command.

"What's up, Man?" Brandon greeted as I closed the door. "Have a seat. I just wanted to talk to you for a minute."

"Okay. What's up?"
"I know y'all didn't know what to expect last night."

"That's an understatement."

"It's all a part of the process. We all went through it. If I could give you one piece of advice to you, that would be; the end justifies the means. Do you understand where I'm coming from?"

"Yes."

"Forget what you've heard or seen in a movie or TV. We're not trying to hurt you. It's all a mind game. Phi Beta Sigma was founded and built on a tradition by who?"

"Big Brothers A. Langston Taylor, Lenard F. Morse and Charles I. Brown."

"Good," Brandon laughed. "See, you learned something last night. What I really wanted to talk to you about is how important you are to your line. You're the #1.

Super Senior

You have to always be on point. You are responsible for making sure your LBs know their shit. You also have to know where they are at all times. Everything goes through you." Brandon reached into his desk drawer. "Put this watch on and have it on at all times. You'll learn why tonight. One more thing…your mandatory library time is for studying your schoolwork not your information. We don't have no dummies in our organization. We've had the highest GPA for the past five years and we intend to keep that up. Any questions?"

"What if one of the Zetas asks us to do something?"
"You do it unless a brother needs you. They can get carried away sometimes but remember that you're pledging Sigma…not Zeta."

"Okay. Anything else?"

"I think that's about it. Same place, same time tonight. Don't be late."

"I don't get off work until 9. I'll be a little late."
"Just get there as soon as you can."

I left the UC and went to the library to get my time in before I had to go to work. Three hours crept by then I headed to work.

While I was working, my boy Snipes came in the store.

"What's up, Dre?" he greeted.

"Tryna get that money like you got," I laughed.

"I called you last night but your roommate said you were gone."

"Yeah…I was out and about."

"You put any more thought into pledging Que this semester?"

"I thought about it but I'm gonna have to pass. I got a lot going on this semester."

"I'm sure we can work around some things."

"I appreciate it but this semester's not good for me."

"I can respect that. Just stay away from the Alphas and Kappas. They recruitin' heavy this semester."

"I know. Damien the Alpha pulled me out the party last week asking me about my GPA."

"You serious?" Snipes laughed.

"The week before, Reno approached me in the UC."

"I don't blame'em though. You're a good dude and I think you'd be a good asset to any organization."

"You just want it to be yours."

"You Damn Skippy!"

Snipes and I shared a laugh as I helped him with some shoes. Snipes was my man fifty grand and it killed me to lie to him but that's just how it was.

Super Senior

The nine o'clock hour found me closing up the store. I didn't know what the night was going to hold when I entered the den of wolves. The only thing I could really think about was how it was going to feel to finally have those letters across my chest. The way the Sigma's and Zetas represented at the Zeta probate, the pool party and every other function fueled my fire to want to be a part of the blue and white family.

Five weeks into the process, Me, Murph and Teddy were inseparable. We were tight before we began but the things we experienced formed a bond that could never be broken. I've heard other Greeks trading war stories about when they were drudging across the "burning sands" and never really put too much stock into it. They would also say that if you didn't pledge, you wouldn't understand. Five weeks in and I understood fully. There weren't a large number of Sigma's and Zetas on the yard at the time that we pledged but it didn't take us long to realize that they had eyes everywhere. Apparently my dear LB thought that it would be okay for him to smoke a Black & Mild behind the library of all places. That night was no good for any of us.

"What the fuck did Big Brother Superstar tell you on the first night, #2?" Big Brother Commando barked as he looked down at Teddy, whom was in a push-up position.

"No smoking, Big Brother Commando."
"And what did you do?"
"I smoked, Big Brother."

While locked up with Murph, I noticed that Teddy's arms were starting to tremble. I had to do something. I let Murph go and went to help my LB.

"Get your ass back in line, #1!"
"No disrespect, Big Brother Commando but I have to help my LB."

Despite the warnings and physical restraint I managed to get free and crawl under my LB so that he could rest on my back for a minute.

"Get your ass up!" Big Brother Predator commanded.

I didn't move until he grabbed me by my ankles and pulled me from under Teddy. As soon as he did, Murph took my place.

"You think you're Mr. Helpful, #1? Commando told you to get back in line."

"Sorry, Big Brother. My LB needed help."
"Well let's see if you're LB is going to help you out. Get in the cut."

The first thing I did was reach into my jeans with my left hand to protect my family jewels. Then I spread my legs, bent at the waist with my head up and my right arm extended while my finger pointed something in front of me.

Big Brother Predator positioned himself behind me while wielding a wooden paddle with the letters burned into one side.

"You better say it like you mean it, #1." With a mighty swing of the paddle, a loud smack filled the room as the wood connected with my ass. Ka-Payow!!

"Feels good, real good!" I yelled.
"You didn't mean that shit." Ka-Payow!
"FEELS GOOD, REAL GOOD!"

After the fourth lick my legs began to tremble. Murph pushed me out of the way and assumed the position.

"What the fuck are you doing, #3?"
"I'm helping my LB, Big Brother Predator."
"Did #1 help you out the other night when you were in the cut?"
"Yes, Big Brother."

In the midst of the back and forth between Murph and Big Brother Predator, Teddy began breathing very heavily while coughing. It seemed like the more he tried to catch his breath, the worse it got. The Big Brothers thought he was faking at first. Shit got real when they tried to stand him up and he passed out. That sent the brothers into full panic mode. I stood in shock as one of my closest friends and line brother lay motionless on the floor. He was barely breathing and unconscious. Brandon instructed everybody to get back and let him breathe. Another one of the brothers brought a washcloth and put it across his forehead. Everything was put on pause.

"Dre, does he have any medical conditions that we don't know about?"

"None that I know of. I remember him saying he used to have asthma but he grew out of it."

"He's not breathing," Tony examined. "Does anybody know CPR." Big Brother Warlord rushed in from the kitchen and began to perform CPR on Teddy.

"Call 911!" Brandon instructed. "We gotta get him to the hospital."

"He might die if we wait for an ambulance to come way out here," Tony pointed out.

When I heard the word die, my body went cold. Just then, Teddy coughed and came to. I was so relieved.

"This is the deal," Brandon began. "You two go back on campus. Tony and I are going to take him to the hospital."

"Why can't we go? That's our LB."
"Hospitals are always on the lookout for situations that look like hazing. If it's just us three, it won't look

suspicious. Now go back on campus and wait for us to get back. Don't say anything to anyone."

Murph and I helped them get Teddy in the car and watched as they sped off. We went back inside to get our hoodies then left.

"You think Teddy's going to be okay?" Murph asked with serious concern in his voice.
"I hope so."

We didn't say anything else until we got back on campus. When we got there we went straight to our apartment. Teddy and I were sitting on the couch when the doorbell rang. It was Alicia.

"Have either of you seen Teddy?" Alicia inquired. "We have to work on a presentation for English."
"I haven't seen him," I lied. Alicia noticed the looks on both of our faces.

"Y'all alright? The two of you look like you just saw a ghost."

"I'm good. I just got some shit on my mind."
"Murph?"
"I'm straight."
"Something's not right here."
"I said were good. I'll tell Teddy to call you when he gets in."

"I'm going to let this one slide cuz I know y'all going through some things. I'll be in my apartment when Teddy gets back."

After Alicia left, we continued to sit and wait. It seemed like things were taking forever. Three hours later, Teddy and Brandon walked in the apartment.

"What did they say was wrong?" I asked.
"They said my blood sugar was low and I just found out that my asthma is back."

"His blood sugar was low," Brandon began "because he hasn't been eating."

"So what now?"

"Y'all chill for the rest of the week and let us sort some things out. We'll let you know what the next step is once we figure it out. I'll talk to y'all boys tomorrow."

"Alright." Brandon left and we helped Teddy to his room. "You sure you alright?"
"I'm good," Teddy responded in a slight whisper. "I just need to get some sleep."

"Let us know if you need anything."
The next day we were all summoned to apartment E-1. That was where Tony, Brandon and a couple of other

Sigmas lived. When we got there, Sigmas and Zetas were everywhere. The table was set and they had food galore.

"You three," Tony called as he paused from his food. "Sit down at the table and eat. Sorors heard that Teddy hasn't been eating so they decided to make sure y'all had some food."

We took our places at the table and were served Sunday Dinner on a Wednesday. The Zetas really put it down. There was fried chicken, corn on the cob, green beans, rice, macaroni and cheese and cornbread. I hadn't eaten like that since my grandmother passed away. Even though we hadn't crossed yet, I could feel the love. While we were eating, drinking and being merry, Brandon came in. He didn't have a good look on his face.

"We have a problem," Brandon stated. "I need the three of you to go back to your apartment and wait for me."

"They haven't finished eating," one of the Zetas interjected.

"Finish your food then go back to your apartment and wait for me."

Once we finished eating, the Zetas gave us some food to take with us. We went back to our apartment to wait for Brandon. He arrived fifteen minutes later.
"Are we the only ones here?" he asked.

"Yes," I answered.

"This is the deal. I just got a call from our grad advisor and he told me that someone called our state director and told him that we were hazing."

"What does this mean?" Teddy asked.
"We gotta shut it down until they come down here and investigate."

"Does that mean you're dropping the line?" I inquired.

"We hope not but we won't know anything until the state director comes down on Monday. They're going to interview you as a group then they're going to talk to you one on one. You have to be flawless in this. Your answers have to match but they can't seem rehearsed. Tony and I will prepare you for this."

"Do you have any idea who could have called in?"
"Probably one of the guys that didn't get picked but we can't worry about that right now. In the mean time, keep this to yourselves. We'll get through this. Our chapter has a stellar reputation and the state director knows us well."

After Brandon gave us all the necessary instructions, he left.

Super Senior

"This is some bullshit!" Teddy barked as he kicked over a chair.

"Calm down," I tried to ease. "We'll be alright."
"I bet it was Mike and his crew of fruitcakes. Fuckin' crab ass niggas."

"Best believe that this shit is comin' out when we cross," Murph added.
"That's if we cross."

"Come on fellas," I began trying to ease the mood. "We haven't come this far for nothing. We just gotta get through the investigation and we'll be back in the cut before ya ass gets soft again."

"Stop tryna make me laugh, Dre," Teddy pleaded trying to hold back his laughter.
"You know what? Now would be a good time to come up with our line name."

"You're kidding me, right?"
"Dude," Murph interrupted. "We don't even know if we have a line right now"

"I'll be damned if we went through everything we've been through for nothing."
"What about Three the Hard Way?" Teddy suggested.

"I like that but I'm feeling like it's probably been done before. It's too obvious."

"Triple Threat?" Murph threw out.
"Still too obvious. We need something that represents us. We'll be the first line to cross since '95."

"Spring, Fall or Christmas?" laughed Teddy.
"You better not let Big Brother Warlord hear you say that shit."

We tossed ideas back and forth for a good hour or so but nothing stuck. We decided to let it go for awhile and get back to it some other time.

18
Certified Intensity

The cool, November air filled my lungs as I took a deep breath. Dressed in blue army fatigues, black hoodies and black ski masks, me and my LBs stood in front of the entrance to the UC. The crowd was frantic. The more I heard the chants and calls of the members of Zeta Phi Beta Sigma, the more I got hype. Throughout the process, we'd done a good job of keeping the fact that we were pledging under wraps. Since all the frats besides the Ques had a line that semester, it was hard to pinpoint who was on what line. A few people speculated but to my knowledge, no one knew about me, Teddy and Murph. The time on my watch read 10:14. It was time to get down to business. The entire time we stood there, numerous frat brothers would get in our faces to hype us up. Through eleven weeks of hell and an attempt by some haters to stop us, our time had finally come.

"BLUE PHI!" Big Brother Predator yelled at the top of his lungs.

You know's and Z-phi's rang out all around us.
"FMU make some muthafuckin' noise!"
Screams and cheers filled the air.

"To the Brothers of Phi Beta Sigma, the Ladies of Zeta Phi Beta, and everyone else under the sound of my voice, I present to you…Certified Intensity!"

More chants and calls filled the air as three Zetas walked up to us, removed our hoods and ski masks. When the crowd saw who it was, they went bananas. Screams of our names came from every direction. The intensity on our faces set the tone for how we were feeling at that moment. My heart pounded in my chest as we waited for the crowd to calm down.

After wiping the sweat from my forehead I began, "P-B-S Step!"

We went into an intricate step that finished with my LBs lined up behind me. Once again the crowd went crazy. Before we went into the next step, the Bruhs and Sorors chanted so that we could catch our breath. From the rear, Murph began.

"To be a Sig-Ma you gotta be…"
"Smooooooth," Teddy and I responded as Murph and I slid in opposite directions.

At the end of the step we were back in our original line. It was time to introduce ourselves to the crowd. With the same intensity on my face, I stepped forward. I looked over the crowd. For a brief moment I locked eyes with Alicia. I could see her mouth the words: "Do ya thing."

"A man came up to me," I began. "He was dressed in black…"

"And old gold!" my LBs responded.

"He spoke of pharaohs, gorillas and being ice cold. I listened to what he had to say then walked away. Then another man approached me dressed in red and white."

"NO! NO!" my LBs responded once again. The chuckles and laughs came from the crowd.

"This one spoke of cane twirlin', diamonds and Playboy Bunnies. I listened to what he had to say then walked away. Another man approached me. This one was dressed in Purple and Gold. This one spoke of dogs, blood and thunder."

Teddy began to growl. I walked over to him and rubbed his head and pretended to give him a treat. The crowd got a kick out of it.

"I listened to what he had to say then walked away."

"Then why pledge Sigma?" Murph asked.

"Cuz I'm too smart to be an Alpha, too pretty to be a Kappa and too nasty to be a Que!"

At the end of that sentence I went down on all fours humped the ground and stuck out my tongue to the ladies that were in the front row causing them to scream. I stood back up and brushed myself off.

"I'm everything they try to be without giving up being me....that's why they call me....Da Chameleon."

I pulled off my hoodie to display my line jersey with my name and number on the back then took my place in line. Once Teddy and Murph introduced themselves to the student body, we did another step then party walked off. There were no words to describe how I felt that night. I had become a part of a family. When they used to say the end justifies the means, I finally understood what it really meant.

The night ended with the three of us at E-1 with the rest of the Sigma's and Zetas. Blue Juice was in everybody's cup. Frat and sorors came from all over the Carolinas to welcome us into the family. Among those in attendance was Tina. She said that she'd be there when I crossed and she kept her word.

"How does it feel?" Tina asked as she placed a Sigma medallion around my neck.
"Feels good, real good," I laughed.
"I wanna give you something else but that comes later. Enjoy your moment. I'll holla at you later."

I watched as her compact frame walked away from me.

"Stop starin' at her ass, you pervert," Alicia laughed as she wrapped her arms around me. "Congratulations."

"Thanks, babe."

"I got you some things but they're in my apartment. I'll give'em to you later."

"It might have to wait 'til tomorrow, if you know what I mean."

"You so nasty. Contrary to popular belief, every female does not want to do you."

"Maybe not every female but there are a few that do."

Alicia noticed me starring at someone. A slim, brown skinned, female was making eyes at me as she sipped her drink. "She don't know no better."

"She doesn't have to. Now if you excuse me."

"Do Dirty!" Alicia laughed.

The rest of the night was spent drinking and laughing with my new family. At around 2am I started getting sleepy because we were up practicing our show until 4am the night before. I said my goodbyes and headed to my apartment. When I got there, Murph and Teddy were already working hard. I could hear music coming from their rooms. I laughed to myself and walked to my room. I paused because I heard slow music coming from the other side. When I walked in, I couldn't believe what was waiting for me.

There were blue and white candles lit all over my room. In my bed, Tina was lying there in a white, lace teddy. The light from the candles reflected off her light brown flesh. She rose to her knees and motioned for me to come to her. Once I was close enough to her, she draped her arms around my neck and kissed me deep and passionately. Before she removed my jersey, she kissed every letter that was across my chest then pulled it over my head and placed kisses on my bare chest. Once she moved back to my lips, I firmly squeezed her soft ass. Every squeeze turned her on even more. As I continued to kiss her, she unbuckled my belt then unbuttoned my pants. When she pushed them down, my dick was so hard it sprung back up like a diving board when my boxers finally let it go.

Tina kissed down my chest, across my stomach then kissed it right on the tip. One gentle kiss led to a lick. The licks lead to her engulfing half my member in her mouth and pulling it slowly out then back in again.

"Mmmmmmm," I moaned.

She took me out of her mouth and then pulled me into the bed. Once on my back, she positioned herself between my legs then went back to work. I continued to moan in ecstasy as I watched her head bob up and down as my dick slid in and out of her mouth. From shaft to balls, she sucked and licked every inch. Once she felt that I was satisfied in that area, she straddled my thighs with my erection standing in front of her. She smiled as she slowly stroked it. Tina reached over to the nightstand and grabbed a condom that she'd brought with her. When she removed it from the wrapper, I noticed that it was blue. How fitting considering the occasion.

Tina did something that I had never seen done before. She placed the condom in her mouth then used her mouth to put the condom on me. Now that was skill.

I was now equipped and ready for action, Tina positioned herself into a squat, placed my head at the mouth of her sexual river then slid all the way down; moaning the entire way down. On my stomach she placed both of her hands and began to bounce up and down. Her vaginal muscles tightened every time she came all the way down. This drove me crazy. Every time I tried to make a motion or try to take control, she stopped me. She was in total control of the situation at that moment.

Without taking me out of her, she repositioned herself with her back to me then continued to ride. I watched as her soft ass jiggled when it came down and hit my pelvis. I reached out and grabbed two handfuls. At one point she decided to flex something she learned as a dancer. Tina came all the way down and stopped. To the beat of the song that played, she made each cheek jump independently of the other. That was something you didn't see every day. This went on for a few minutes then she slid me out of her. She was now on her hands and knees looking back at me. She didn't have to tell me twice. When I got to my knees, she started to make her ass clap. I placed one hand on her hip and with the other I grabbed my dick and slid it back inside her. I didn't have to move because once I was inside; she bounced her ass on me sliding me in and out of her. About five minutes into this position, I felt my orgasm coming on. I tried to slow her down but she knew what was going on and sped up. With both hands, I grabbed her hips and stopped her while I erupted into the condom. I grabbed it by the base and pulled out of her, took the condom off and tossed it in the trash can beside my bed. I was still erect when I laid back on the bed.

"Did you enjoy your present?" Tina asked in a sultry voice as she kissed me on my shoulder.

"Honestly, I don't know what I enjoyed more; coming out tonight or coming just now."

"I'm glad you liked it. Can I tell you something?"
"What's up?"
"I've always wanted to be with you."
"Why didn't you ever say anything?"

"When we met that night at the skating rink, I was feeling Eric but when we all started hanging out and practicing for shows, I really started feeling the kind of guy you were. Vicki didn't deserve a guy like you. I never said anything because we had a good thing going with the group."

"To be honest, I always had my eyes on you. It was something about the way you moved when you danced. It was always sexy to me."

"Here we are…seven years later."
"Better late than never."

I never thought that joining a fraternity would change my life in the ways that it did. Some days I felt like a rock star; especially when we took road trips to other college campuses. Because we came out so late in the semester, I had to wait until the spring to really represent like I wanted to. After the Christmas holiday was over and we were back on campus, A whole new world was opened up to me.

I never had problems with the ladies but it was something about having those three Greek letters across my chest. Women came out of the woodworks! People always referred to Teddy, Murph and myself as the road trip crew before we pledged. Once we crossed, we were gone almost every weekend. My first full semester of being a Sigma was a nonstop party. If we weren't going to another chapter's party or probate show, we were doing something on our own yard. With all that was going on around me, I forgot about a few things…class and grades. Around the end of the Spring semester, I got a very rude awakening.

Troy Pendleton was my financial aid advisor. The Monday before exams started, he called me into his office to sit down and have a serious discussion. When I arrived he was his usual cheerful self. We shot the breeze for a minute and then we got down to business.

"This isn't easy for me," Troy began. "I was looking over your grades for this year and we have a serious problem."

"What's that?" I enquired with a nervous tone.

"Even if you get all A's on your final exams, your GPA is not going to be high enough for you to qualify for financial aid next year."

A cold numbness shot through my body. I sat in silence for about five minutes before I spoke.

"What do I have to do to qualify?"

"The only way to become eligible again is to raise your GPA. If you go to Summer school, you have to take one class during Maymester, and 2 classes in Summer I and Summer II. Not only do you have to pass them, you have to get at least 3 A's and 2 B's."

"Do I at least qualify for any financial aid for Summer school?"

"I'm afraid not. Everything is going to be out of pocket."

I sat back in the chair and released a huge sigh.

"Listen, man. I've always been straight up with you. It's not just you. It happens to a lot of people after they pledge. Hell…it happened to me. You get caught up in being a part of something new and something different, school becomes the furthest thing from your mind. You can get through this but you have to realize that you came to school for an education first. Everything else is second."

"I have no idea how I'm going to explain this to my grandfather."

"Just be honest. He may get upset with you at that moment but eventually it'll pass and he'll help you do what it takes to get back on track."

"I guess you're right."
"If you need anything, just call me or stop by. I'll do everything I can for you but for now, you have to do your part."

"Thanks, Troy."
I shook Troy's hand and exited his office. I had no Idea what I was going to do. I couldn't afford all three summer sessions. I had some serious thinking, planning and grinding to do.

When I got back to my apartment, Murph and Teddy where sitting at the kitchen table studying for their finals.

What's up, Fellas?" I greeted in a quiet tone.
"What's wrong, #1?" Murph asked.

"I fucked up bad. All this partying and road tripping we did this semester caught up to me. My grades are down and now I don't qualify for financial aid. The thing is, I have no one to blame but myself. Even Alicia tried to tell me to slow down but I didn't listen."

"What are you gonna do?" Teddy interjected.
"I have to figure out a way to pay for Summer school so I can get my grades up or sit out until I can afford to pay for school on my own."

"I have a suggestion. Don't go to Summer school. Use this summer to grind and work as much as you can. Save up enough money to pay for your tuition in the fall."

"What about housing?"
"Housing and tuition is going to run about $3000. If you can't come up with it all at least pay for tuition. You'll just have to commute. I'm sure you can find some place to crash on some of those nights."

"You know Blue and White will look out as much as they can."

"I don't know man. I need some time to think it over. I'm already behind because I sat out after my grandmother passed away."

Super Senior

"Nobody said anything about you sitting out. You just have to get ya grind on and make it happen."

"Do you know how long that commute is?"
"That's an excuse and excuses are?"

"You're right. I'll figure it out. Just do me a favor. Don't say anything to Alicia. You know how she gets. I'll talk to her when I get time. For now, I gotta hit the books."

I did the best I could on my finals. Out of 5 classes, I managed three A's and two B's. It wasn't enough to save me but at least I finished strong. With school out and Maymester starting in a week, I had a decision to make.

19
Reality Check

The summer arrived and I decided to take Murph's advice. After talking to my manager at Foot Locker, she adjusted my schedule so that I could work 40 hours a week during the day so I could pick up a second job at night. I wasn't going to have the summer that I'd planned to have but I had no one to blame for that but myself. About two weeks into May, I managed to get a job working 3rd shift at a plant in Florence. From Monday to Friday I put in sixteen hour work days and slept all weekend.

In a month I had already managed to save a thousand dollars. It looked like I was moving in the right direction to reach my goal. At the pace I was going, I could afford to pay for tuition and housing or I could pay tuition and get my own place off the yard. It was still too early to make any solid plans but at least I had options.

It was difficult being a college student working at the plant. The guys gave me more of a hard time than respect. In their eyes, they thought that I thought that I was better than them. I had no idea why it was like that. I've never looked down on anyone or perceived myself to be better than them. I was merely trying to make a better life for myself like my grandfather always pushed me to do.

Super Senior

Since I was the new guy, I didn't know anyone so I sat by myself most of the time. The majority of the guys that were on my shift had been there for years. They were mostly middle-aged men. The majority of them were Black. One night while on our lunch break, an old head decided he wanted to start with me. Rick Jordan was the team leader for my crew because he had the most years in. He was a Black male in his late 40's. Rick seemed to have a problem with me from the first night I showed up on his crew. I knew it was going to be a problem when he came in that night running off at the mouth.

"Look at this ol' college ass nigga right here," Rick began as he sat down two tables away from me.

I didn't say anything. I kept eating and reading my magazine.

"Leave that man alone, Rick," one of the guys on our crew interrupted.
"Nah, Reg. He think he better than us cuz he in college and shit."

"What makes you say that?" I asked as I looked up from my magazine.
"It's everything about you. You act like you too good for us. Every night you sit by yaself and don't say nothin' to nobody."

"No disrespect but I don't fuck wit people that don't fuck wit me. I've been here for a little over a month and nobody has done anything to make me feel like a part of the crew. When y'all go out for breakfast after work, I don't get invited. When y'all order food, nobody asks me if I want anything. I'm not begging anybody for friendship. I'm cool."

"He is right," another crew member interrupted. "You just assumed that because he's in college he thinks he's better than us. He's actually a pretty cool dude. He went to school wit my niece."

"He went to school with my niece, too. She told me all about him. Does the name Chelsea Bridges ring a bell?"

"That's what this is about? You got beef with me because of what happened between me and Chelsea? Now that's some high school shit."

"Yeah, she told me about how you thought you were too good for her because she didn't go to college."

"That's what she told you?"
"That's exactly what she told me."

"Did she also tell you how I helped her get her place when she got tired of driving back and forth to Florence? Did she tell you that I paid her rent for her when she got sick and could work for almost a month? She didn't tell you that. Did she? She probably told you about another girl, too. Did she tell you that girl was my best friend since we were 9 and the first time I saw her was three years after I moved from Fayetteville to here was when she transferred to my school? Of course she didn't tell you that part. I'm a man and you're a man so I'm going to tell you this man to man…Before you try to loud me out talking about some shit that you don't know anything about, you might want to check ya source."

"Who the fuck this lil' nigga think he talkin' to?"
"I'm talkin' to you, Old Man. You may think you the shit because you got seniority but that don't mean shit to me. I was taught by the old school. You gotta give respect to get respect. If you don't like me, that's cool…but dislike me for reasons other than that high school shit you brought up tonight."

"I will bust yo ass up in here."
"If that's what it takes to make you feel like a big man, bust a move. I promise you I'll teach you a lesson I didn't learn in school."

It got so quiet in that break room; you could hear a rat piss on cotton. I later found out that nobody has ever stood up to Rick like that. I try to avoid confrontations but I will not sit quietly while somebody is trying to punk me. My grandfather taught me better than that.

The next night when I arrived to work, Rick was waiting for me in the locker room. He apologized to me for what transpired the night before and I apologized to him because I felt that I was out of line as well. After we got the air cleared, we went to work. After that day things changed. I was no longer "college boy." I'd become one of the crew. With the tension gone, it made working there a little but easier.

The end of July was nearing and the fall semester was approaching. Due to a setback I had to dip into my school money to buy another car leaving me short by about a thousand dollars. I had a decision to make. I could sit out another semester and get my money right so I could afford housing and tuition or I could just pay tuition and commute. The decision got a little harder to make when I was offered a permanent position because the entire time I worked at the plant, I was working through a staffing agency. The permanent position would move me from 3rd shift to 1st shift working 7am-3pm. The position also came with more money. If I took the position it would only be until the spring semester and I wouldn't be able to return to school in the fall. The upside to it would be that I would be able to pay tuition and housing or get my own place and just pay tuition. I had one week to make up my mind.

The next morning was Saturday and I was off. I sat down with my grandfather and talked to him about it. After hearing what he had to say, I was still unsure. I needed to talk to someone else. I took a shower, went to sleep for about six hours then hopped in the car and headed to the one place to talk to the one person that I felt could help me come to a decision.

I arrived in Fayetteville around 4 o'clock that afternoon. When I pulled into Alicia's driveway, she was running out of the house before I could turn the car off. She wrapped her arms around me and squeezed me tight when I got out of the car.

"Hey!" Alicia squealed. "What are you doing here?"

"Do I need a reason to come back to my hometown?"

"Well…the fact that this is the first time you've been here all summer and the summer is almost over…yes!"

"I'll take that," I laughed. "I came up because I need to talk to you."

"You could have called me."
"This is kinda important."
"Come on in the house."

Once in the house I was greeted by Mr. and Mrs. Burroughs. We engaged in small talk for about thirty minutes then Alicia and I moved into the den so that we could talk in private.

"So what's up?"
"I'm having a hard time making a decision concerning school. I need your input but I also need you to be objective."

"Okay...what is it?"

"You know I've been working two jobs to get my money together so I can go back to school this semester. Well, I had to get another car and that means I had to dip into my school money. I have enough to pay tuition, just not housing."

"Then just pay tuition and commute for a semester."

"That's not everything. My other job offered me a permanent position and a raise. If I take the position, I'll have to sit out for the semester and return in the Spring."

"You can't do both?"
"The hours are 7am-3pm. The upside is that once I return in the Spring, I can pay for housing and tuition or get my own place in Florence and just pay tuition."

"You can't afford the place now?"

"Not by myself. I asked Murph and Teddy if they wanted to get a place off campus but they said they wanted to wait until next year."

"Why didn't you ask me?"
"The thought never crossed my mind."

"So you're saying that you wouldn't want me as a roommate."
"I'm not saying that. I'm saying that the thought never crossed my mind."
"Let me get this straight...you ask Murph and Teddy whom you've only known for five minutes to get a place but you don't even think about me...a person you've known almost your entire life."

"Why are you making this difficult?"
"I'm not making this difficult. I'm just making an observation."

"So you're saying if I would have asked you, you'd be cool with that."
"Yes."
"Are you serious?"
"Yes, I'm serious. When you first told me about your financial aid situation what did I tell you?"

"You said that you would help me in any way you could."

"This is a way for me to help you. I don't want you to have to sit out and I'd rather you not have to commute all the way to FMU. I start working as soon as I get back and I've wanted to live off campus but like you, I can't afford to do it by myself."

"What would your parents say?"
"It's not like we're shacking up. We'll be roommates. I'm pretty sure my parents would be cool with it because it's you."

"I've never lived with a female before."
"And I've never lived with a guy before."
"Can I think about it?"
"I have to mail my housing check by Tuesday. If you decide to do it, I can use that money for my half of the deposit and 1st month's rent."

"What about furniture?"
"We have an extra bed out back in the shed and my Aunt Ruby has some furniture she's trying to get rid of. We can get that. All you need is a bed for you."

"I have a bed."
"Then what is the problem?"
"I'll be here until tomorrow night. I'll give you my answer before I leave."

"Alicia!" Mrs. Burroughs called from the kitchen. "Telephone."

"I'll be right back."

Alicia trotted off into the kitchen to answer the phone. Five minutes later she came back.

"You'll never guess who that was."
"Who?"
"Teddy. He's having a birthday party tonight at the Red Roper. I told him you were here. You wanna go?"

"Hell yeah! You know I gotta go show my LB some love on his birthday. Wait a minute; has Teddy met Monica or Danielle?"
"No."
"Are they in town? Danielle is. Monica stayed in Raleigh for Summer school."
"Call Danielle and tell her about it. I've been telling Teddy she's right up his alley."

"I will do no such thing."
"Why not?"
"Teddy is not going to dog my girl out."

"First of all, watch your mouth talkin' about my LB. Second of all, I just said I wanted to introduce him to her. Danielle is a grown woman."

"And Teddy is a dog."
"But Teddy's your boy just as much as he is mine."
"And I watch you and Teddy runnin' around campus humpin' everything moving."

"What about Murph?"

"Murph has a girlfriend now. He's the good friend."

"Wow! Seriously?"

"You know Murph was never out there like you and Teddy to begin with."

"You're kidding me, right? Just because you don't see it doesn't mean it's not happening."

"I will sit here and have you taint my image of Murph. He's an angel."

"More like a light-brown eyed devil."

"Anyway…go see your family and be back here to pick me up at ten."

"When do we go to parties so early? Never mind…it must be ladies free before 11."

"You know!"

I said my goodbyes to Alicia's parents and headed across town to see my family. Later on that evening I picked Alicia up and we went to Teddy's birthday party at the Red Roper. I hadn't partied in Fayetteville since we crossed and went to a probate at Fayetteville State. The night was just what I needed. Because I was working two jobs I didn't have time to party. Since it was summer, a lot of students were home. Once we ran into some Sigma's and Zetas from other schools the night really got wild.

When it was all said and done, I dropped Alicia off and went back to my Aunt's house. The next day, I took a cruise through my old neighborhood. As I drove around Rivers Circle, I could see me and my friends running wild as kids. We truly had some good times. While riding, I thought about Alicia's offer. It had me nervous. I didn't want anything to jeopardize our friendship. Though we were best friends, Alicia was a beautiful girl with an amazing body. I didn't I know if I can handle watching her walk around an apartment scantily clad and be cool with that. Maybe if we set some ground rules from the beginning, things would be okay.

The scorching, afternoon sun began to lower in the sky as I made my way toward Alicia's house to give her my answer before I headed back to South Carolina. Even as I drove, I still hadn't made up my mind. When I arrived Alicia came out of the house to meet me. She gave me a hug then escorted me to the patio in her backyard. Her mother greeted me with a motherly hug and lemonade then left the two of us to talk.

"Have you made your decision?" Alicia asked with a certain tone of anxiousness in her voice.

"I know this decision shouldn't be that hard to make but it is. This is a huge step."

"It really is. I've been thinking about it since the subject first came up."

"It would help a lot but I'm so scared."

"What are you afraid of?"

"I don't want anything to happen to our friendship. You know how we are. We're always draped on each other. We sleep in the same bed sometimes. What happens if we cross the line?"

"I thought about that, too. To be honest, would it really be so bad? We've known each other for so long. So what if something happens between us unexpectedly? I think our friendship is strong enough to handle anything that life throws at us. We've done a good job maintaining so far."

"It's a lot to think about."

"I need an answer today. I have to send my check for housing no later than Tuesday."

I sat back in my chair and gazed into the sky. I took a deep breath then exhaled. Nothing was said by either of us for a good five minutes. As my mind raced, the birds sang the evenings song. I sat up and gazed into Alicia's eyes.

"Let's do it."

"For real, Dre?"

"Yes. I think we can handle it." A huge smile spread across Alicia's face.

"Let's go talk to my parents."

"Hold on," I laughed. "Back ya bus up. You tryna get me shot."

Just like when we were kids, Alicia took me by the hand and led me into her house. If it were anyone else, her parents probably wouldn't have been cool with the idea. Because it was me and they know the friendship that we've always shared, they didn't protest. Well at least her mother didn't protest. Her father didn't care who I was. Once Alicia hit him with the "please Daddy eyes" and his wife gave him that look, he jumped on board.

After gaining her parents approval, I said my goodbyes then hit the road back to South Carolina. For some reason, I wasn't as nervous about the whole thing as I was before. The more I drove, the more I warmed up to the idea of Alicia and I living together. It was cool that her parents approved but there was no way in hell I was telling my grandfather.

Early Monday morning I got up and went apartment hunting. I was trying to find the nicest, most affordable place that was as close to campus as I could find. Not too far from campus there were about three apartment complexes that a lot of FMU students resided. They were close to the school and affordable but weren't up to par for my taste. I rode around all day looking at apartments and getting applications. By the time all of the leasing offices were closing, I wrapped up my search then headed to work. When I arrived home after work, I walked in the house surprised to see my grandfather sitting in the kitchen. The reason I was surprised was because he was there but his truck wasn't.

"Where's your truck?" I asked as I opened the refrigerator.

"It went out on me. I tell ya, if it ain't one thing, its anotha."

"Do you know how much its going to cost to get it fixed?"

"Whatever it cost, if it ain't free, I ain't got it."
"I have some money saved up. If you need something, you know it's yours."

"I couldn't do that. That's your money for school."
"I know but that's okay. I can make a sacrifice to make sure that you can still put a roof over your head. You can't do that without your work truck."

"I have faith and I believe God will make a way. He hasn't brought us this far to leave us now."

"Where is the truck at?"
"I had it towed to Jimmy's."

My grandfather and I continued our conversation. I knew that even if I offered him the money he wouldn't take it. That's why I asked where the truck was so I can take care of it myself. The next morning I went by the garage to get the estimate for my grandfather's truck. It was a little more than I'd expected. If I took care of it, I had to either sit out that semester or not move in with Alicia. Since Alicia already had her heart set on getting the place, I couldn't disappoint her. I really didn't want to sit out again but my grandfather has done so much for me, I couldn't leave him without means to work. I told Jimmy to go ahead and fix it and that I would take care of the bill. I also told him not to tell my grandfather that I paid for it. Even if he doesn't tell him, I know he's going to know it was me. That was just a chance I was willing to take.

20
Thunder Buddies

At the beginning of the third week in August, Alicia and I moved into our apartment. It took us forever to decide on a place but we finally came to a compromise. We were ten minutes from campus and both of us were close to our jobs. In all the excitement of getting the place, I hadn't brought myself to tell Alicia that I was going to have to sit out for the fall semester and that I'd taken the position they offered me at the plant. The first night in our new place, Alicia and I were sitting on the floor in the living room eating pizza. We both had a bed but we had no couch and no kitchen furniture.

"I can't believe it," Alicia began as she wiped her mouth. "My first place."
"I bet you didn't think in a million years that we'd be living together."

"Not in two million. It's going to be a slow process but we'll get it just right."

"I'm leaving that all on you. With the exception of my bedroom, you can do whatever you want, just remember that a guy also lives here."

"I guess a pink bathroom is out."

Super Senior

"All the way out," I laughed. "My Aunt said that her new living room suit is coming one day this week and that we can have her old set."

"What color is it?"
"Navy blue leather."
"I can work with that."
"It's not worn out or anything like that. She just wanted something different. If I'm not mistaken, it's only a couple of years old."

"Cool. I guess we'll go half on a kitchen set."
"That sounds like a plan to me."
We continued to eat and talk. Before long I felt it was time to come tell Alicia the truth.

"Alicia," I began. "I have something to tell you."
"What's up?"
"First, you have to promise me you won't get mad."
"What did you do?"
"Promise me."
"I promise…now what did you do?"
"I'm not going back to school this semester…"
"Andre Marcellus Marshall!"
"You promised…remember?"
"I'm sorry," Alicia paused and took a deep breath. "Why aren't you going to school this semester?"

"Right after we agreed to do this, my grandfather's work truck broke down on him and he didn't have the money to have it fixed. I offered him the money but he wouldn't take it so I just paid for it without him knowing. It was a huge sacrifice but that's my dad."

"Why didn't you say anything to me about it? We could have put this off and you returned to school."

"I saw the look on your face when I told you that I was down with us getting a place. I couldn't bear to take that way. Besides, I had options. I took the new position at the plant. With the money I'll make full time, I'll have more than enough to go back to school."

"You are too much, Andre Marshall. You're always willing to look out for others even if it means putting your needs aside. I don't know what I'd do without a person like you in my life. Come here."

Alicia wrapped her arms around me and gave me a big hug. Still holding on we pulled back and stared into each other's eyes. The moment was perfect. As soon as I saw Alicia begin to bring her face closer to mine, I had to stop it.

"Okay! Let's get these boxes unpacked."
"That sounds like a good idea. Let's do it....I mean that."

We shared a laugh then continued to get our apartment together. A moment like that is what scared me

Super Senior

about Alicia and me living together. I didn't know if I could stop it the next time. Since elementary school, she's been my world. I lost her then got her back. Now we're two grown-ups under the same roof. If I ever needed strength, now was definitely the time.

School started that Wednesday for Alicia. My new position started on the following Monday. It felt good to go to work in business attire instead of old jeans, a t-shirt and work boots. In my new position, I was put in charge of shipping and receiving. The only time I had to go down on the floor was if there was a problem with an order. It was a change of pace but I missed the guys on my old crew. There were times I ran into a couple of them that stayed for the next shift to get overtime. When I arrived home from the first night in my new positon, there were a couple of visitors at my place. Alicia invited Teddy, Murph and his girl, Denise, over for a house warming dinner. Cheers and jokes rang out as I entered the door.

"Ladies and gentlemen," Murph began. "I present to you, Mr. Corporate America!"

"You got jokes," I laughed as Alicia greeted me with a beer. "What's good, #3?"

"You already know what it is. A new semester filled with new adventures."

"Sign me up cuz I'm ready to roll out!" Teddy added.

"Back ya bus up you two," Alicia interrupted. "We had our fun but now it's time to get serious. Let Dre be an example to what can happen when you party too hard."

"That's cold blooded. Out of all the people in the world I could expect that from…but you? I'm so hurt."

"You know I'm just playing with you, Baby." Alicia hugged me and kissed me on my cheek.

"Get off me! I don't know where your mouth has been."

"I had no idea this is how the four of you act when you're together," Denise laughed. Denise was about 5'3", light-skinned with long curly hair and dark brown eyes. She was a Mulatto from San Diego. Denise didn't go out with us or road trip with us but she was cool people. She was good for Murph and they were good together.

"This is nothing. Wait until Murph makes his world famous *Kingstree Kool-Aid*."

"I don't know, Dog. My girl wants me to retire my recipe."

"That's blasphemy!" Teddy objected as he stood up. "You cannot deprive the future of FMU of this. I'll not stand for it!"

"Number 2…sit yo ass down!"
"Yes Big Brother Da Chameleon."

"But on the real…I missed the hell out of y'all over the break. I hate that I'm not in school this semester."

"It has happened to the best of'em," Murph interjected. "You came from New Grove. The way ya boy, Nick talked about how much of a prison that place was, nobody blames you for gettin' buckwild."

"If you only knew how that place was. Words can't describe it. You have to experience it to really feel my pain."

"I think I'll just take your word for it. Speaking of Nick…have you talked to him lately?"

"Nah…I ran into his brother in the mall a couple weeks ago. According to him, Nick is selling mobile homes in Pageland."

"That sounds about right," Murph laughed.

We continued our conversation then had dinner. It felt good to be around my LBs and Alicia again. They kept me grounded. I really wished I would have heeded their warnings when I was partying so hard but it was all good. Some people just have to learn the hard way.

The next morning I awoke to the smells of all of my favorite breakfast treats. Alicia didn't have class until 9:55 but she was up. When I walked into the kitchen she was in her pjs…if that's what you want to call them. She wore a pair of super short, pink satin shorts and a tight fitting tank top. I was mesmerized at how her ass jiggled as she moved around the kitchen. When she finally turned around, my eyes were quickly drawn to her erect nipples poking through her top.

"Hey Sweetie," Alicia greeted. "Sit down. Breakfast is almost ready."

"You didn't have to do all of this."
"Do all of what? I eat breakfast every day and so should you."

"Who am I to turn down some good food?"
"Your work clothes are ironed and hanging on the back of the bathroom door. I didn't know what shoes you wanted to wear with them but I guess you'll figure it out."

"Come on, Alicia. All of that is really not necessary."

"It was no trouble at all. You know I'm a morning person. I was up and bored."

"You're too good to me."
"I know…now eat."

It didn't take long for Alicia and I to fall into a routine. Every morning we got up at the same time. She cooked breakfast and laid my clothes for work out. In the evenings she would be in the kitchen cooking dinner. If she worked late she would always bring home some take out. She even did our laundry. From the outside looking in, one would think that Alicia and I was a couple. All of the things she did for me were the same things my grandmother did for my grandfather. I can't lie, I enjoyed having her there. It seemed to make life so much easier. Despite my reservations about us living together, things were going well.

The only thing that had me worried was how Alicia would react the first time I brought a girl home. Since Chelsea and I parted ways, I hadn't been in a relationship and neither had she. I'd partake in some no strings attached, miscellaneous activity with Alexandria and Tina from time to time but nothing serious. Alicia knew about both of them but it was never right in her face like it would be if I brought a female to our home. I was hoping that Alicia would be the one to break the ice by bring a guy home. That way she could see how cool I would be about the situation and give her no reason to trip when I did the same. Before that happened, Alicia and I were put through a serious test.

It was an unusually warm October night. I'd been working overtime because of a new account we'd acquired at the plant. After a twelve hour shift, I came home exhausted. With all of the energy I had left, I took a shower and went to bed. Around 11:30 a loud thunder clap woke me out of my sleep. As I gathered myself, I heard footsteps running through the apartment. Before I knew it, Alicia burst through my door, and in my bed. She put her arms around me and held on for dear life. Like a frightened child, Alicia's body trembled.

"Are you serious?" I laughed. "You can't be afraid of thunder."

"Shut up, Dre. It's not funny."
"I bet your roommates flipped the first time you jumped in bed with them."

"I'm serious. Stop joking about it."

I reached over and turned on the lamp that was on the nightstand beside my bed. When I looked into Alicia's eyes, I could see that she was genuinely terrified.

"Have you always been like this?"
"Not until the accident."
"Was it storming that night?"
"Yes. I shouldn't have been behind the wheel in the state of mind I was in."

"You never told me the story of how that happened."
"I can't talk about it right now. I promise that I'll tell you the story…just not tonight."

Another loud thunder clap caused Alicia to scream and pull herself further into it. Alicia continued to tremble.

I couldn't imagine what she was going through. All I could do was hold her close. The thunder lasted for about an hour. When it was finally over, Alicia was able to calm down enough to hold a conversation.

"You know what this reminds me of?" Alicia began.
"Hurricane Hugo."
"I can't believe that I got stuck out at your aunt's house with you and your family."

"Do you remember what else happened that night?"
"We shared our first kiss."
"Can I ask you a question?"
"Sure."
"How can two people be so close but never find themselves together?"

"I don't really know. I guess we didn't want to run the risk of getting into a relationship and it not work out. That would have put our whole friendship in jeopardy."

"I feel that argument but this is us though. We've been through so much together."

"So how would you have handled the situation back in the day when me, Ty and Eric first got down with Vickie and the twins? That almost killed our friendship."

"I think that if we were together at that time, things would have been different. She would've just been a girl that you performed with. With me in your life, you wouldn't have looked at her like that."

"I guess you're right. I've always had it bad when it came to you."
"Really?"
"After I got to South Carolina, everybody I dated or tried to date, I compared to you and nobody could hold a candle to you personality wise. The only thing I could do is find a light-skinned girl with pretty eyes, a beautiful smile and good hair."

"Are you serious?" Alicia laughed.
"I'm dead serious. If I couldn't have you in my life, I tried to have someone in my life that at least reminded me of you. As a matter of fact...I think you're the reason I'm hooked on light-skinned women."

"You are not going to put that on me, Dre."
"Let me show you something."

I got out of the bed and walked into my closet. From the top shelf, I pulled a Nike shoe box full of pictures down and brought it back to the bed. I rifled through the pictures until I found pictures of Tommy Girl, Jocelyn and Vickie. I placed the pictures side by side.

"What do all three of these girls have in common with me?"

"Pretty smiles, good hair, beautiful eyes and light skin."

"That's just coincidence."

"Coincidence my ass….all of these girls remind me of you in some type of way. That's how much you always meant to me. If I couldn't have you, I needed someone as close to you as possible."

"Awww…that is so sweet."
"That's not sweet. You're like a virus I can't get rid of."

"Shut up!"

Alicia hit me in the face with a pillow. I retaliated by diving on her and tickling her. Like two big kids we rolled around on my bed laughing and wrestling. This went on for a good fifteen to twenty minutes. We ended with Alicia on top of me straddling my waist trying to hold my arms against the bed. What started off as innocent fun got serious very quickly when Alicia started playfully kissing my neck like some people do with babies. I don't know whether her actions were or purpose because she knew that was my spot. Things got hectic when the kisses went from playful kisses to real kisses. At one point, she paused and gazed into my eyes. All the willpower I thought that I had begun to leave my body.

Alicia laid her soft, full lips right on mine. I was doing a good job maintaining until her tongue slid into my mouth. Our tongues wrestled each other like they were in a WCW championship match. Hearing her sensual moans as I rubbed her back and squeezed her body drove me crazy. I could feel her erect nipples through her tank top on my bare chest. As this was happening, the Good Dre and the Bad Dre popped up like in the cartoons and began to argue.

"You cannot let this happen," Good Dre pleaded. "You're going to ruin your friendship."

"Shut up, Punk!" Bad Dre interrupted. "Do you know how long it's been since we got some action? Do ya thing, Dre."

"One night of passion can cause you a lifetime of pain."

"Can somebody get this *Thin Line Between Love and Hate*, movie quotin' ass scrub up outta here!"

"This is not some random female, Andre. This is Alicia. If this goes bad, that's twelve years down the drain."

"Did she or did she not tell you that if something happened, your friendship was strong enough to withstand it. It's just sex!"

"When it comes to Alicia…its never "just" anything."

As all of this was going on in my head, I failed to realize that Alicia was headed south of the border. As she licked and kissed down my chest and stomach she was also raking her nails down my chest. My dick was harder than college trigonometry. As bad as I wanted her to keep going I had to stop her.

"Wait," I commanded as I put my hands on top of hers that were on the waistband of my boxers. "We can't."

"Boy," Alicia giggled. "Stop playin'."
"I'm serious, Alicia. Please?"
"What's wrong?"
"I know we were getting caught up in the moment but I'm not ready for this."

"Come on, Andre. Now that things are getting physical between us, you're not ready? I see you with these random chicks…"

"That's just it," I interrupted. "You're not just some random chick. You're Alicia. You mean so much more to me."

"Then why am I not yours!"

A deafening silence filled the room. The look Alicia had on her face was one of anger, desire and confusion. I'd seen that look before but never from her. For the first time, I was speechless. I watched as her beautiful, brown eyes fill with tears.

> "Please don't cry."
> "I can't help it."

I pulled her down onto my chest and wrapped my arms around her. Nothing more was said that night. When she finished crying, she returned to her room. I was so confused. I've never in my life turned down sex. It was just something about it being Alicia. She wasn't a random female to have casual sex with. She meant so much more to me.

When I woke up the next morning, I had an uneasy feeling. I didn't know what to expect after the previous night's encounter. Smells of breakfast floated through the air as they did every morning. Alicia was putting breakfast on the table as I entered the kitchen.

> "Good morning, Sleepyhead."
> "Good morning."
> "Orange juice or apple juice?"
> "Orange juice is okay."

Alicia poured me a glass of juice and sat down at the table with me.

> "About last night…"

Super Senior

"Don't even worry about it," Alicia interrupted. "We're cool. What happened was supposed to happen."

That was the thing that that I always loved about Alicia. I never had to read between the lines with her. If she said we were cool, then we were cool.

"Are you working late tonight?"
"I got everything caught up yesterday. I'll be home regular time tonight."

"Are you going to the AKA party in the UC tonight?"
"I didn't know there was a party tonight."
"That's what happens when you sit out. You're fall out of the loop."

"Seriously?"
"C'mon Dre," Alicia giggled. "You know I'm just messin' with you."

"I might go. I don't have anything else planned for a Friday night."

"You know if you don't go Melissa is going to put out an APB on you."

"You're just on fire this morning, aren't you?"

"Stop acting like you and Melissa are a secret. FMU isn't but so big. I've seen your car parked in front of her apartment a few times."

"How do you know I was with Melissa? You spying on me?"

"In case you didn't know, Melissa and I have a Psychology class together. She talks about you 24/7. Besides, she's cool people. I say go for it."

"I'm sorry but when did I need your approval?"
"Judging by your past skeezer, you need someone's approval."
"That's cold."

Alicia and I fell into the AKA party around 10:30pm. DJ Shi C, one of the areas prominent DJs, had the party rockin'. We never went to parties that early but the ones on campus ended at 1am. Since there were no after parties that we knew about, we figured we'd get in a couple hours of partying. I didn't realize how much I was missed on campus. People hailed me as soon as I stepped through the doors. Alicia found a couple of her friends and I was off to search for frat and sorors.

As I made my way through the crowd to the dance floor, the AKAs were doing one of their strolls. When I got to the dance floor, they were just getting to my side. When Melissa got in front of me, she smiled at me, winked and blew me a kiss. Once the stroll was finished, Melissa grabbed me by the hand and led me out on the dance floor. The UC was no Sweat Box but it did get hot in there. Melissa and I made our way outside to get some air and cool off. I sat down on the steps leading to the entrance.

"You know I can't sit down sit down there with this skirt on."

"Come sit on my lap."
I grabbed Melissa's hand and helped her down the steps and onto my lap.

"You look good tonight," I complemented as I wrapped my arms around her waist.
"Thank you. I wore this especially for you."
"Stop lying," I laughed.
"I'm serious. I remember you telling me how much you liked these shoes so I had to put an outfit together to set them off."

"What if I didn't come tonight?"
"Then you would've missed out but I'm glad you came."

"I figured I'd come out and show you and your girls some love since you always show us love."

"Are you coming back to school next semester?"

"You know it. That's why I'm working and saving now."

"What about your job?"

"I'll probably have to resign my position."

"That sucks."

"It does but getting my degree is more important to me."

"Not too many people are willing to give up a good job for school."

"I made a promise to my grandmother before she died. I can't see breaking that. I think it will be better for me in the long run."

"That's true."

"Yo Dre!" Teddy called from the door. "We gettin' ready to get it in."

"I'm on my way."

"I knew it wouldn't be long before they came and got you," Melissa giggled.

Melissa stood up so that I could get up. I grabbed her hand once again and helped her up the steps. Once she was on level ground, she didn't let my hand go as we walked back into the party. In the back of the room, I could see frat teaching some frat brothers from out of town one of the hops we learned at Benedict. I hugged Melissa before I ventured to join my brothers.

"Make sure you find me before you leave," she whispered in my ear.

Super Senior

I assured her that I would then caught up with my brothers.

Ten minutes before every on campus party ended, the lights came on. People continued to dance and the frats and sororities began to chant. While acting up with my blue and white family, Alicia found me to get my keys so that she could get her bag out of the car and to tell me that she was staying on campus that night with her homegirl since her roommate went home for the weekend. Once I gave Alicia my keys I found Melissa and told her I would be waiting for her outside. I stood in front of the UC laughing with Murph and Teddy as I waited for Alicia to return with my keys and for Melissa to come out. Twenty minutes later, Murph and Teddy left and I was sitting on the steps once again waiting for Melissa.

"Hey Big Head," Melissa greeted as she raked her nails across the nape of my neck.

"What you gettin' ready to get into?" I asked as I stood up and faced her.

"A few sorors are going back to Katrina's apartment with some Alphas that came up from Charleston but I'm not feelin' it."

"You hungry?"
"I could eat."
"You wanna change first?"

"Nah, I'm cool. I can go like this."
"Is Venus cool?"

"We don't have to go all the way to Venus. You'll be close to home. Then you'll have to drive all the way back here then go home."

"Who says I'm bringing you back?"
Melissa stood there with a surprised expression on her face. I took her hand and led her to the car.

21
Settled Down

Venus was one of my favorite places to go after a party. The local clubs hadn't let out so it was fairly dead. We found a booth in a cozy corner and sat down. Melissa and I engaged in small talk as we looked over the menu. A couple of times she caught me staring at her as she decided what she wanted to eat. Once the waitress came and took our order, we continued to converse.

"What's it like for a guy having a female roommate?" Melissa inquired as she poured cream into her coffee.

"That's a hard question to answer."
"Why so?"
"Alicia is my best friend, you know? I kick it with her like I kick it wit' da homies."

"I guess it is different since you two have been friends for so long."

"You know that song by R Kelly, *Homie, Lover, Friend*?"
"Yeah…"
"Alicia is like a homie, sister, friend."

"I like that. That's cute. I can tell you two are close. She talks about you all the time. To be honest, I had to ask her if you two were seeing each other."

"Really?"
"Yes. I didn't want to step on another sistas toes."
"How so?"

"Are you serious? Come on, Dre. We've been tipping around this for months. We like each other. So what's the issue?"

"To be honest, there is no issue."
"All this time we've spent together and you have yet asked me out on a real date."
"What do you call this?" I laughed.

"Breakfast at Venus during booty call hours is not a date. Is it because of Alicia?"
"No."
"Then what is it?"
I took a deep breath then exhaled.

"Since I've started dating, I've never taken time to heal after a relationship breaks up. I jump right into the next one. When we first met, I was in a relationship. You know that. That relationship ended because she couldn't deal with the fact that Alicia was back in my life. About a month before school started that semester, she and I had a conversation about how she would handle it if Alicia ever came back into my life. She said she would deal with it if it ever came up thinking that that day would never come. Fast forward a month and who do I run into on my way to the registrar's office?"

"That was the day after we met."
"Yes it was. When I told her about it, she felt that I knew about it the entire time. She called me all types of motherfuckas."

"That's when the relationship ended."
"Not at that point. We managed to work things out. I was so excited to have my best friend back after not seeing her for three years, I went a little overboard."

"What do you mean?"
"It wasn't like I left my girl hanging but I was so consumed with catching up with Alicia that I spent more time with her than I spent with my girl. You know how me, Teddy and Murph used to road trip and party. Alicia was a part of the crew."

"Did you ever try to introduce the two of them?"
"On a daily basis but Chelsea was never willing to do it. She always came up with an excuse. Eventually, I stopped trying."

"How did the relationship end?"
"That was my fault and I take full responsibility for it. After State's homecoming, I said that I was going to

chill out and get my relationship right with Chelsea. On the weekend I promised Chelsea that I would be all hers, I let Murph and Alicia convince me to go to one last party in Kingstree. Instead of being straight up with Chelsea, I lied to her. I told her I had to go to Fayetteville to handle some family business. To make a long story short, she showed up at the same party."

"Cold busted."
"To add insult to injury, when I was outside trying to talk to her, Alicia comes outside looking for me."

"That was the straw that broke the camel's back."
"Indeed it was. She told me that one day I would eventually have to choose between her and whoever I was in a relationship with. Is that true? Will I eventually have to give up my best friend?"

"It sounds to me that she was insecure."
"I never gave Chelsea any reason to doubt my loyalty or fidelity to her."

"It takes a strong woman to accept when a man has a best friend of the opposite sex. The only thing most women will see is the fact that she's a female. They'll never see the friendship no matter how long you've been friends or how deep the friendship is."

"How would you have handled the situation?"

"Which part? Your friendship with Alicia or the lying part?"

"The friendship part."

"If you and I were together and you told me that your best friend had come back into your life, after we'd had the previous conversation, the first thing I would have done was make it my business to meet her. I would want to talk to her so that I could feel her out in order to see if you two were genuinely friends or if she was really an ex-girlfriend. Once I found out the friendship was legit, there would have been no problems as long as she respected our relationship."

I sat back in the booth and rested my chin in my hand and stared at Melissa for about five minutes. In that time, the waitress brought our food. Once the food was on the table, I continued to stare.

"Stop staring at me and say something."

"Marry me."

"Shut up," Melissa giggled.

"I'm serious. I will never find another woman that will understand my situation. I can't let you get away."

"Remember the night we met?"

"Like it was yesterday."

"That night you said that you prided yourself on being a different breed of man. Well…I'm a different breed of woman. What's mine is mine and no woman can take that away from me."

"You are so hot right now. I could jump over this table, pour syrup all over your body and lick you from head to ankles."

"I thought it was head to toe?"

"I don't suck toes."

"You know what? Eat your food."

We shared a laugh as we ate and continued to talk for the next few hours. The more she and I talked, the more I realized that Melissa was the type of woman I needed in my life. Alicia meant the world to me and I would never let a woman make me choose, however; I needed a woman that was going to understand and believe me when I tell her that Alicia and I are just friends.

"What time is it?" Melissa asked.

"A quarter after four."

"Are you serious?

"You got somewhere you need to be?"

"No. I just didn't realize it was so late. I really hate for this night to end."

"Don't get the wrong idea when I ask you this next question."

"What is it?"

"Will you stay with me tonight? I will take you back on campus if that's what you want but I would really like for you to stay with me tonight."

"Promise me you'll behave?"
"I promise."
"Okay. I'll stay at your place tonight."
"I just have to stop by the store on the way home."
"What could you possibly need from the store at this hour?"
"Condoms."
"Take me back on campus."
"I'm just playin'," I laughed.
"You better be."
"I have condoms at home."
"You know what?"
"You should know me by now."
"You're right. I set myself up for that."

It seemed like it took forever but the spring semester finally arrived. Once again I was an active student. It felt so good to be back. In all the time that had passed, Melissa and I had taken the step and became an item. I felt like I had finally made the impossible happen. I had my girl and I had my best friend. Melissa never questioned me about Alicia and Alicia was cool when Melissa would be at the apartment. They weren't besties but they had a pretty good friendship. I was the happiest man alive.

That spring was the first semester of Melissa's senior year. She and I came to an agreement. I knew that her last couple of semesters where going to be hectic for her and she knew that I had a lot of ground to make up. We kept the partying to a minimum and road trips were out if I hadn't got my studies done. I resigned my position at the plant and went back to working nights at Foot Locker.

It took about two weeks for me to get back used to being a student again. Murph and his girl moved off of the yard for Murph's last semester before graduation. Priyah hung in there for so long and Teddy finally made things exclusive between the two of them. Looking back on everything, I was proud of all of us. We'd grown so much over the past years. It seemed like yesterday that we were all just graduating from high school.

In high school and the beginning years of college, you get into relationships without thinking about the long term. As Melissa's graduation was on the horizon, it brought up a few questions about our relationship. One night while studying for mid-terms a conversation about the future came up. Melissa and I were in her room. I was lying on her bed on my stomach and she was draped on me with her book on my back.

"Boo," Melissa began, "Can I ask you something?"
"What's up?"
"I'll be graduating next semester and you have a year to go after that."
"That wasn't a question, Babe."
"Where are we headed with this?"
"This as in us?"
"Yes. We've never talked about a possible future."

"I haven't really thought about it. Where do you see us going with this?"

"That's the thing. Once I graduate, I plan to go to law school in Maryland. What about you?"

"I'm pretty much wide open. I would love to work in broadcast once I finish. You know how much I love music. I can see me as a radio personality somewhere."

"With the success of that play you put on last month, I could see you as a writer for a hit TV show."

"That would be hot."

"Do you see us being together after we graduate?"

"I can see us together. It just depends on how things work out. We both have dreams that we want to follow. The question is: will the following of those dreams allow us to be together?"

"That's the million dollar question."

"I know we want to look ahead and try to plan a future but let's enjoy the time we have now and concentrate on graduating."

"You know what? You're right."

"We don't need any more pressure on us than what we have now. What is supposed to happen will happen."

Melissa laughed to herself.

"What's so funny?"

"The last time I had this conversation with a guy was the last time I saw that guy."

"That guy had to go…to make room for me."

Lorenzo "El Gee" Gladden

"You're too much Andre Marshall."
"That's what they tell me."

22
Ain't that a Snitch

The days sped by like race cars on a track. Before I knew it, one semester was over and another one was beginning. Melissa's final semester as an undergrad had arrived and this was the last semester before the start of my senior year. Everything was going good until financial issues started to happen. Instead of reapplying for financial aid when the time came, I decided to continue to pay my tuition out of pocket. With my savings depleting rapidly, the Foot Locker money wasn't going to be enough. As I sat at the kitchen table surrounded by bills and other papers, Alicia noticed that my mood wasn't a good one.

"What's wrong?" She asked as she approached the table.

"I think I'm going to have to find another job. Foot Locker isn't cuttin' it anymore. Times like this I wish I hadn't given up my position at the plant."

"You ever thought about waiting tables? That's what I do when I'm home for the holidays and during the summer."
"I never thought about that. I have a couple of sorors that work at Applebee's. They say they make pretty good money."

"You should look into it. I make pretty good cash at the restaurant I work at."

"I'll talk to soror and see if she can get me on."
"In the meantime, do you need anything?"
"I'm okay right now but thanks for asking."
"You know I got ya back, MC Cataract!"
"You silly. You do know that right?"
"I get it from you."
"Touché."

The next day I ran into one of my sorors in the UC and asked her if her job was hiring. She told me that they were and she would see if she could get me an interview. A week later I had my interview and was hired on the spot. I started the next day.

Once I finished my training and got onto the floor, things didn't jump off to a good start. The restaurant stayed busy but the money just wasn't right. It was decent but I thought there would be more. Waiting tables was not that big of a change from retail. You still had to deal with customers, the only thing was that I had to rely on those customers to pay me.

Quite a few of my coworkers were FMU students. We knew each other and we had a lot of fun at work. On Friday nights, the restaurant was bananas. Everybody came in to eat and drink before they went out to party. The clientele wasn't the greatest but I enjoyed the atmosphere and the pretty ladies that came in.

On particular Friday night, something happened that would later change my life. At the close of another hectic night, I was sitting at a table with Kelly, one of the veteran servers. She and I were doing our nightly cash out.

"How much did you make tonight?" I asked.
"$165.00"
"How in the hell did you make that off of the crowd that was just here?"
"I make that or more almost every night."
"How?"
"You must not know."
"About what?"
"I can't tell you right now," she began as the closing manager walked into the dining room. "Do you work tomorrow?"
"I come in at five."
"Come in at 4:30 and I'll show you how to make some real money."

The next day I came in thirty minutes early as I was instructed to do. Kelly was at a computer station when I walked in. She saw me and motioned for me to come to her. When I arrived she told me to watch what she was doing on the computer terminal. I observed as she moved a couple of things around and then closed the check.

"There," Kelly said. "I just made an extra four dollars plus the five they left me."

"I don't understand."

Kelly explained to me a scam that was just as old as the company. Servers had been manipulating the system to benefit their own pockets. After she broke everything down and explained it to me, I still had no clue on how it was going to help me make money. Regardless of my understanding, I put Kelly's instructions into action. At the end of the night I walked out with $175 in five hours.

I was hooked like an addict. I found myself hooked on the oldest drug known to mankind…money. In everything that you do, discretion must be in there somewhere. As the money grew, I lost sight of everything. All I knew was that I was trying to make as much money as I could. I ran the scam so much that it became a part of my training process when new people were hired. The way Kelly passed it on to me; I passed it on to others. In a flash I went from making anywhere from $300-$450 a week to around $700-$800 a week.

Like a man possessed, I became blinded by the money. I needed to slow down but I couldn't. The signs were all around telling me to slow down. I ignored them all. Even after a crew of servers at the same restaurant in another state got busted, I kept going. Unbeknownst to me, my restaurant was getting ready to undergo an investigation of its own.

Super Senior

Apparently, all of the franchise owners gathered and decided that they were going to put an end to it at all costs. They sent informants in posing as new hires. I didn't train the guy that came to my store but someone had passed it on to him. The more I watched him and the way he caught on so quickly, I started to have my doubts about him. He even went as far as to show us new ways to skate money off of the top. Had I not been distracted by the money, I would have been able to pay more attention to him.

The new guy hung around for about three months. Two weeks later, one of our own servers got busted for scamming. We all know how our judicial system works, the first one to snitch, gets the deal. In order for her to walk, she had to give up some names. Unfortunately for me, my name was one of the names on the list along with three others. Three days after she got caught and mysteriously lost her job, my manager asked me to work on one of my days off because the owner was coming for a visit. He gave me some bullshit story about wanting to have his best workers in the building while he was there. I blindly agreed to work and walked right in to a trap.

When I go to work that day, my manger got me as soon as I walked through the door. He led me into the kitchen and into the office. The owners and two detectives were waiting. I was arrested and charged with Breach of Trust with Fraudulent intent. Because of greed was facing a felony charge that carried up to fifteen years in prison. At that moment the only thing I could think of was: How in the hell was I going to explain this to my grandfather? I had plenty of time to think about it because the four of us were on our way to the courthouse to get prepped to be sent to the county jail. Lucky for me there was a bail bondsman in the courthouse that followed us to county to get us after we went through central booking.

During the long ride back to school, my rage began to grow. I wanted to end the lives of the owner, the manager, the bitch that snitched and the punk ass informant. As I neared school, I realized that I was the only person to blame. That day that Kelly showed me the scam, I had a choice. Greed tainted my thought process and I opted for the money. By the time I got back to my apartment, the word had leaked. Alicia, my LBs and a couple of sorors that were coworkers were at my place. Everybody was there to make sure that I was alright. Once I assured them that I was, I thanked them for coming by and retired to my room. Later on that night, I was lying in bed starting at the ceiling when Alicia came in.

"Dre?" she called from the other side of the door. "Are you okay?"
"Come in," I commanded.

Alicia walked in and sat on my bed. She didn't say anything for about five minutes. The only thing she could do was stare at me as I stared at the ceiling fan.

"You know my life is over, right?"

"Your life is not over. You made a mistake. It's not like you killed anybody or was busted for drugs."

"Here I am, this close to graduation and I blow it. I might as well drop out of school. No one is going to hire a felon…even with a degree."

"You know you can't do that as hard as you've fought to get to this point. You're a semester away. People make mistakes. What you've done doesn't define who you are? Someone will overlook this and take a chance on you."

"What if they don't? Then what?"

"You'll find a way. You always do and you always have. It may not happen for you here in Florence but it will happen for you somewhere. I believe that."

"I guess you're right. It all seems surreal right now."

"It just happened. Give it time."

For six months I was caught up in the court system while I awaited my day in court. Every Monday for those six months I had to report to the courthouse just so they know that I was still in town. Believe me when I tell you that running away crossed my mind several times. I decided to stand up and own up to what I'd done.

The semester closed for the summer and my day in court came. When it was all said and done, I plead guilty and was sentenced to five years of probation. I was also ordered to pay a restitution to the owner. I glimmer of hope came that day for me.

"Mr. Marshall," the judge began. "Before I close this case, is there anything you'd like to say?"

"Yes Your Honor. I have made a terrible mistake and I'm deeply sorry for what I've done. At the time, I didn't realize the severity of it all. Now I do. This experience is going to be a very hard lesson learned for me about being a leader instead of a follower."

"Mr. Marshall, what is your highest level of education?"

"I'm a high school graduate and a graduating senior at Franklin Memorial. I graduate in December."

"What is your major?"
"Mass Communications with a focus in broadcasting for television and radio."

"In light of the proceedings, I believe that you are a good, young man that truly made a mistake. I can't make all of this go away but I can help you out. I'm issuing you what is called a PTUP. Do you know what that is?"

"No, Your Honor."
"PTUP stands for probation terminates upon payment. This means that once you've paid the restitution

in full, you will no longer be on probation and you can move on with your life."

"Thank you, Your Honor."
"Being a graduating senior says a lot about who you are as a person and as people, we make bad choices. Let this be the last one you make. Court is adjourned."

With the bang of the gavel, court was dismissed. After what the judge did for me, I had a change in attitude. I decided that I wasn't going to let the situation get me down. Once I graduated, I was going to do everything that I could to pay off my restitution as soon as I could so that I could move on with my life. I didn't know where I was headed but I'd get there…some way, somehow.

24
Movin' On

At the close of the semester prior to my day in court, with the exception of Alicia, all of my people graduated. Both of my LBs and Melissa were gone. Melissa was still in town because of a job she took to pass the time before she left for law school. Other than her, all I had was Alicia. Because of my financial situation, Alicia and I were forced to move back into the apartments on campus. It hurt to move back on the yard but we had no choice.

Alicia was cool with it but I know that deep down inside, she would miss having her own place. There was an upside to it though. In my last semester, I didn't have to work as hard. I could focus on my course load and get the hell out. I thought that the job situation would be difficult but it wasn't. I moved on to a popular seafood restaurant in our city. I was completely honest with the managers and they gave me a job.

When the semester started, I'd just turned twenty-five. I was a lot older than most that were there. I really got a reality check when I met a group of freshmen girls. When they asked how old I was and I told them. One of the girls replied, "Damn you old!" At that moment I knew that it was time for me to move on.

I felt like an outcast in a familiar territory. Old faces had moved on and the new ones were piling in. I couldn't

Super Senior

believe that after everything I'd endured since graduating high school, I was finally in my final semester. The finish line was getting closer and closer as each day came and went. One evening while Alicia and I were studying for tests, we had a very interesting conversation.

"Can we talk for a minute?" Alicia asked as she closed her marketing book.
"Yeah…what's up?"
"Something has been weighing heavily on my mind."
"Is something wrong?"
"Nothing is wrong." Alicia paused and looked at me. "I've never just taken the time to tell you thank you."

"For what?"
"Thank you for always being there for me no matter what."
"We're best friends. That's what I'm supposed to do."

"It's deeper than that. You've held me down like no one else has ever done. You even sacrificed a relationship for me. No matter what you say, you and Chelsea broke up because of me."

"You're my girl. If a woman can't understand our history and everything we've been through, then she's not the woman for me. For the first time, I have my best friend and a girlfriend that understands our friendship and isn't intimidated or jealous by it."

"What's going to happen after you've graduated? I'm going to be here by myself finishing up my degree."

"I'll still be here. Other than paying this money back and getting off of probation, I have no idea what my next move is. I can't take the traditional route because now I'm a felon. You know companies are going to frown on that. I have to figure out a way to use my talents to get me to where I want to be."

"The other night I was thinking about the play that you wrote and we produced and directed. I thought about how you were during the entire process. You were in your element. Maybe that is your calling. I've read tons of things that you've written. You have a way with the written word that is uncanny."

"I've thought about writing for TV but that would take me to either New York or LA. I'm a country boy. I don't think I'm ready for those cities just yet."

"I was reading an article the other day. There is a new television network that just opened in Atlanta. They're looking for writers."

"What's the name of it?"

"The network is called Black Reign. It's owned by Joseph and Jonathan Conrad, two brothers from Chicago. They started out with Oprah when she first started Harpo."

"Sounds very interesting."

"You should really look into it. I know you could do well there. You just have to get your foot in the door."

"I'll definitely look into it. My cousin, Jerome would love it if I came to Atlanta."

"Jerome's down there?"

"Yup...he's been down there for about three years now."

"Are you kidding me? Jerome is in Atlanta and we've never been down there. You're slippin'."

"I know. So much has been going on around here. It never really crossed my mind."

"Look at it like this; if you do get the job down there, you have somewhere to crash until you get on your feet."

"That's true. I just don't know if I want to get mixed up in his lifestyle. Jerome runs one of the hottest clubs in Atlanta according to him."

"You're a grown man. You know how to say no. You tell me no all the time."

"When do I tell you no?"
"I can recall a certain thunderstorm….."
"Okay…point taken."

"But on the real, look into it. I think you have the talent to really make some noise there. They said they are a new network looking for fresh new faces and ideas. That's you all day long."

"Thanks, Alicia. I really appreciate all your support and faith in me. It really means a lot. You've always pushed me to do my best and for that…I'm truly grateful."

"Just don't get to Atlanta and forget about ya girl."
"I'll try not to. From what I hear, the ratio of men to women is very one-sided. Cuz said there is scattered ass everywhere!"

"You know what? Never mind….I don't think you and Jerome back together is a good idea."

Time continued to march on. Before I knew it, graduation day had arrived. I stood on the stairs with my fellow graduating classmates. We were all draped in black caps and gowns. I could hear the chatter from the gymnasium. The moment was surreal to me. Everything that I'd endured on my road to pursue higher education had come to an end. I was the first grandchild on both sides of my family to graduate from college.

Super Senior

Once the moment passed and all the celebrations were over, it was back to the reality of the entire situation. I was a twenty-five year old, college graduate with a felony. I had beaten the odds of finishing school but the real world stood in front of me. That night, I returned to my grandfather's home. As I sat in the room that I'd left some years ago, a strange feeling took over my body. In my head I kept hearing a voice saying, "Now what?" I had no clue.

The next morning I went to the library and began to research jobs in my field. As expected, everything was either in New York or in Los Angeles. There were a couple of opportunities in Chicago but that was just as bad. I was a southern born and bred guy. The big city would consume me. Further into my search, I came across the network Alicia spoke of. There were tons of openings in my area of knowledge as well as others. I gathered the necessary information that I needed to apply and left the library.

That night I sat in my room going through my writings and scripts trying to find the best material to send as samples along with my resume. I chose a couple of good scenes and then decided to write an original scene. It was harder than I thought it would be. After an hour of being blocked, I turned on the television and began to click through the channels. I landed on an unfamiliar channel showing a drama with all black actors. The show really caught my attention. During the commercial break I found that the station was the very one that I was interested in…Black Reign.

After watching the show in its entirety, I knew what my sample piece would be. I would write an episode for that show. I was excited to get to work. Two scenes into my writing, reality hit me like a ton of bricks falling from atop a building. Why was I rushing? I still had to serve my probation and get the money that I owed paid.

For a year and a half, I worked double shifts, when I could at the restaurant. Knowing my situation, Kim let me come back to Foot Locker during the day. My television stayed locked on Black Reign Networks. I learned everything about every show that they produced hoping that my knowledge would pay off.

The day before I was to make my last payment to release me from probation, I got a phone call. I didn't recognize the number.

"Hello?" I answered.
"May I speak with Andre Marshall?" a female voice asked.

"This is Andre."
"Mr. Marshall, my name is Karen Union. I am an executive producer at Black Reign Networks."

"Hello Ms. Union. I was hoping to hear something from you."

Super Senior

"I'm going to get right down to business. I looked over your resume and read your sample pieces. I'm very impressed."

"Thank you, Ma'am."
"I would like for you to come to Atlanta for an interview. When can we set that up?"

"I have a prior commitment on tomorrow but any time after that will be great."

"How about this coming Monday at 1pm?"
"That works out fine for me."
"That's great. Before I go, are you familiar with our show, Tryin' Times?"

"Yes. I watch it faithfully."
"Then as you know, the show comes on tomorrow. I want you to write a follow up episode as if you were writing it to be aired next Friday. Can you do that?"
"Yes I can."
"That's wonderful. We'll see you on Monday."
"I'll see you then. Thank you so much."

When I hung up the phone I yelled "YES!" at the top of my lungs. I was so happy for the opportunity to interview for Black Reign. My grandfather came running around to my room to see what was going on.

"Boy," he began. "What da world is wrong with you?"

"I'm sorry, Dad. I just got some good news."

"What is it?"

"I have an interview with a TV station in Atlanta on Monday."

"Doing what?"

"Hopefully writing for one of their shows."

"Ain't God good?"

"Yes he is."

"I'ma send up some serious prayer for you."

"I need all the help I can get."

"You know what I always tell you…what God has for you, no man can take it away. You claim it and it's yours."

Thanks to some wiggling and favors I had to call in, I got Monday off for my interview. I left South Carolina at 5am that morning. I arrived at Jerome's place around 10am. He wasn't there but he's left his key for me. Once inside, I showered and got my clothes ready. Before I got dressed I printed out the directions to Black Reign from Jerome's computer. Luck for me, it wasn't that far away. Still not wanting to take any chances, I left Jerome's apartment at 11:45.

Around a quarter past twelve, I arrived at Black Reign. Once I received my visitors pass from the front gate and directions to where I needed to be, I headed to the

Super Senior

parking deck. With over thirty minutes to kill, I sat in my car and meditated. Right before I got out heading to my interview, I said a quick prayer and I claimed it.

When I arrived to the floor in the building I was supposed to be in, I was greeted by a gorgeous, young woman sitting at the receptionist desk. Her eyes were bright and a dark shade of brown. Her hair was black, long and straight. The smile that spread across her face when she noticed me approaching was wide, toothy and beautiful.

"Hi," she greeted. "What can I do for you today?"
"My name is Andre Marshall. I have a 1 o'clock interview with Karen Union."
"We've been expecting you. Have a seat. Ms. Union will be with you shortly."

I took a seat in the lobby to wait. I skimmed through my notes for the interview as well as the questions that I had prepared to ask. Out of all the resumes that I'd sent out, Black Reign was the first to respond and give me an interview. I didn't know what the future held for me but I was ready. My Dad told me to claim it and that's exactly what I'd done every day since I spoke to Ms. Union for the first time. My thoughts were interrupted by the young lady at the desk.

"Mr. Marshall…Ms. Union will see you now."

Lorenzo "El Gee" Gladden

Thank you for reading Super Senior by PRINTHOUSE BOOKS: Author; Lorenzo 'El Gee' Gladden. Please leave a review; we would love to know what you think.

Other titles available from Lorenzo "el Gee" Gladden.

PRINTHOUSE BOOKS

Read it, Enjoy it, Tell a Friend!

Atlanta, Ga.

www.Printhousebooks.com

Lorenzo "El Gee" Gladden

www.ingramcontent.com/pod-product-compliance
Lightning Source LLC
Chambersburg PA
CBHW030515230426
43665CB00010B/628